FOUNDATIONS OF LIBRARY AND INFORMATION SCIENCE

FOUNDATIONS OF LIBRARY AND INFORMATION SCIENCE

By

Rakeshkumar Shantilal Prajapati

B.Lib., M.Lib.
Librarian
Swami Vivekanand Sarvoday Bank Education College
Mehsana (Gujarat)
(India)

DPH

DISCOVERY PUBLISHING HOUSE PVT. LTD.
NEW DELHI-110 002

Published by:
Tilak Wasan

DISCOVERY PUBLISHING HOUSE PVT. LTD.
4383/4B, Ansari Road, Darya Ganj
New Delhi-110 002 (India)
Phone : +91-11-23279245, 43596064-65
Fax : +91-11-23253475
E-mail : discoverypublishinghouse@gmail.com
sales@discoverypublishinggroup.com
parul.wasan@gmail.com
web : www.discoverypublishinggroup.com

First Edition: **2013**

ISBN: 978-93-5056-384-7

Foundations of Library and Information Science

Printed at:
Dynamic Printers
Delhi

Content

Preface *ix*

1. **Library and Society** **1**

The Role of Libraries in Modern Society, New Lines in the EU-AND in the United States, Earlier Actions in EU, Decisions of the EP Concerning Library Policy, Traditions and New Forms of Work in the Same House, The Public Libraries in the Knowledge Society, The Libraries in a State of Flux, The Political Basis for the Committee's Work, The Commission's Assignment: Mandate for the Committee on the Public Libraries in the Knowledge Society, Digital Libraries and Society, Books, Libraries, and the Socially Disadvantaged, What are Digital Libraries, Using Digital Libraries to Disseminate Humanitarian Information, Universal Access

2. **Historical Overview of Library Development** **39**

Growth of Libraries in India, Growth and Development of Oriental Libraries in India, Academic Libraries in India: A Historical Study, Saraswathi Mahal Library, History, Efforts, The Collection, Some of the Rare Books and Manuscripts, Library Museum, Khuda Bakhsh Oriental Library, History, Collection, Bhandarkar Oriental Research Institute, The Institute, The Manuscript Collection, The Critical Edition of the Mahabharata, Vandalism in 2003, Asiatic Society Library, Manuscript Collection, Rare Book Division

3. **Information and Information Science** 84

Information, Etymology, Information Theory Approach, As Sensory Input, As Representation and Complexity, As an Influence which Leads to a Transformation, As a Property in Physics, Technologically Mediated Information, As Records, Information and Semiotics, Characteristics of Information, Nature of Information, Information Science, Scope and Approach, Definitions of Information Science, Philosophy of Information, Ontology, History of Information Science

4. **Dr. S.R. Ranganathan** 122

Birth and Parentage, Family Life, Education, Teaching Career, Towards Librarianship, Activities at Madras, Activities at Banaras, Activities at Delhi, Towards Zurich, Activities at Bangalore

5. **Types of Libraries** 132

Public Library, Services Offered, Digital Divide, Origins as a Social Institution, Public Libraries in India, Ancient Period, Medieval Period, The British Period, Post-Independence Period, Library Legislation in India, Model Public Libraries Act of Dr. S R Ranganathan, Model Public Libraries Bill of Ministry of Education, Model Public Libraries Bill of the Planning Commission, Model Public Libraries Bill of Indian Library Association, Model Union Library Act, States with Library Legislation, States/ UTS without Library Legislation, Contribution of Raja Rammohun Roy Library Foundation, National Policy on Library and Information System, National Knowledge Commission, Library Associations, National Library of India, Aims, History, Collection, Conservation Activities, Academic Library, Academic Libraries in India: A Present-Day Scenario, School Library, History of School Libraries, The Purpose of the School Library, The School Library Collection, Staffing of the School Library, Research

Libraries, Reference Libraries, Special Libraries, Archive, Museum and Records Management, Archive, Museum, Records Management

6. **Library Co-operation** 234

Resource Sharing, Resource Sharing: Need of the Time, Problems, Prospects and Prerequisites, Characteristics of a Networked Library Resource Sharing System, Library Networking, Delnet, Calibnet, Malibnet, Mylibnet, Bonet, Punenet, Adinet, Inflibnet, Conclusion

7. **Professional Association in Library and Information Science** 251

Indian Library Association (ILA), Indian Association of Special Libraries and Information Centres (IASLIC), Indian Association of Teachers of Library and Information Science (IATLIS), Formation of the Organization, The Revival, Aims and Objectives, American Library Association (ALA), Membership, Governing Structure, Political Positions, Special Libraries Association, Chartered Institute of Library and Information Professionals, Functions, Role in LIS Education, International Federation of Library Associations and Institutions, Mission

Bibliograpy 269

Index 271

Preface

Libraries are now universally recognized as important social institutions, no community is considered complete without a library. The gradual spread of the concept of democracy, education, the intensification of search activities, the rapid increase in production of recorded knowledge, have led to the expansion of libraries and the development of their services.

A library is an important element of a community; an academic library is an essential part of an educational institution school, college or university; a business and industrial organization.

Librarianship is a growing field, which has by now attained the status of a separate discipline in the universe of knowledge. It presents challenges and interesting situations to library personnel.

The management of these libraries needs persons with good academic and professional qualification proficiency in one the natural sciences, social science or the humanities is helpful in the professional development of a librarian. Library work is primarily a social service, and therefore, needs young men and women with a sense of dedication and a spirit of service.

Those intending to enter the library profession should satisfy themselves that they possess the academic qualification and the sense of vocation that would enable them to work successfully as librarians.

The objective of the book is to bring together a balanced selection of core concepts as well as new perspectives that collectively articulate a knowledge-based view of foundations of library and information science. This book covers a wide range of foundations of library and information science issues, and attempt to introduce the subject in a comprehensive way. It avoids the narrow focus and considerable complexity of many other books in this area where in depth treatment is required.

—Author

1

Library and Society

THE ROLE OF LIBRARIES IN MODERN SOCIETY

First, the general development of the information society is pushing to re-evaluation of all the institutions which work with information, data, and knowledge-indirectly also with culture. In this connection the roles of education and media have been discussed already quite largely also in the European Union. But libraries-as well as other memory institutions like archives and museums-have not been considered.

Still, there is a clear need in the information society to maintain an institution which is concentrating in collecting and organizing information and offering general access to it. Until now, this work has been underestimated, but I argue the situation will change!

Libraries are especially important now when the whole idea of education is stressing more and more independent learning and acting. All citizens must be able to find and use information. It is the key raw material-but it is a zero resource, if there are no access points to it and if documents are in chaotic order.

Here we can see libraries enter the stage:

* The unique function of libraries is to acquire, organize, offer for use and preserve publicly available material irrespective of the form in which it is packaged in such a way that, when it is needed, it can be found and put to use. No other institution carries out this long-term, systematic work. Culture must be nominated especially: it has an important and unique role in mobilizing resources of human beings. It has been

> described: To some extent, culture makes its influence felt more indirectly than knowledge, but it is impossible to imagine how people's creative powers could be fully activated without the impact of culture, which extends into the depths of the mind.

The challenge to modern societies is that the basic resource, knowledge, is developing from information in very individual, capricious and unpredictable process. It cannot be commanded. Still, societies can support this development, *e.g.* by offering access to cultural and knowledge treasures.

This can even be translated into economic language: to get out the best from the human resources in Europe, this resource must be feeded up with rich and various cultural and information contents! I would like to stress especially the idea of organizing information by libraries.

It is often shadowed by the second important side of library work: offering access. But in the life-long learning and new technology context just all forms of organizing documents are getting more to the focus. This is clear to anybody who has tried to find something from not-so-often-used Internet websites.

NEW LINES IN THE EU AND IN THE UNITED STATES

In accordance with these phenomenons, there are new political lines in the European Union: The Maastricht Treaty in 1992 launched the cultural aspects. This was only after a long discussion, which made it clear that we have to remember to separate the national view and the European view. The Amsterdam Treaty in 1997 declared citizenship as an important theme.

A significant part of this are a.o. granting information skills and access to information to every European. In addition to this, the European future strategies need to meet the democratic aspects of the information society development. One of the crucial points is again general access to information. Libraries, especially public libraries, are a good tool in all of these new areas. But the European union does not support whichever cultural or citizen concentrated projects in Europe.

In the interests of the European Union there is always to find the European element. So, what can be done in library policy on the European level, taking in account that libraries are primarily a part of national education and cultural policies? The own-initiative report "The role of libraries in modern societies," adopted by the European Parliament in October 1998, is the first effort to answer these questions.

The same topics have been discussed in the United States. They have reached the point where especially the problems of those lacking access to digital resources have been studied. The report Falling Through the Net: Defining the Digital Divide by the U.S. Department of Commerce was released earlier in July 1999.

The report finds that minorities, low-income persons, the less educated, and children of single parent households, particularly when they reside in rural areas or central cities, are risk groups. The report calls for public policies and private initiatives to expand affordable access to critical information resources.

But it also shows, for the first time as far as I know, that libraries and community centres really can diminish the information gap between haves and not-haves. The 1998 data from the U.S. demonstrate very clearly that community access centres, primarily public libraries, are particularly well used by those groups who lack access at home or at work: *e.g.* unemployed groups used Internet in libraries three times as often as an average citizen.

EARLIER ACTIONS IN EU

In the European Union, there have been some efforts to mobilize "the treasures of the European libraries" since the mid-80's. These discussions and resolutions led to two special library programmes under the 3rd and 4th Framework programmes of research and development. The later programme has been known as "Telematics for Libraries". They have been strongly concentrated in IT, because it has been seen as a good tool to produce better access to the existing, underused library resources.

These programmes have had a clear impact in the European library co-operation and development. Benefits of this work come to public libraries indirectly: common standards and working methods help in the end all kind of libraries. But a fact is, that nearly all the libraries active in these EU projects are national libraries or big research and university libraries. Two main exceptions are Publican, a network of European public libraries, and ECUP, which was a copyright awareness raising project, and reached public libraries as well.

A new beginning was the so called Morgan report in 1997. In this report libraries were for the first time put clearly onto the place where they belong in the information society. As one result of the Morgan report, the European Commission informed that it will produce a Green Paper about the role of libraries in the information society.

For one or another reason, this was made quite ready but was never published. In this situation the Committee on Culture, Youth, Education and the Media in the European Parliament decided to produce an own-initiative report about libraries.

The main reason was that they wanted to influence the big issues under work in the EU, first of all the copyright directive and the 5th framework programme, which will have a direct impact to libraries. I was nominated the rapporteur of the own-initiative report. The report was adopted almost unanimously and with a very encouraging discussion in the Plenary session of the Parliament in October 1998.

DECISIONS OF THE EP CONCERNING LIBRARY POLICY

In short, when adopting the own-initiative report, the EP was calling the Commission and/or the member states to following actions:

* Libraries must be taken in account in national and EU information society strategies and in the respective budgets.
* Libraries need more resources for acquiring expensive books.
* The Green Paper on libraries by the Commission must be completed.
* The users position must be taken in account in the copyright directive process, the balance must be

maintained-this was politically the most important decision in short run.

* Support to libraries was demanded from the 5th Framework programme of research and development, *e.g.* for networking, drafting standards, preserving, and transferring information; there is no more named library programme under the 5th framework programme
* A clearing-house to solve problems of long-term conservation should be founded.
* Studies concerning permanent paper should be done on European level.
* The member–states should take care of digitizing their cultural heritage for future.
* There should be studies and concrete support to libraries in licensing matters, which are–will be the next big issue in library work.
* The EU cultural and information budget should be opened to libraries as well, libraries and their co-operation should be taken in account in planning new programmes.
* Problems of legal deposit in international and multinational materials, especially in electronic materials should be solved.
* The member states should provide all types of libraries with modern equipment, particularly with Internet connections.
* Free of charge use of public libraries, in the spirit of the UNESCO Public Library Manifest, was demanded.
* Free and easy access via libraries to material produced with the aid of tax revenues was demanded.
* The members states should organize for their library professionals up-dating education and training.
* A European Union focal point for libraries should be set up
* The member states should found European information points at libraries in countries where they do not yet exist.

* Library statistics should be better and more comparable both on national and European level.
* The national Parliament libraries should be opened to the MEP's in countries where this is not yet the practice.

In addition to these, the report strongly stresses that the library financing must be re-thought in the information society. Without new resources libraries are unable to do everything they are expected to do! After the EP adoption of this report, the European Commission informed that it will next prepare a communication about actions to do. It was stated that the report had already served as a discussion paper, and so the need for the Green Paper had disappeared. The communication is in summer 1999 still under work in the Commission DGXIII/2.

TRADITIONS AND NEW FORMS OF WORK IN THE SAME HOUSE

The European Commission R&D framework programmes have concentrated in IT matters. The three cultural programmes, Caledoskope, Ariane and Raphael, have not been very useful for libraries, because their scope has been quite narrow. *E.g.* the books and reading programme Ariane has concentrated in translations. In the coming framework programme Culture 2000 libraries will have more possibilities to get support also for their cultural actions. What then will be the fate of the traditional tasks of libraries in general? Will the information society wipe out book loaning and poems?

THE PUBLIC LIBRARIES IN THE KNOWLEDGE SOCIETY

THE LIBRARIES IN A STATE OF FLUX

The municipal reform in 2007 had major consequences for the library service. The number of libraries decreased and the remaining libraries grew in size. The reform thus underlined and intensified various tendencies in library development over the past many years.

The public library is in a state of flux. *Library service to children* from 2008 that chose as its point of reference the changes in children's use of the library. Thus this report had a strong focus on one target group and on how the library can develop new services to that group.

The present report also focuses on the target group, but slightly more on the institution–the public library. Based on a number of societal needs and new opportunities the report also considers how the library can be developed as an institution. The library offer is changing rapidly, but it continues to be much sought after.

Two out of three Danes use the public library, and 29% of the adult population visit the library at least once a month. In 2008 the public libraries registered more than 34 mil. visits. This makes the library one of our most popular, public cultural offers, and this has been the case for many years. But the way we use the library is undergoing a change. On the one hand the loan of physical materials – books, CDs etc. – is falling.

In the period 2000-2008 the public libraries' loan of physical materials has thus fallen by 22%, from ca. 62 mil. to app. 48 mil. materials. On the other hand the use of digital offers is growing, an offer that spans from downloads of music and e-books to renewals of loans via the library's homepage. Bibliotekernes Netmusik, where as a library user you can via your municipality download music for free, experienced over 2,5 mil. downloads in 2008 – an increase of 48% compared with 2007.

One explanation of the change in borrowing patterns could be that the technology and media development has resulted in new media habits on behalf of the library users. At the same time the libraries' consistently high visiting figures show that they have succeeded in reorganizing and revitalizing themselves and continue to be attractive.

This happens by developing new library services, particularly digital services, but also by turning the library into something more than just a collection of materials, so that the physical library maintains its desirability.

Today the library is also a place for being and meeting, where one for example gets instruction, uses the Internet or gets help in the local citizen service centre. However, borrowing books remains the main reason why Danes visit the library. The latest cultural habits survey from 2004 shows that 85% of adult library users visit the library to borrow books and journals. The same tendency becomes apparent in more recent studies.

In a Gallup poll conducted on behalf of the Danish Library Association, the Union of Danish Librarians and HK Kommunal (white collar workers' union (municipal) in 2009, "borrowing books" is the most frequent reason for visiting the library, followed by "borrowing electronic media", "taking the children to the library" and "watching events".

There is in fact also a growing interest in the library's non-users, as can be seen from the large number of new initiatives, which the libraries participate in at municipal level. In many cases these have a social aspect, and the library is here used as a partner in a targeted initiative towards certain target groups.

This effort is particularly relevant in the light of the challenges that globalization presents to less resourceful citizens. The focusing on non-users also has another angle, which is i.a. clearly expressed in former minister for culture, Carina Christensen's strategy Culture for everybody from 2009. Here the emphasis is on the value of participating in a cultural community and the individual citizen's benefit from cultural offers. The strategy suggests that all citizens should be able to take advantage of the cultural offers and consequently–that the cultural institutions focus more purposefully on non-users.

THE POLITICAL BASIS FOR THE COMMITTEE'S WORK

The appointment of the Committee on the Public Libraries in the Knowledge Society was decided by the minister for culture in connection with several consultations in Folketingets Kulturudvalg (parliamentary cultural committee), which took place in the wake of a large number of public library branches being closed down during the first year of the municipal reform. The discussion fuelled by this naturally included the media and technology development.

A suggestion for a more extensive, interdepartmental committee work was rejected by the minister, who referred to the work that had already been done by the Globalisation Council. The committee's work builds on the report *Future library service to children* from 2008. The report contains a number of recommendations as to how to make sure that a strong library offer continues to be available to all Danish children.

In 2008 the Danish Agency for Libraries and Media also published the report *The public libraries after the municipal reform,* which analysed the development within the public library area with particular focus on any consequences due to the municipal reform. The report concluded that the closure of the branches in 2006-2007 was a natural adaptation of the library service, and that at the same time it demonstrated a prioritisation in order to deliver a more up to date and value-enhancing library offer.

With the report from the Committee on the Public Libraries in the Knowledge Society we now have a number of recommendations as to how this prioritisation can be made so that the public libraries also in future will be able to meet the public's need for enlightenment, education and cultural activity. The committee presents its recommendations within an expenditure-neutral framework with the perspective that it may be both necessary and correct with local changes of priorities within the library field in order to support and strengthen the public library in the knowledge society.

THE COMMISSION'S ASSIGNMENT: MANDATE FOR THE COMMITTEE ON THE PUBLIC LIBRARIES IN THE KNOWLEDGE SOCIETY

The committee must focus on continuous development of the public libraries in Denmark. This includes the public libraries' interaction with other libraries and relevant institutions. Focus must be on the libraries as an easily accessible offer to everybody. The committee must build on the report *Future library service to children* and pay particular attention to service to youngsters and adults.

The committee must assess the public libraries' role in relation to the challenges facing the knowledge society, the globalisation strategy's focus on education, lifelong learning and societal cohesive force. The committee must assess to which extent there is basis for establishing new concepts for a library service that meets the public's needs in terms of enlightenment, education and cultural activity, and close to the citizens.

Likewise the committee must asses the possibilities for continuous development of traditional core services such as literature dissemination. In particular, the committee must asses the need for further development of the libraries' digital infrastructure and the interaction between digital and traditional services.

The committee must furthermore describe models for the mediation of digital cultural heritage and licensed digital media and models for various forms of learning and inspiration activities (*e.g.* in relation to citizens with poor reading and IT skills). The committee must likewise give examples of new partnerships, including inter-institutional cooperations and binding networking commitments.

Finally the committee must assess the need for competence development of library staff. On the basis of its analyses the committee must put forward recommendations and suggestions as to how the strategy's objectives can be realised within the present legislation and existing division of labour between state and municipalities. The committee's suggestions must be expenditure-neutral.

The committee is composed upon appointment, so that the minister for culture appoints three members, while Local Government (KL), Danish Library Association, Association of Library Directors, Danish Research Library Association, the Regional Libraries, Union of Danish Librarians and Børne-og Kulturchefforeningen each appoints a member. The Danish Agency for Library and Media's director general is chairman of the committee, and the Agency is the committee's secretariat. The committee must have completed its work primo 2010.

DIGITAL LIBRARIES AND SOCIETY

Digital libraries are large, organized collections of information objects. Whereas standard library automation systems provide a computerized version of the catalog—a gateway into the treasure-house of information stored in the library—digital libraries incorporate the treasure itself, namely the information objects that constitute the library's collection. Whereas standard libraries are, of necessity, ponderous and substantial institutions, with large buildings and significant funding requirements, even large digital libraries can be lightweight.

Whereas standard libraries, whose mandate includes preservation as well as access, are "conservative" by definition, with institutional infrastructure to match, digital libraries are nimble: they emphasize access and evolve rapidly.

The five stages in this part provide an excellent illustration of the huge variety of interesting issues in digital library research that impacts the Asia Pacific region. Unlike the New World, where most of the research on technological aspects of digital libraries originates, Asia has an exceptionally rich cultural heritage. This manifests itself in a huge legacy of documents, in various forms—from paper to palm leaves—and in various different conditions.

The need to preserve this legacy is particularly pressing in today's world, where political instability is rife and climate change is beginning to have an effect. As recent events have shown, disasters, both manmade and natural, can have a devastating effect on fragile cultural artifacts.

S.M. Shafi from the University of Kashmir, India, surveys the many issues involved with digital archiving of medieval manuscripts in Asia. Libraries are pillars of education, and it is natural to expect that digital libraries will provide new opportunities for innovative educational practices.

These will be particularly relevant to the Asia Pacific region because of the huge disparities in access to education between the different communities there. Peer-to-peer learning has always been a crucial factor in personal development, although it is frequently ignored in educational studies.

Natalie Lee-San from Nanyang Technological University, Singapore, describes her studies of how digital libraries can provide an innovative, perhaps revolutionary, environment for peer-to-peer learning amongst youths. She touches on many practical issues: gender differences, different learning styles, different levels of media and computer literacy, and age-related differences.

Many economies in the Asia Pacific region are agriculturally-based. Modern agriculture is a knowledge-based activity that can benefit greatly from digital libraries. Mila Ramos from the International Rice Research Institute in the Philippines describes a large-scale digital library system designed to support the growth, nurturing, harvesting, and distribution of that most Asian of staples, rice.

This digital library supports an institute whose goal is to improve the well-being of present and future generations of rice farmers and consumers, particularly those with low incomes. The institute's library houses the world's most comprehensive collection of technical literature on rice, and provides a widely-used international reference service.

As in many specialized libraries, digital library technology is seen to have special advantages in a world of shrinking library budgets. Intellectual property issues are a central driving force behind the market in information of which libraries are a part. And the questions become more complex as the nature of today's information shifts from a primarily book-based culture to one that embraces all types of multimedia objects, and large, carefully-curated, collections of such objects.

The stage on *"Multimedia digital library as intellectual property"* by Hideyasu Sasaki and Yasujshi Kiyoki at Keio University in Japan clarify the copyright situation as it affects multimedia collections and compilations. They go on to discuss the patentability of particular retrieval mechanisms, an essential component of digital libraries. The fifth stage in this part on how digital library research impacts the Asia Pacific region is the present one, on digital libraries in society.

Most existing digital library projects, being research-oriented, are predicated on state-of-the-art equipment and interfaces, academic and research institutions, special collections. In contrast: digital library technology can and should be available to everyone, on all platforms, in all countries; and it can and should enable ordinary people to exercise their creative powers to conceive, assemble, build, and disseminate new information collections that are designed not just for western academics but for a wide diversity of different audiences throughout the world. Though less glamorous, this may, in the end, be a more important goal for society.

Digital libraries pose an inherent tension between the technologist's desire for advanced solutions that use the latest and greatest hardware and software, and the librarian's desire for wide, crossplatform availability and long-term preservation—as epitomized by the sustained success of paper as a delivery medium.

To achieve universal access for both information consumers and collection-builders is really a problem for HCI. We examine the social need for digital libraries, particularly in developing countries, by briefly sketching some trends in commercial publishing and contrasting them with a growing international perspective of information as a public good. We draw out the implications for the user interface, which is the principal bottleneck in allowing non-specialist people to make public information available in focused collections that are universally usable.

Then we introduce digital library technology and illustrate it with a particular example, the Greenstone digital library software, which is designed for a broad user base and is in widespread use in many corners of the world—from Uganda to the US, Kazakhstan to Canada, Nepal to New Zealand. Following that, we review a project that is applying digital library technology to the distribution of humanitarian information in the developing world, a context that is both innovative and socially motivated.

Next we discuss issues of universal access and illustrate them with reference to the Greenstone software. We include a brief demonstration of a prototype system that is intended to allow anyone to build and disseminate information collections, and illustrates some human interface challenges that arise when providing necessarily complex functionality to a non-computer-oriented user base.

We close with the hope that future digital libraries will find a new role to play in helping to reduce the social inequity that haunts today's world, both within our own countries and between nations.

BOOKS, LIBRARIES, AND THE SOCIALLY DISADVANTAGED

Today, the long-standing three-way tension between the

commercial interests of publishers, the needs of society and information users, and the social mandate of public libraries, is being pulled and stretched as never before. First, the very notion of a "book" is evolving in many different directions: books become more interactive; publishers rent content; books are distributed under restrictive conditions that mechanically prohibit sharing.

While it would be premature to make specific predictions, it seems likely that these trends will further disadvantage the disadvantaged—particularly those in poorer countries who have yet to benefit from ready access to ordinary books. Second, a huge body of information is becoming freely available on the Internet.

Much is of questionable quality, but some is very good indeed. In many cases the information is provided for the "public good" rather than for commercial profit, and the redistribution of such information is likely to be encouraged, rather than prohibited, by those who make it available.

Initiatives like UNESCO's "Information for all" programme and the upcoming World Summit on the Information Society highlight the importance of public information; they are founded on the belief that information literacy will help alleviate many of the problems confronting human societies.

Third, the implications for libraries are mixed. Whereas new controls by publishers over how the content they own may be used presents libraries with significant problems, the ready availability of "public good" information meshes well with library philosophy.

A new role is emerging for information professionals who can select material, index it, add appropriate metadata, and redistribute it in added-value form for the good of society. Suitable technological infrastructure is being provided by the open source movement, which is making available high-quality software for repackaging and distribution of information (and not just on computer networks).

Books

What future has the book in the digital world? The question

is a complex one that is being widely aired. Authors and publishers ask how many copies of a work will be sold if networked digital libraries enable worldwide access to an electronic copy of it.

Their nightmare is that the answer is *one*: how many books will be published online if the entire market can be extinguished by the sale of one electronic copy to a public library? To counter this threat, the entertainment industry is promoting new *"digital rights management"* (DRM) schemes that permit a degree of control over what users can do that goes far beyond the traditional legal bounds of copyright.

Indeed, the acronym is more aptly expanded as "digital restrictions management" because it is concerned solely with content owners rights and not at all with user's rights. It is, in effect, a "private governance system in which computer systems regulate which acts users are and are not authorized to perform".

Anticircumvention rules are sanctioned by the *Digital Millennium Copyright Act* (DMCA) in the US. The DMCA has been used, for example, to prosecute a Norwegian teenager for writing software to play a DVD that he had purchased on a computer for which no commercial playback systems exist.

Can DRM be applied to books? The motion picture industry can compel manufacturers to incorporate encryption into their products because it holds key patents on DVD players. Commercial book publishers are promoting e-book readers that, if adopted on a wide scale, would allow the same kind of control to be exerted over reading material.

Basic rights that we take for granted—such as the ability to lend a book to a friend, resell it on the second-hand market, keep it indefinitely, continue to use it when your e-book reader breaks down, donate it to charity, preserve it for your grandchildren, copy excerpts without resorting to a handwritten transcription—are in jeopardy.

DRM allows such rights to be controlled, monitored, and withdrawn instantly, and DMCA legislation makes it illegal for users to seek redress by taking matters into their own hands.

Fortunately, perhaps, lack of standardization and compatibility issues are delaying consumer adoption of e-books.

In the realm of scholarly publishing, digital rights management is more advanced. Academic libraries license access to content in electronic form, often in tandem with purchase of print versions too. They have been able to negotiate reasonable conditions with publishers—probably because they represent the lion's share of the scholarly market.

However, the extent of libraries' power in the consumer book market is moot. One can envisage a scenario where publishers establish a system of commercial, pay-per-view, libraries for e-books and refuse public libraries access to books in a form that can be circulated. These new directions present our society with puzzling challenges, and it would be rash to predict what society's response will be. But one thing is certain: they will surely increase the degree of disenfranchisement of those who do not have access to the technology.

Public Information

In parallel with publishers' moves to reposition books as technological artifacts with refined and flexible control over how they can be used, an opposing trend has emerged: the ready availability of free information on the Internet. Of course, the world-wide web is an unreliable source of enlightenment, and undiscriminating use is dangerous—and widespread.

As early as 1996 complaints arose that the Web's contents are largely unattributed, undated, unannotated, unreliable; information about author and publisher is unavailable or incomplete; far too many resource catalogues are chasing far too few original or non-trivial documents—complaints that are very familiar today. But one thing has changed: search engines and other portals have enormously increased our ability to locate information that is at least ostensibly relevant to any given question.

Teachers complain bitterly that students view the Web as a replacement for the library, harvesting information indiscriminately to provide answers to assignments that are at best shallow and at worst incoherent and incorrect. One consolation is that the very same search facilities can be used to detect plagiarism.

Nevertheless, the Web abounds with accessible, high-quality information. Many social groups, non-profit societies and charities make it their business to create sites and collect and organize information there. To take a single example at random, a Google search for *diabetes* returns three national diabetes associations in the top ten hits, and of course many more exist.

Each of these sites offers a cornucopia of valuable information on the disease, which is not commercial and provided for the public good. Widespread use is strongly encouraged, and it seems likely that arrangements could be made for re-distribution of the material presented there, particularly it was intended as a not-for-profit service and appropriate acknowledgement was made.

One of the key problems with information distribution via the Web is that it disenfranchises developing countries. Although the Web does not extend into the homes of the socially disadvantaged in developed countries either, various national programmes are working to provide access.

But network access varies enormously across the world. Whereas in 1998 more than a quarter of the US population were surfing the Internet, the figures for Latin America and the Caribbean was 0.8%, for Sub-Saharan Africa 0.1%, and for South Asia 0.04%. Schools and hospitals in developing countries are poorly connected.

Even in South Africa, the bestconnected African country, many hospitals and 75% of schools have no telephone line. Universities are better equipped, but even there up to 1,000 people can depend on just one terminal. The Internet "is failing the developing world".

Prompted by this inequity, the importance of information, and particularly public information, is today being highlighted by prominent international bodies. For example, UNESCO's "Information for all" programme was established in 2001 to foster debate on the political, ethical and societal challenges of the emerging global knowledge society and to carry out projects promoting equitable access to information.

It reflects a growing awareness that information is playing an increasing role in generating wealth and human capital, and that participation in the "global knowledge society" is essential for social and individual development.

Information literacy is described as "a new frontier" by the Director of UNESCO's Information Society Division. The International Telecommunications Union has established a World Summit on the Information Society, held in Geneva in December 2003 and Tunis in 2005, to promote a global discussion of the fundamental changes that are being brought about in our lives by the transformation from an industrial to an information society, and to confront the extreme disparities of access to information between the industrialized countries and the developing world.

Libraries and their Role

What is the librarian to make of all this? The mandate of today's public libraries, in sharp contrast to that of publishers, is to facilitate the open distribution of knowledge. Librarians strive to enable the free flow of information. Their traditions are liberal, founded on the belief that libraries should serve democracy.

To help fulfil their mission as resource centers for citizens, public libraries maintain collections of records, policy statements, government documents, and so on. A recent promotional video from the American Librarian's Association exults that "the library is democracy's place of worship".

Clearly, the impending redefinition of the book as a digital artifact that is licensed rather than sold, tied to a particular replay device, with restrictions that are clearly laid out and mechanically enforced, is an innovation that goes right to the heart of libraries.

The changing nature of the book may make it hard, or even impossible, for libraries to fulfill their mandate by providing quality information to readers. And on the other hand, the emergence of a vast storehouse of information on the Internet poses a different kind of conundrum. Librarians, the traditional gatekeepers of knowledge, are in danger of being bypassed, their skills ignored, their advice unsought.

Search engines send users straight to the information they require—or so users think—without any need for an intermediary to classify, catalogue, cross-reference, advise on sources. The ready availability of information on the Internet, and its widespread use, really presents librarians with an opportunity, not a threat.

Savvy users realise they need help, which librarians can provide. A good example is Infomine, a cooperative project of the University of California and California State University. Infomine contains descriptions and links to a wealth of scholarly and educational Internet resources, each of which has been selected and described by a professional academic librarian who is a specialist in the subject and in resource description generally.

Participating librarians see this as an important expenditure of effort for their users, a natural evolution of their traditional task of collecting and organizing information in print. What kind of technical infrastructure is needed to support and promote this kind of work?

Open source software is a powerful ally for librarians who wish to extend liberal traditions of information access. These systems make the source code freely available for others to view, modify, and adapt; and the very nature of the licensing agreement prevents the software from being appropriated by proprietary vendors. But the open-source movement is more than just a vehicle for librarians to use: its link with library traditions goes much deeper.

Public libraries and open source software both enshrine the same philosophy: to promote learning and understanding through the dissemination of knowledge. Both are pervaded by a sense of community, on the one hand the kind of inter-institutional cooperation exemplified by interlibrary loan and on the other teams of designers and programmers that frequently cross national boundaries.

New trends in information access present librarians in developed countries with difficult and conflicting challenges. Meanwhile, however, the situation in the developing world is dire. Here, traditional publishing and distribution mechanisms have failed tragically.

For example, whereas a US medical library subscribes to about 5,000 journals, the Nairobi University Medical School Library, long regarded as a flagship center in East Africa, last year received just 20 journals. In Brazzaville, Congo, the university has only 40 medical books and a dozen journals, all from before 1993, and the library in a large district hospital consisted of a single bookshelf filled mostly with novels.

Digital Libraries and the Challenge for HCI

Traditional libraries are substantial institutions that occupy physical space, present a physical appearance, and exhibit tangible physical organization. When standing on the threshold of a large bricks-and-mortbar library you gain a sense of presence and permanence that reflects the care taken in building and maintaining the collection inside. Digital libraries, in contrast, are lightweight. But they provide potentially far greater accessibility, which means that they will have even greater social effects.

Once created, they can, without significant institutional support, continue to serve users. They can be distributed throughout most of the developed world over the Internet. In developing countries and remote corners of the developed world they can be circulated on removable media—CD-ROM, DVD, or 100 Gb disk units the size of videocassettes—and updated over radio. Issues of copyright pose difficult problems, but they are manageable.

For example, there is plenty of non-copyright material, or material whose owners are prepared to donate copyright for socially useful purposes, and trends towards more open access to academic and humanitarian information are visible. Not everyone sees digital rights management and the DMCA as the way forward, and in the longer term publishers, to remain viable, will have to investigate alternative revenue models for the information they own.

No wonder international organizations such as the United Nations, along with many smaller *non-government organizations* (NGOs), are keenly interested in digital library technology. Advances in digital library technology are radically lowering the bar for the design and production of richly-organized, coherent, focused collections of information.

Now, anyone with access to sufficient source material can use public-domain software to build large, fullysearchable, collections the size of traditional personal or institutional libraries—in minutes. Let the minutes stretch to hours and the collection can be polished, organized, branded, distributed. It can include fully-illustrated text, images, video, music.

It can present attractively-designed pages with consistent use of icons. Keywords, key phrases, even acronyms and their definitions, can be extracted—automatically—and used to underpin novel means of access. Let the hours stretch to days and metadata can be manually added that permits further levels of organization. Given access to programming skills, creative new facilities that stretch the imagination can be rapidly integrated into the system. All this, one might say, can be done with ordinary Web sites: there is no need for digital library technology.

However, bitter experience has shown that all but the most rudimentary sites do require significant institutional support—for organization and maintenance. The Web is littered with incomplete, unfinished, unmaintained, out-dated, inconsistently-organized, useless information collections.

Just as traditional library cataloging procedures integrate new works into existing collections with minimal overhead so that they immediately become first-class members of the collection, so digital libraries allow new documents to be added completely automatically.

In the case of traditional libraries this is done through the small but nonnegligible overhead of generating a new catalog entry. With ordinary Web sites it requires inserting links manually into index pages and the like, and may involve adding links not only into the new document but also into existing ones that ought to reference it—it's like rewriting the book, and maybe revising all other books in the library too!

In contrast, digital libraries bring access structures instantly and effortlessly up to date whenever new documents are added. The challenge for HCI is to design and build digital library systems that fulfill the potential of digital libraries as a "killer app" for computers in developing countries, which will bring concomitant benefits in almost every other sphere of application.

For the information consumer we need access to information that is guaranteed across space, time, and culture. We need flexible distribution mechanisms for documents, and for information objects of all types, that can be accessed on all computer platforms—including the lowliest. We need a choice of distribution over the Web or on removable media such as CD-ROM or DVD.

Digital libraries can incorporate flexible presentation that caters to individual differences, such as large-font displays or spoken output for the visually impaired. Libraries are places where information is preserved, not rendered obsolete, and digital libraries must instill confidence that information prepared today can be accessed next week, next decade, next century—regardless of technological changes.

An important aspect of digital libraries is their ability to work in local languages, promoting pluralism and reducing the risks of homogeneity. Because language is the vehicle of thought, communication, and cultural identity, this will encourage diversity and strengthen individual cultures. But there is a long way to go: even Unicode is woefully incomplete in certain areas, such as African languages.

Naturally, today's digital library systems focus principally on the reader: the consumer of the material stored in the library's treasure-house. But digital libraries make a more radical, and perhaps ultimately more important, contribution by empowering ordinary users to conceive, assemble, build, and disseminate new information collections themselves.

In principle, modest computing resources are quite sufficient to enable users to build new collections by gathering together material in local files or on the Web; augmenting it with appropriate metadata that supports convenient search and browsing operations; incorporating advanced features like key-phrase extraction, document summarization, and metadata extraction; designing an attractive and functional interface; and publishing the collection on a variety of different media that are suitable for the intended readership.

The HCI challenge is to realise this potential for users—such as most librarians—who have a strong understanding of information and its organization, but no more interest in computers than they have in papermaking technology, last millennium's vehicle for information dissemination.

WHAT ARE DIGITAL LIBRARIES

A digital library is an organized collection of information:

A focused collection of digital objects, including text, video, and audio, along with methods for access and retrieval, and for selection, organization, and maintenance of the collection.

This definition deliberately accords equal weight to user and librarian. The latter functions are often overlooked by digital library proponents, who often work from a technology perspective rather than from the viewpoint of library or information science, but it is precisely these aspects that allow digital libraries to be used to democratize information dissemination.

As a concrete example, consider the Humanity Development Library, a collection of some 1200 authoritative books and periodicals, produced by many disparate organizations—UN agencies and other international organizations—on various areas of human development, from agricultural practice to economic policies, from water and sanitation to society and culture, from education to manufacturing, from disaster mitigation to micro-enterprises.

It contains 160,000 pages and 30,000 images, which if printed would weigh 340 kg, cost $20,000, and occupy a small library book stack. Instead, it takes the form of a digital library and is distributed on a CD-ROM throughout the developing world at essentially no cost.

The Humanity Development Library is produced using the Greenstone software, a freelydistributed open-source project whose aim is to create novel digital library technologies and make them available for others to use. Greenstone digital libraries are arranged in *collections*. A collection comprises several documents, and a library may include several collections, each organized differently.

Collections built with Greenstone offer simple but effective searching and browsing facilities based on metadata and the full text of electronic documents. Each collection is individually designed to take advantage of whatever metadata is available.

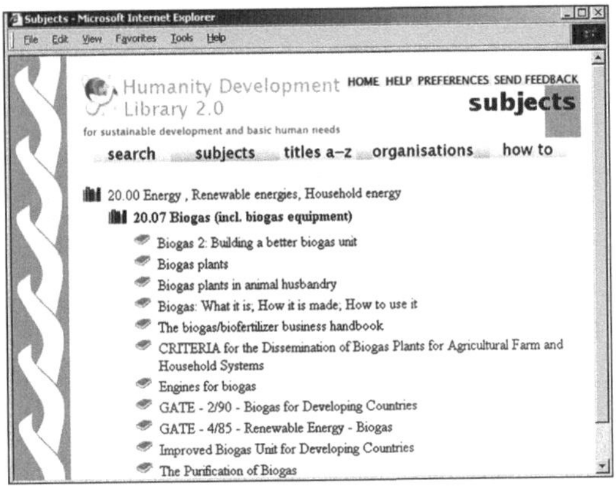

(a)

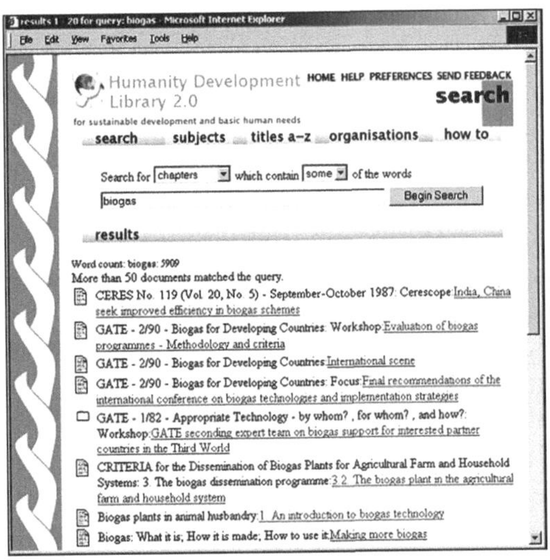

(b)

Fig.1.1 (Contd.)

All collections support full-text searching and most provide several different browsing options, although they differ depending on the collection design and the metadata available. Typically you can search for particular words that appear in the text, or within a section of a document, or within a title or section heading. A variety of interfaces exist for browsing collections by *title, subject, date,* or any other metadata chosen by the collection designer.

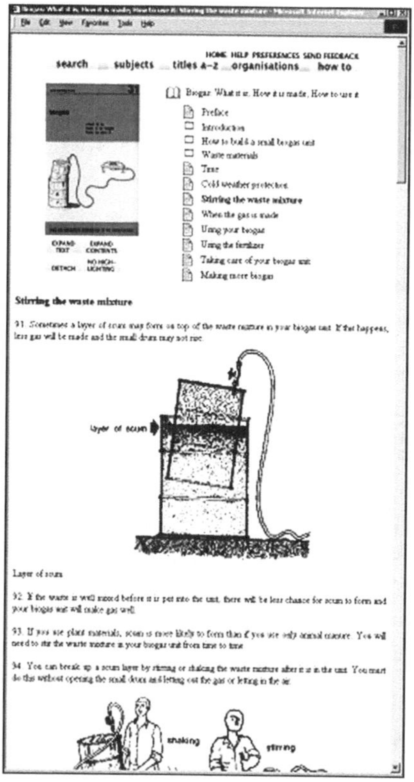

Fig 1.1. The Humanity Development Library: (a) Searching for *Biogas;* (b) Browsing by Subject; (c) Reading a Document.

Figure shows snapshots of the Humanity Development Library. In figure documents are being searched for stages containing the word *biogas.* In figure the collection is being browsed by subject: *Energy, Renewable energies, Household energy.* Pursuing an interest in energy from biogas, the user selects a book by clicking on its book icon. All the icons in the screenshots of figure are clickable.

The navigation bar beneath gives access to the searching and browsing facilities, which differ from one collection to another.

This particular collection can be searched by book, chapter, or section, and browsed by subject, title, organization, and "how to" metadata as indicated by the navigation bar. Documents are presented as Web pages generated by Greenstone from the source material.

In figure, the book's cover is displayed as a graphic on the left, and an automatically constructed table of contents appears at the start of the document. The current focus, *Stirring the waste mixture,* is written in bold in the table of contents; its text starts further down the page.

Incidentally, the material in this collection on building household biogas plans is fascinating, though it is not directly relevant to this chapter. Greenstone collections present documents as automatically-generated Web pages.

This allows documents in different source formats to be presented in a consistent manner, and lets users view the entire collection with a standard Web browser—no special viewing applications are required. However, the collection maintainer may choose to present the original source document instead of, or as well as, the HTML version, and rely on the user's web browser to select a suitable application to display the document. In general, Greenstone deals well with documents and metadata in a wide variety of different formats.

USING DIGITAL LIBRARIES TO DISSEMINATE HUMANITARIAN INFORMATION

Digital libraries provide perhaps the first really compelling *raison d'être* for computing technology in the developing world. Priorities in these countries include health, agriculture, nutrition, hygiene, sanitation, and safe drinking water. Though computers *per se* are not a priority, simple, reliable access to practical information relevant to these basic needs certainly is.

In an article entitled "*The promise of digital libraries in developing countries*" Witten mention ten information collections, available on the Web and CD-ROM, from organizations ranging from UN agencies to small NGOs, in which Greenstone is being used to deliver humanitarian and related information in developing countries.

For example, the Humanity Development Library described is a compendium of practical information aimed at helping reduce poverty, increasing human potential, and giving a practical and useful education. We describe four new ones that have been created recently, and distributed in the same way.

Fig 1.2. A Selection of Recent Humanitarian Digital Library Collections on CD-ROM.

The Researching Education Development library is a project of the *Department for International Development* (DFID), a British government department responsible for promoting development. Its central focus is a commitment to an internationally agreed target of halving the proportion of people living in extreme poverty by 2015.

Associated targets include ensuring universal primary education, gender equality in schooling, and skills development. It works in partnership with other governments and multilateral institutions, with business and the private sector, with civil society and the research community. It has created a CD-ROM library containing many education research papers and other documents.

Each one represents a study or piece of commissioned research on some aspect of education and training in developing countries. The Energy for Sustainable Development library was initiated as part of the outreach phase of the World Energy Assessment, which was initiated jointly by the *United Nations Development Programme* (UNDP), the *United Nations Department of Economic and Social Affairs* (UNDESA), and the *World Energy Council* (WEC), along with funding from the United Nations Foundation. This library contains a broad and valuable collection of 350 documents from UNDP, UNDESA, WEC and many other organizations.

It includes titles that all these organizations have published on the subjects of energy for sustainable development—technical guidelines, journals and newsletters, case studies, manuals, reports, and other training material. The documents are in English, Spanish and French, and one document has Arabic, Russian and Chinese translations as well.

The UNAIDS Library contains publications in the "Best Practice" collection which form a unique resource for those working in planning and practice. It is produced by the Joint United Nations Programme on HIV/AIDS, whose global mission is to lead, strengthen and support a response to the AIDS epidemic that will prevent the spread of HIV, provide care and support for those infected by the disease, reduce the vulnerability of individuals and communities to HIV/AIDS, and alleviate the socioeconomic and human impact of the epidemic.

The Health Library for Disasters is the result of a collaboration between the emergency and disaster programmes of the *World Health Organization* (WHO) and the *Pan American Health Organization* (PAHO), with the participation of many other organizations: the *United Nations High Commissioner for Refugees* (UNHCR), the *United Nations Children's Fund* (UNICEF), the International Strategy for Disaster Reduction (EIRD); the Red Cross Movement (ICRC and IFRC); the SPHERE Project; non-governmental organizations such as OXFAM; and national organizations such as the National Emergency Commission of Costa Rica.

It contains more that 300 technical and scientific documents on disaster reduction and public health issues related to emergencies and humanitarian assistance. A follow-up to the Spanish-language Biblioteca Virtual de Desastres discussed by Witten *et al.*, it includes technical guidelines, field guidelines, case studies, emergency kits, manuals, disaster reports, and other training materials.

UNIVERSAL ACCESS

Universal access to digital libraries presents huge challenges to software engineers and HCI practitioners. The Greenstone digital library software allows us to glimpse some of the issues, although it certainly does not yet effectively address them all.

Platforms and Distribution

Most digital libraries are accessed over the web, using any

web browser. However, in many environments, particularly in developing countries, web access is insufficient and the system must run locally. And if people are to build and control their own libraries, a centralized solution is inadequate: the software must run on their own computers.

Thus digital library systems intended for broad access should run on a wide variety of computer systems, particularly low-end ones. Developed under Linux, the Greenstone server runs on any Windows, Unix, or MacOS/X system. All versions of Windows are supported, from 3.1 up.

Supporting primitive platforms poses substantial challenges of a rather mundane nature: for example, Microsoft compilers no longer support Windows 3.1 and it is necessary to acquire obsolete versions. Under Windows, pre-built collections can be viewed on any system with at least 8 Mb RAM, but collections cannot be built under Windows 3.1/3.11—for this at least a Pentium processor is generally required, except for very small collections.

The fact that Greenstone does not run on early Macintosh systems is a serious drawback in certain environments. In an international cooperative effort established in August 2000 with UNESCO and the Belgium-based Human Info NGO, Greenstone is being distributed widely in developing countries with the aim of empowering users, particularly in universities, libraries, and other public service institutions, to build their own digital libraries.

UNESCO recognizes that digital libraries are radically reforming how information is acquired and disseminated in its partner communities and institutions in the fields of education, science and culture around the world, and particularly in developing countries. Their hope is that this software will encourage the effective deployment of digital libraries to share information and place it in the public domain.

The UNESCO distribution of Greenstone is a CD-ROM that contains the full source code and executable binaries for Windows and Linux, along with all necessary associated software. Full documentation and five demonstration collections are included.

The current CD-ROM is trilingual, with complete interfaces, instructions, and documentation in English, French and Spanish. For those with Web access, the same package is also available for download from the Greenstone Web site, often in a form that is slightly ahead of the CD-ROM version—for example, many other language interfaces are included and full documentation is available in Russian and Kazakh too.

Providing accessibility in different languages is more difficult than one might at first realise. As well as the manuals, installation instructions and installation prompts, the licensing agreement, and the readme files have to be translated too.

Access for Readers

Greenstone collections like the Humanity Development Library can be published as standalone collections on removable media such as CD-ROM, or presented on the Web. CD-ROM is a very practical format in developing countries.

Any Greenstone collection can be converted into a self-contained Windows CD-ROM that includes the Greenstone server software itself and an integrated installation package. The installation procedure has been thoroughly honed to ensure that only the most basic of computer skills are needed to install and run a collection under Windows.

Even standalone Greenstone users interact through a Web browser: Netscape is supplied on each CD-ROM for those who do not already have a browser. In standalone mode the software runs locally but incorporates a Web server so that if the system happens to be connected to a network—say a hospital or school intranet—information is available to other machines that may not possess CD drives.

This happens automatically: no special configuration is necessary. Another difficult engineering challenge is checking for the existence of a network. While installed network software is easily detected, it is hard to determine non-intrusively whether it is operational. Incorrectly installed or configured software is endemic in developing countries, because computers there are often cast-offs whose software is inappropriate to their present environment, yet system support to rectify the problems is unavailable.

It is essential for universal access that such problems are addressed properly and solved satisfactorily without involving the user, even though they are mundane and timeconsuming. Greenstone provides some support for the visually impaired by incorporating a "textual" mode of access that replaces all images by textual prompts. This output is suitable for users with speech synthesizers or other specialized access devices. However, the facility is not well advanced: in particular, we have not yet refined it through usability testing and interface improvement.

Building New Collections

Effective human development blossoms from empowerment rather than gifting. As the Chinese proverb says, "Give a man a fish and he will eat for a day; teach him to fish and he will eat for the rest of his days." Disseminating information originating in the developed world, like the Humanity Development Library, is a useful activity for developing countries.

But a more effective strategy for sustained long-term human development is to disseminate the capability of creating information collections, rather than the collections themselves. This will allow developing countries to participate actively in our information society, rather than observing it from outside.

It will stimulate the creation of new industry. And it will help ensure that intellectual property remains where it belongs, in the hands of those who produce it. Users whose skills resemble those of librarians rather than computer specialists should be able to build and distribute their own digital library collections. As an initial step in this direction, Greenstone includes an interface called the "Collector" that is intended to help people build their own library collections.

Collections may be built and served locally from the user's own web server, or remotely on a shared digital library host. End users can build new collections styled after existing ones from material on the Web or from their local files—or both, and collections can be updated and new ones brought on-line at any time.

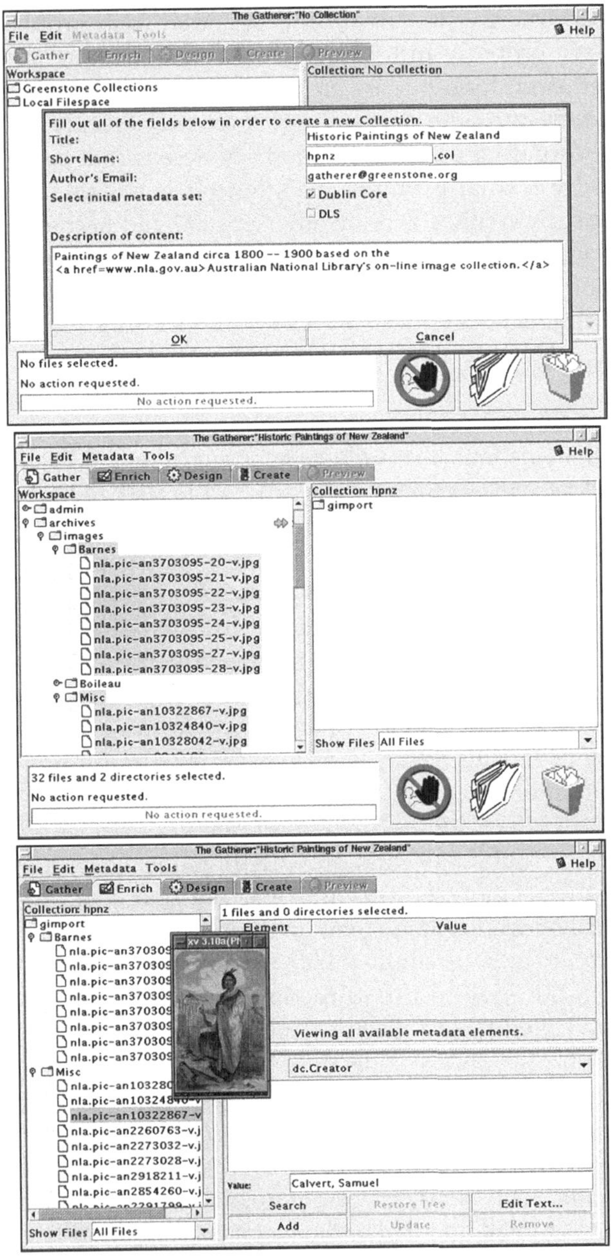

Fig. 1.3 (Contd.)

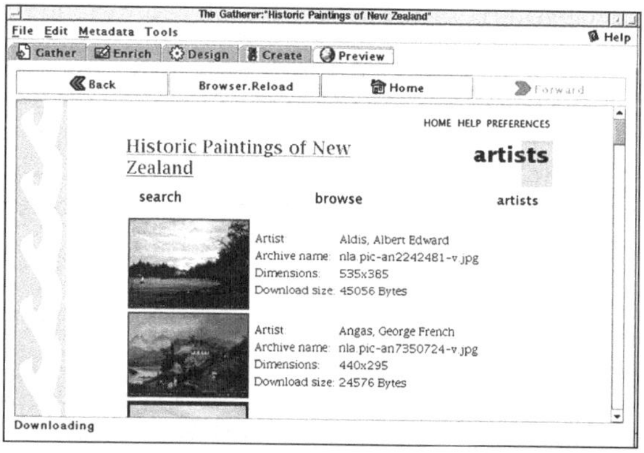

Fig 1.3. Building a Collection with the Gatherer.

The interface, which is intended for non-professional end users, is modeled after widely used commercial software installation packages, frequently called software "wizards"—a term we deprecate because of its appeal to mysticism and connotations of utter inexplicability. We chose this interaction style because it simplifies the choices and presents them very clearly.

Figure 1.3 shows a new Greenstone librarian interface, currently undergoing beta testing by UNESCO at sites in Argentina, India, Kazakhstan, Mexico, and South Africa, which builds on lessons learned from the Collector. It incorporates a great deal of additional functionality, particularly the ability for users to associate metadata with any item or group of items, and to reuse metadata elements without retyping them.

In figure, it is being used to collate a selection of images for a digital library collection, augment these source documents with textual metadata and then build and view the collection. From here, it is a matter of a few further clicks to produce a self-installing CD-ROM version of the collection.

In this illustration the user is developing a digital library collection of historic paintings of New Zealand. The user creates a new collection using the file menu, and a resulting popup window prompts for some general information about the collection. Once the user has filled out this form the main window becomes active. A series of panels guide the user through the processes required to build the collection.

The left-hand pane of the *Gather* panel shows the file system and the right-hand one represents the contents of the collection, initially empty, which the user populates by dragging and dropping files. In figure, the user has moved to the *Enrich* panel and is adding textual metadata to the selected documents. The next two panels, *Design, Create,* help the user structure the collection, control its appearance, and build it.

On completion the result is viewed in the *Preview* panel. Figure shows a page from the newly built collection, in which source documents are alphabetically listed by artist. Shown alongside each thumbnail are the artist's name, its catalog number, image dimensions, and its download size.

The full-size image is shown by clicking on the thumbnail. The user may skip backwards and forwards through the panels using them to augment and enhance the collection, perhaps adding further source documents, editing metadata values, and altering the collection's appearance.

Customization

An important component of access is allowing people to control the appearance of the collections they create. Many who build digital libraries want to brand them to ensure that they with an appropriate personal, institutional, or corporate image, and some can only contemplate software solutions that allow them to do so.

Although Greenstone comes with the standard appearance shown in figure—a distinctive bar down the side of all pages except those that show documents in the library, a green access bar with yellow buttons, etc.—the interface is highly configurable. Greenstone creates all pages that appear on the screen on the fly: none are stored in advance. They are generated using macros, written in a simple language specially designed for the job, that perform textual replacement.

One reason is that Greenstone accommodates a large number of different interface languages and macros help cope with this. All text fragments are couched as macro definitions. To add a new language, just the macro contents need to be translated—no web pages need be reworked.

Every page displayed by the system is passed through a macro interpreter that expands all the macros on the page. The interpreter checks a language variable and uses the macro definitions pertaining to it, which loads the page in the appropriate language.

Macros can have parameters. In this case, the parameter is the language variable: it causes the appropriate text fragment to be used for the macro's expansion. If there is no Arabic version for a particular macro, the interpreter will automatically substitute the default version.

This lets system developers experiment with the interface without having to worry about translating every little bit of new text immediately. Defaulting to English is not ideal—it reflects an Anglo-centric mindset—but it seems better than displaying nothing. Macros are also used to deal with display variables. When-ever a web page contains information that is not known in advance—like the number of documents returned by a search, or the value of a particular metadata item, or the content of a document page—a macro name is used in the page description.

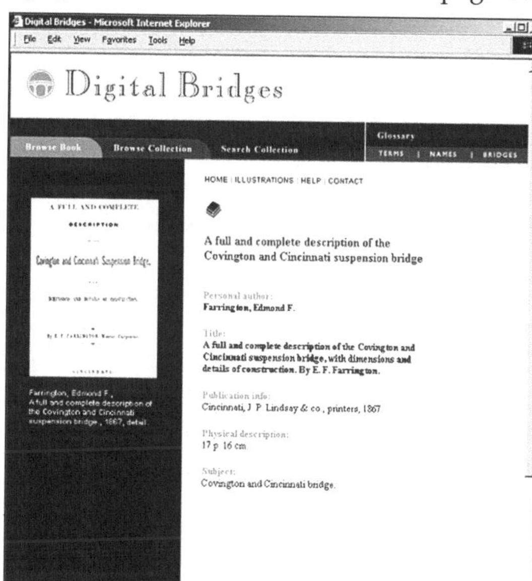

Fig 1.4. A Customised Interface to Greenstone.

Unlike language macros, these macros are *dynamic*: their content is not stored in advance but generated by the system in accordance with the value of the variable in question. Users can completely alter the form of the user interface by rewriting the macro files—or even by writing their own web pages which embed the dynamic macros that generate bits of Greenstone output.

Figure 1.4 shows a Greenstone interface that has been heavily customised by Lehigh University Library, Pennsylvania. The standard Greenstone appearance has been completely obliterated in favour of an in-house style, yet all the Greenstone functionality is available. Figure shows a thumbnail of a book cover on the left, and full bibliographic information on the right. Entering a book displays facsimile images of its pages.

Internationalization

The international Unicode character set is used throughout Greenstone, and documents in any Unicode-supported language and character encoding can be imported. Collections of documents in Arabic, Chinese, Cyrillic, English, French, Spanish, German, Hindi, and Maori are publicly available.

The New Zealand Digital Library Web site hosts many of these, and the Greenstone Web site links to sites that contain further examples. It makes little sense to have a collection whose content is in Chinese or Russian, but whose supporting text—instructions, navigation buttons, labels, images, help text, and so on—are in English.

Consequently, the entire Greenstone interface has been translated into a range of languages, and the interface language can be changed by the user as they browse from the *Preferences* page. All the language fragments in the interface are stored in macro files. These have been translated by Greenstone users in other parts of the world and contributed back to the project.

Figure 1.5 shows an example: a Russian collection. Currently, interfaces are available in Arabic, Czech, Chinese, Dutch, French, Galician, German, Hebrew, Indonesian, Italian, Kazakh, Maori, Portuguese, Russian, Spanish, Turkish, and English. Managing the organizational and software complexity of any comprehensive and evolving open source software system presents a significant challenge.

Fig 1.5. A Russian Digital Library Collection.

However, the challenge is greatly magnified when the interface is available in different languages, for enhancements to the software and changes to the interface must be faithfully reflected in each language version. No single person knows all interface languages; no single person knows about all modifications to the software—indeed there is likely no overlap at all between those who translate the interface and those who build the software.

Currently, Greenstone has about twenty interface languages and there are around 600 linguistic fragments in each interface, ranging from single words like *search*, through short phrases like *search for, which contain, of the words*, to sentences like *More than... documents matched the query*, to complete paragraphs like those in the on-line help text.

Maintaining the interface in many different languages is a logistic nightmare. The solution adopted by Greenstone is to incorporate a language translation facility, which allows authorized people to update the interface in specified languages. A standard version control system is used to manage software change, and from this the system automatically determines which language fragments need updating and presents them to the human translator.

2

Historical Overview of Library Development

GROWTH OF LIBRARIES IN INDIA

GROWTH AND DEVELOPMENT OF ORIENTAL LIBRARIES IN INDIA

Libraries have always had a pivotal role in the storage, processing, and dissemination of information. Some may serve general needs, but special libraries serve the needs of a particular community of users. Among special libraries, Oriental libraries hold an important place because they preserve the cultural heritage of a nation or a civilization.

Oriental Libraries

"Oriental Libraries" are those libraries that have literature pertaining to Oriental studies and languages. "Oriental" in this context refers to the ancient Near East, including India, Persia, and ancient Arabia, among other places, and the languages and literatures of those places and peoples.

Growth and Development

India is a vast repository of different cultures, both because it was invaded by a number of foreign countries and peoples, and because of its contacts with people from the East. The languages from those Eastern countries are part of Indian literature. The literature in those Eastern languages created India's Oriental libraries.

Their history can be traced back to the Vedic period, when the written literature was kept in Ashrams or Gurukuls. Gurukuls were mostly located peaceful forest environments. With the passage of time, Gurukuls were also established in cities.

Jain and Buddhist Era

Taxila was one of the famous educational centres where students came from different parts of the country. Varanasi also distinguished itself by having a large number of Gurukulas. During this period, the literature was preserved in the Sutra style of composition.

Buddhist and Jain Monastries acted as repositories of knowledge, for religious literature as well as other types. Monastic Oriental Libraries were also called Viharas. Over time, these Viharas developed into institutions of higher learning. A federation of Viharas constituted a Mahavihara, which was a larger educational institutional institution.

Nalanda Mahavihara is the best example. Fa-Hien, a Chinese traveller, also found a number of monastaries in India. Kanyakubja, Sravasti, Kusunagara, Vaisali, and Patliputra were centres of Oriental literature according to Fa-Hien. Hiuen-Tsang, another Chinese traveller, visited India during A.D. 629-645.

He left a detailed account of his visit, which gives us significant information about Buddhist educational institutions possessing a rich variety of Eastern literature. Taxila was a center of learning in Ancient India and a large number of people from all over the world and the subcontinent itself visited this place to gain knowledge.

Literature related to medicine and archery enriched the library at Taxila. Rahula Sankrityayana, Angiris set up a seminary with a Granthakuti attached to it at Taxila, which later flourished in to an academy or university. Nalanda University is the best known of ancient India's universities. It has been called the treasure house of information by European archeologists. The information there helped locate Buddhist shrines in India.

It is believed that King Kumara Gupta built the first monastery at Nalanda to train Buddhist monks. Nalanda University was an expansion of this seminary. King Buddha Gupta, Jagatha Gupta, Baladitya, and Vijra made additions and expansions to the building.

There were three large libraries with vast amount of literature in Oriental languages on subjects such as science, medicine, astrology, fine arts, literature. The University of Valabhi was built by the Maitraka Kings during the years A.D 475-775. Its library had a variety of Eastern literature. This great university and its library lasted until the 12th century, when they were completely destroyed by Arab invaders.

Odantapuri University was founded by King Gopala and was a well-known center of learning. It had a library that was rich in Brahmanical and Buddhist works. Mohammad Bakhtiyar Khilji destroyed this monastic university along with its library. Somapuri also possessed a wealth of Oriental literature, but it was destroyed by fire in the middle of the 11th century.

Vikramasila monastery, built by King Dharmapala, had a variety of literature on metaphysics, tantras, grammar, ritualism, and logic. The library fulfilled the demands of outsiders, especially those from Tibet, by providing them copies of manuscripts in a most liberal way. Another University with a significant Oriental collection, especially in Tantric Buddhism, was Jagaddala, founded by King Ramapala.

Another monastery with a rich wealth on different aspects of Oriental literature was Kanheri University, built during the reign of Amoghavarsha. By the 10th century, the corpus of Jain literature had increased many times, and Jain monks had contributed substantially to nearly all branches of knowledge known at that time. The Jayendra monastery of Kashmir had a good library where the Chinese traveller Hiuen–Tsang spent two years copying manuscripts.

Similarly, he spent fourteen months at the Chinapati monastery. Several Hindu kings and their ministers, who flourished between 10th and 12th centuries AD, are credited with establishing libraries and supporting the library movement. Among them was King Bhoja of Dhara, who flourished in the

11th century, and was a distinguished scholar with a rich library. King Kumarapaladeva of the Chaulakyas is said to have established 21 Jain Libraries. He kept a copy of Kalpasutra written in golden ink in each one of them.

Mughal Empire

When the Muslims established their rule in India at the beginning of the 13th century, Muslim emperors paid special attention to libraries, taking care to establish libraries in educational institutions. They constructed no separate library buildings; rather, books were deposited and preserved in educational institutions, mosques, and Khangahs.

Many Muslim rulers were from the East, and they helped enrich libraries with Oriental literature. Paper began be used as a writing material in the 12th century, and this helped book production in this periods. Mughal sovereigns and their courtiers were educated and accomplished, and some maintained personal libraries.

The Muslim sovereigns collected and preserve the Vedas, the *Ramayana*, and other Hindu religious books. They also translated a variety of books in Hindi in to Persian and Arabic, and helped disseminate Hindu art and culture. After the establishment of Sultans of Delhi in 1202, a new period in the history of Oriental libraries came in to existence. These minor Muslim rulers and nobles encouraged Islamic learning and established *maktabs* (primary schools), *madrasas* (schools of higher learning), libraries, and mosques.

They encouraged Arabic and Persian literatures in all branches of learning, and enriched Oriental literature in the libraries. They gave shelter and protection to scholars, who brought literature from other parts of the world to India. The Library of Khwajah Nizam-ud-din Auliya was an important Oriental library.

It was the property of the *Waqf* (religious board) and was open to every man of letters. During the reign of the Khilji dynasty the number of Oriental libraries increased. Jala-ud-din Khiljee established the Imperial Library at Delhi and appointed Amir Khusru as its librarian.

The Tughluq Dynasty opened a new chapter in the history of Oriental libraries in India. Mohammad Tughluq built one thousand madrasas, each with a library with collections in Arabic and Persian. Humayun ascended the throne in 1530 and a library known as Khan-i-Tilism.

Humayun's library played a significant role in Mughal history. Akbar, the greatest of Mughal emperors maintained a very rich library. He added a sizable number of books, obtained from his conquest, from libraries in Gujarat, Jaunpur, Kashmir, Bihar, Bengal, and the Deccan.

His library was unique in its collection of rare books, among which was the Persian *Divan of Human Shah.* By the time of Akbar's grandson, Shah Jahan, the library was a complex organization with a large staff, and headed by Nazim, a noble of the court. In Kashmir, a picture of the first library is found in the Shrine of Hazrat Bulbul Shah, which was established by Muslims.

A magnificient monastery and mosque were constructed by the emperor of Kashmir, Sultan Sadruddin, for Hazrat Bulbul Shah. A library was attached to this mosque. Amir Kabir Syed Hamdani, a theologian and scholar had a well established personal library that contained Oriental literature. He established a number of libraries in Kashmir which added to the wealth of the Indian Oriental libraries.

The Sultans of Kashmir had given funds to establish madrasas and libraries. Each madrasa had a library. Sultan Zain-ul-Abedin-ul constructed a library which historians tell was one of the best in the world. Among the other libraries built by Budshah, Darul-ul-Uloom Nausherah was the best.

Another library, by the name of Madrasa-i-Sher, was built by Budshah near modern Islamabad. During the Chak Sultanate many libraries thrived and brought Oriental literature to the limelight. Akbar conquered Kashmir in 1587 and established many madrasas and libraries there. In Gujrat and Malwa, a number of libraries were introduced by Ahmad Shah I and Dilawar Khan.

Shah Jahan, like his predecessors, patronized learning and education and built a library with a rich collection of Arabic and

Persian manuscripts. Dara Shikkoh, Aurangzeb, and Bahadur Shah Zafar also contributed to the development of Oriental libraries. Mughal rule was a period of literary excellence. Most of the emperors were themselves scholars, and also extended their patronage to scholarship and learning.

Other Kingdoms

There were kingdoms in other parts of India that also had libraries enriched by Oriental literature. The kingdoms of Bahmani and Deccan had independent kings who reigned for 340 years, and who were patrons of learning, as were the Bahmani kings, who continued their rule up to AD 1526 and had an empire that stretched from coast to coast.

They founded many colleges and libraries. Ahmad Shah built a magnificient college near Gulbarga. Muhammad Shah Bahmani II built another imposing college at Bidar that is one of the many beautiful remains of the grandeur of the Bahmanis. All these colleges had libraries that possessed an enormous amount of Oriental literature.

Arabian and Iranian literature brought by visitors and travellers were added to the libraries of Bahmanis. The Urdu language was at its zenith during the reign of Firoz Shah Bahmani, and a vast amount of Urdu literature enriched the Bahmani Libraries.

The library of Gesudaraj was distinguished among the libraries of Deccan. Books on Sufism and religion were available in this library. The emperors of Qutub Shahi also established a good number of libraries during their reign, and a vast amount of literature in Persian was included. Tipu Sultan, son of Haider Ali and emperor of Mysore established a number of libraries.

"Zaimul-Umoor" was the great university of Seringa Patnam in his reign. He collected books from many countries including Europe. The library had a copy of the Holy Quran which was written by the hand of Aurangzeb Alamgir. It is estimated that the library had nearly 2,000 volumes of Persian, Arabic, and Hindi manuscripts from all branches of Islamic literature.

After the downfall of the Mughals, and with the invasion of Ahmad Shah Abdali, the literary wealth of the Indian libraries was looted away. In 1857, after the Sepoy mutiny, thousands of books were destroyed and thousands of important, valuable, and rare books were siphoned to England.

British and other Europeans

The growth and development of Oriental libraries was regenerated again during European and British rule. The interest shown by the British and European scholars in Oriental Learning and Indology, along with the social, cultural and religious movements spearheaded by eminent Indians, resulted in new Oriental libraries. These institutions established libraries for Oriental scholarship. The result of this renaissance is a number of special libraries devoted to Oriental and Indological collections in various parts of the country.

Rampur Raza Library, very rich in Indo-Islamic studies and arts, was created by Nawab Faizullah Khan in 1794, and has tremendous manuscript wealth. One can find manuscripts in Arabic, Persian, Urdu, Sanskrit, Sinhali, Tamil, Kannada, and other Oriental languages.

The Asiatic Society Library, Kolkata, a premier and leading oriental institutions of the country was established in 1784 by Sir William Jones. Colonel Mackenzie, an Englishman and an engineer by profession established an Oriental Library by the name of " *Government Oriental Manuscript Library* (GOML) " in Chennai.

Contemporary Libraries

Khuda Baksh Oriental Library was founded in 1842 by Maulvi Khuda Baksh Khan, who donated his entire personal collection. Since 1977 it has been issuing regularly a multi-lingual research quarterly *Khuda Baksh Library Journal.* The library has been recognized as a research center by seven Indian universities. The collection has a rich repository of Persian and Arabic manuscripts. Maulana Azad Library, Aligarh Muslim University was initially founded as "Anglo Oriental College (MAOC) at Aligarh in 1875 and raised to the status of a university in 1920.

The personal collection of Maulana Azad also enriches the library. The library has a total collection of over 1 million volumes and 14,571 manuscripts. The Maulana Azad Library has the largest collection of Urdu books in the Indian subcontinent, which is perhaps largest in the world as well.

The collection includes:

* Urdu
* Arabic
* Persian
* Sanskrit
* Hindi
* Sir Syed Collection
* Gandhian Collection
* Aligarh Collection
* Thesis Collection
* Archives
* Microfiche
* Manuscripts

Hakim Mohammad Syed Library, Jamia Hamdard, New Delhi is a leading university founded in 1906.

It has a well known Oriental library, which has a number of special collections:

* Nazaria Collection
* Abdul Sattar Siddiqui Collection
* Maulana Abdul Salam Niazi Collection
* Jaffri Collection
* Shafi Ahmad Collection
* Dr Tanveer Alvi Collection

The library has 4,500 rare manuscripts. Osmania University Library was established in 1918 and is considered seventh oldest in India, the third oldest in South India, and the first to be established in state of Hyderabad.

The library has a collection of rare books and manuscripts including Palm Leaf manuscripts. The National Library of India, which came in to existence in 1948, is the largest library in India. Previously it was known as the Imperial Library which was formed in 1891 by combining a number of Secretariat libraries.

It has a wide range of collections in a variety of national and international languages. A good number of Arabic and Persian documents are also available here. The Oriental library initiative that took place in ancient India reached its zenith in the period when the British and other Europeans came to India. The Mughals also contributed a great deal to the development of Oriental libraries. Eventually, their extravagant ways caused the libraries to deteriorate, but social and political conditions eventually led to better libraries with larger collections.

ACADEMIC LIBRARIES IN INDIA: A HISTORICAL STUDY

Research in library history in India has remained largely neglected area which has resulted into availability of very limited and scanty literature. Commenting on the status of library history in India, Donald G. Davis, Jr. of the University of Texas at Austin, writes that "although a core literature on Indian library history exists, it has many imbalances and gaps. The scholars are very dispersed in their interests and their geographical location. With one person rarely contributing more than one work. There is little pattern to existing research efforts."

In this context, the role of historian happens to be much more crucial and significant to make an assessment of the growth and development of libraries in India, the factors responsible for their development and the impact of those factors on the library progress. Rajgopalan, in his 1987 presidential address to the Indian Library Association rightly said, "it is generally acknowledged that our libraries are underutilized in relation to investments being made in them.

Non-use and low-use of libraries amount to wastage of facilities being made available. Maybe the literacy rate, lack of reading habits, etc., are the causes for low use from the side of patrons... User education programmes must be organized by libraries in a way that libraries are fully utilized." He further remarked that, "if library historians would address the roots and trends of library issues, they would provide a valuable service to the profession and society."

The Father of Library and Information Science in India,Padmashri Dr. S.R. Ranganathan while giving a radio talk in April 1956 said: "an account of the libraries in the first four periods must necessarily depend upon the historical research. This has not yet been done. The library profession is too small in India to spare a person to fill up this antiquarian gap. Those trained in the scientific method of tracing history are too preoccupied with dynastic and political history to spare sufficient time for cultural history in general and library history in particular."

Thus, an historical study of the growth and development of academic libraries in India, is a desideratum, the fulfilment of which should go a long way in removing the imbalances and gaps. Such a study becomes significant not only in view of the tremendous activity concerning the growth and development of libraries in India, but also because their growth has been shaped in the first phase by the phenomena that have shaped the historical course of this period and, secondly, the rise of library as an important instrument in the advancement of knowledge and socio-economic transformation.

Source Material for Writing History of Libraries

For the purpose of scientific writing of history of libraries, an understanding of the nature of existing source material and knowing the art of using it is essential. The sources for writing the history are available in Pali, Sanskrit, Chinese, Arabic, Persian and European Languages and most of them have been translated into English. These exist in various formats, such as Manuscripts, inscriptions, copper plates etc.

They are either indigenous or foreign. The contribution of foreign travelogues such as Tibetan, Chinese, Muslim, Portuguese, English and other Europeans is highly useful. Some noteworthy foreign travelogues are Itsing, Fahien, Hieun Tsang, Alberuni, Ibn Batuta, Minhaj, Firishta, Badauni, Afif, bernier, mandelso, Manrique de Lara, Martin, Count Noer.

In addition to the contribution of the travelogues, the contribution of historians like Henry M. Eliot, John Dawson, Stanley Lane-Pool, Ishwari Prasad, R.C. Majumdar, Jadunath Sarkar, V.D. Mahajan, Mohammed Muhammed Zubair, J.S. Sarma and N.N. Law etc. is also significant.

Though scanty, yet there are articles written by the library professionals on history of libraries. A few efforts have also been made for conduct of research in the area of history of libraries and such like works have been consulted for the purpose of writing this paper.

University Libraries in Ancient India

In the Vedic age instructions were imparted "orally, without the medium of books." Taxila from 700 B.C. to AD 300 was considered to be the most respected seat of higher learning and education in India but still there is no evidence found so far in the archaeological excavations at Taxila that there had been a good library system in the Taxila University.

Fa-Hien noticed such libraries at Jetavana monastery at Sravasti. In A.D. 400, there came into being one of the biggest known universities, the Nalanda University, which by A.D 450. became a renowned seat of learning, its fame spreading beyond the boundaries of India.

Nalanda near Patna grew to be the foremost Buddhist monastery and an educational centre. Most of what we know of the Nalanda University during the 6th and the 7th centuries A.D. is due to the accounts left by Hiuen-tsang, who lived in the institution for three years in the first half of the 7th century, and I-tsing who also stayed there for ten years towards the latter part of the same century.

Information on the Nalanda University Library is also found in the Tibetan accounts, from which we understand that the library was situated in a special area known by the poetical name the Dharmaganja, which comprised three huge buildings, called the Ratnasagara, the Ratnodadhi and the Ratnaranjaka of which the Ratnasagara was a ninestoried building and housed the collection of manuscripts and rare sacred works like Prajnaparamita Sutra etc.

The library at Nalanda had a rich stock of manuscripts on philosophy and religion and contained texts relating to grammar, logic, literature, the Vedas, the Vedanta, and the Samkhya philosophy, the Dharmasastras, the Puranas, Astronomy, Astrology and Medicine. The University of Nalanda and its library flourished down to the 12th century A.D. until Bakhtiyar Khalji sacked it in A.D. 1197-1203. and set fire to the establishment of Nalanda.

The world famous universities, such as, the Vikramasila, the Vallabhi and the Kanchi were coming up in other parts of the country during the period from the 5th century A.D. to the 8th century A.D. All these universities possessed rich libraries and in the hall containing such books there used to be an image of the goddess Saraswati with a book in her hand.

The Nalanda and the Vikramshila universities were under the control of the king Dharmapala. He founded the Vikramshila monastery in the 8th century A.D. It had a rich collection of texts in the Sanskrit, the Prakrit and the Tibetan languages.

Regarding the library of the university, the *Tabaqat-i-Nasiri* informs us that there were great number of books on the religion of Hindus there; and when all these books came under the observation of the Mussalamans, they summoned, a number of Hindus that they might give them information regarding the import of these books; but the whole of the Hindu community was killed in the war.

Muslim vandalism caused the disappearance of the excellent collection at Vikramashila. The Jaggadal Vihara in Varendrabhumi was also an important centre of learning with considerable collection of the reading material. It was established by the king Kampala, who ruled from A.D. 1084 to 1130.

The provision of facilities for reading, writing, editing and translating manuscripts shows that this library was in no way less than its contemporary libraries in importance. Though not as large as the library of Nalanda, it abounded in private collection of texts.

Likewise Mithila had been famous for its scholars since the days of Rajrishi Janaka and had a rich collection of various commentaries on the different branches of the Hindu *Shastras.* The library of its university played an important role in teaching and learning. A needle *(Shalaka)* was pierced through the manuscript on the subject of the student's specialization and he was expected to explain the last page pierced.

In this way the student's all-round mastery of the subject was tested. Mithila continued to enjoy its all India importance in the field of learning till the end of the 15th century AD. The university at Sompuri, like that of Vikramshila, occupied a significant position since the days of Dharampala.

Like Nalanda, this university also had its own library. Atisa Dipankar, a noted scholar, lived there. He with the help of other scholars, translated into the Tibetan the *Madhyamkaratnapradipa* of Bhavaviveka. This university was destroyed by fire in the middle of the 11th century A.D. Efforts were made by the monk Vipulsrimitra to renovate the university but it could not regain its past glory.

At a time when Nalanda was famous for its *Mahayana* courses of study, the Maitrakakings provided their patronage to the Mahavihara of Vallabhi. This university was famous for its *Hinayana* studies. The fact that this university had a good library is supported by a reference in a grant of Guhasena, dated A.D. 559, wherein a provision was made out of the royal grant for the purchase of books for the library.

This important seat of learning at Kanheri, on the West Coast, flourished during the reign of Amoghavarsha in the 9th century A.D. The library occupied a significant position within the establishment, and the donors provided money to buy books for the library.

The last of the famous seats of learning in Eastern India was Navadwipa in Bengal. It reached its height of glory from 1083 to A.D. 1106 as a centre of intellectual excellence as well as its rich library facilities, when Lakshman Sen, a king of Gauda, made it his capital. However, this library was also destroyed along with the centre by Bakhtiyar Khalji.

Situated in South India at Amaravati, on the banks of the Krishna, the Nagarjuna Vidyapeeth flourished in about 7th century A.D. Its library housed in the top floor of the five storyed building of the university had an enormous collection on the Buddhist philosophy, particularly of the *Mahayana* school that Nagarjuna had founded, science and medicine.

There is enough archaeological evidence that supports the existence of this 7th century university and its library. The enormity of the collection in this library is borne out by the fact that it not only had works on the Buddhist literature and the *Tripitakas,* but also works on several branches of scientific knowledge, such as, Botany, Geography, Mineralogy and Medicine. It was a great attraction for scholars from the different parts of India and from countries, like, China, Burma and Ceylon.

University Libraries in Medieval India

The existence of academic libraries during the medieval period of Indian history is not known, though the Muslim rulers did patronize libraries in their own palaces. A lone exception, however, was a library attached to a college at Bidar, having a collection of 3000 books on different subjects. Aurangzeb got this Library transferred to Delhi to merge it with his palace library. During the medieval period, due to Muslim invasions and political troubles, the powerful empires and kingdoms of Indian rulers fell one by one. This affected higher education and the development of academic libraries as well.

Libraries in Modern India

During the British rule in India, number of academic institutions were established by the East India Company, and by the Christan missionaries. Some of the worth mentioning events which led to the growth and development of higher education in India during this period were the establishment of the Calcutta College in 1781, Jonathan Duncan, then a British agent, founded the Benaras Sanskrit College in 1792. The Calcutta Fort William College was founded in 1800. All these colleges were having their own libraries.

The Charter Act of 1813, the foundation of Fort William and Serampore Colleges, Calcutta, Madras and Bombay universities and their libraries, Hunter, Raleigh and Calcutta University Commissions, library training programmes, the establishment of Inter University Board, Sargent Report and appointment of the University Grants Committee, the establishment of Madras University, University of Bombay, University of Calcutta and their libraries, the constitution of Inter-University Board, the appointment of Hartog Committee, the Montague-Chelmsford reforms of 1919, the Government of India Act of 1935, and the Sargent Committee Report etc. laid foundation for establishment of libraries in various parts of the country.

The Fort William College was founded in Calcutta on 18th August 1800 by the Marquis of Welleselay, the Governor-General of India during 1798-1805. Reverend David Brown, Provost of the college was instrumental in setting up the library which had a well rounded collection of Eastern manuscripts.

In the absence of adequate financial support, the library could not survive for long and in 1835 it was decided to close the library and its valuable collection was transferred to the Asiatic Society Library in Calcutta between 1835-39. The Charter Act of 1813 passed by the British Parliament gave the East India Company complete responsibility for educating Indians.

The establishment of C.M.S. College in Kottayam, Hindu College in Calcutta in 1816 and Raven Shaw College in Cuttack in 1816 was the immediate result of the Charter Act 1813. These and other colleges came into existence thereafter had their own libraries the day they were established. Serampore College during this period was founded by the Danes in 1818 and the King of Denmark in 1927 agreed to give this college an academic status by providing equivalence to the Danish Universities with power to confer degrees.

The library of this college too was established along with its foundation and at a later stage the college was given affiliation to the University of Burdwan for the purpose of conferring degrees. The 7th March 1835 decision of the British Indian Government to promote English literature and sciences in India was resulted into the spread of number of colleges in India and by 1839 there were over forty colleges with attached libraries in the British territory in India.

For their establishment, lots of money was made available by the Indians in the form of donations. In 1840 Presidency College was founded in Madras, followed by a medical college in Bombay in 1845. This progress in education was instrumental in establishing universities in India.

The Charles Wood dispatch of 1854 popularly known as the 'Magna Carta of English Education' in India also paved the way for the establishment of the universities in the presidency towns. Sir John Colville introduced the Bill to establish universities in India and it was passed by the Governor General of India Lord Dalhousie on 24th January 1857, paved the way for the foundation of three universities based on the London Universities Model in the Presidency towns of Calcutta, Madras and Bombay.

Indian Education Commission, popularly known as Hunter Commission was appointed by the British Indian Government in 1882 to study the progress of education under the new policy adopted in 1854 by the East India Company and transferred to the Crown and accepted by the Secretary of State in 1859. Sir William W. Hunter in his report had clearly stated that the conditions of the libraries was in a very poor state and declared them "hardly creditable." The Commission paid special attention to the colleges and their libraries and other facilities.

The direct result of the Commission was the establishment of Panjab University, Lahore and Allahabad University in 1882 and 1887 respectively but still the condition of the education and libraries remained in a poor state.

The Raleigh Commission 1902 appointed by Lord Curzon to investigate the conditions and prospects of the Indian universities and to recommend measures to improve their constitution and working and standards of teaching also paid special attention to the academic libraries and found that, "the library is little used by graduates and hardly at all by other students." Further, the Commission commented, "In a college where library is inadequate or ill arranged, the students have no opportunity of forming the habit of independent and intelligent reading."

Thus, the Commission specifically recommended that reference services must be made an integral part of all libraries in colleges and universities, and that one of the prerequisite conditions for the grant of university affiliation to a college be the accessibility of students to the library of the institution.

The recommendations of the Raleigh Commission were included in the Universities Act of 1904 and provided the power to all universities to require that all colleges applying for affiliation maintain proper libraries, equipment, library building, and lend books to all students but the situation and the status of libraries could not be improved much simply because the recommendations made by the Commission and the provisions made in the act could not be implemented properly.

The Calcutta University Commission popularly known as Sadler Commission was appointed by the government in 1917 to study the situation and the status of education in the country and to make recommendations to solve the existing problems.

The Commission noticed that "one of the greatest weaknesses of the existing system is the extraordinarily unimportant part which is played by the library" and found that "in some colleges the library is regarded not as an essential part of teaching equipment but merely as a more or less useless conventional accessory." The Commission made the recommendations regarding the libraries that college libraries be strengthened and that training should be given to the students and occasionally to the teachers about use of the library.

One of the immediate result of the Calcutta University Commission was the establishment of a few new teaching-cum-residential universities at Patna in 1917, Osmania in Hyderabad in 1918, Dacca, Aligarh, and Lucknow in 1921, Delhi in 1922 and Nagpur in 1923 and all of them were established along with the establishment of libraries as an integral part of the university system.

As stated earlier, the impact of the Commission could very well be seen in the establishment of several universities along with their libraries. This was the period when in the libraries scenario, a person appeared who at a later stage turned the entire scene and become the father of library science in India.

The man was none other than Dr. S.R. Ranganathan. The University of Madras appointed Dr. S.R. Ranganathan as its Librarian in 1924. He was trained at the University of London Library School before joining his duties at Madras. Things did change rapidly after his joining. For example, he introduced the lending and reference services at the Madras University Library and extended the library hours for the benefit of the readers.

Whereas the hours had previously been 7 a.m. to 4 p.m., they were changed to 7 a.m. to 6 p.m. He delivered a series of lectures to about two thousand teachers at the conference of the South Indian Teachers' Union in 1929 regarding the use and importance of the library services.

The Madras Library Association started a summer course in librarianship and the lectures for this course were mainly delivered by Dr. Ranganathan. The main objective of the course in its beginning was to spread the ideas of the value of good library services and modern library methods among potential users of the library. The budget of the university library of Madras had been very poor from the beginning and it was really a difficult task to manage, run and administer the library effectively within it.

Ranganathan brought this poor financial position to the notice of the then Chief Minister, Dr. P. Subbaroyan, when he delivered a speech during an educational conference held at Madras in 1926. In his speech, Ranganathan "gave a graphic account of the library network in Europe and the United States of America and compared it with the poor, appalling facilities existing in India.... added that paucity of funds prevented him developing his library."

The Chief Minister was highly impressed by Ranganathan's speech and promised to give more State help to the University Library. Its immediate result was a grant of rupees 6,000 which was added to the annual grant from the State, and, in addition, rupees 100,000 in lump sum were sanctioned by the Madras State Government in the same year to buy books and periodicals in pure sciences, humanities, and social sciences.

Provision was also made for additional grants to the library, as and when new departments of study and research were established. In the words of Ranganathan, "This was the first time when such a forward financial step in the history of the university libraries in India was taken in the second quarter of the 20th century."

The University of Madras library made a good start under Ranganathan's effective leadership and administration. In 1930, the library had five well-trained reference librarians to help the readers, and they "carried the work to a high pitch of efficiency."

This was the first time in the history of Indian libraries that a special reference service was introduced in a university library. The library collection increased to 93,000 volumes in 1935 and on September 3, 1936, the library was shifted to its first new and permanent functional building. By 1944, when Ranganathan resigned from the position of the Librarian, to become the University Librarian at the *Banaras Hindu University* (BHU), the collection of the Madras University Library had augmented to 1,20,000 volumes.

The contribution of Dr. Ranganathan to the growth and development of libraries in general and the Madras University Library in particular is undoubtedly tremendous and unforgettable. It will not be wrong to say that the Library School of Madras and the Madras University Library were the laboratories of Ranganathan to propound his ideas in library science and to test them practically.

Some of the important and major ideas of Ranganathan were the Five Laws of Library Science which were enunciated by him in 1924, and their formulation and publication in 1929 and 1931 respectively. These laws are still considered a unifying theory for all library practices and services, and set of guidelines for the dynamic development and study of library science as a whole.

The University of Bombay Library received a special grant of rupees 50,000 from the Central Government in 1939 to strengthen its collection for graduate studies. During the period from 1931 to 1939, a few more special grants were given to the library for its collection development. A very special grant of rupees 10,000 was given by Kikabhai and Maniklal, sons of the late Premchand Roychand, in 1931 to replace the electric clock of the library tower.

The collection, which stood at 4,504 volumes in 1900, rose to 70,000 in 1939 and 73,582 in 1947. Though higher education and academic libraries made some progress during the first quarter of the present century, yet their growth and development was not very well organized.

Academic institutions and their growth after 1916 created a few problems also and the general feeling was that the "quality of Education was being sacrificed for quantity." While such a situation prevailed, the Indian Statutory Commission, popularly known as the Simon Commission, was appointed by the Government in 1927 to study the conditions prevailing in India.

The Simon Commission appointed an Auxiliary Committee to look into the growth of education in India. Sir Philip Hartog, a former member of the Calcutta University Commission, and a former Vice-Chancellor of the University of Dacca, was appointed its Chairman.

In its report, submitted in 1929, the Committee stated that "the dispersal of resources for university teaching among a number of colleges had made it difficult to build up university libraries of the type required for advanced work both at the Honours and the research stage majority of the university libraries were inadequate and all needed great additions."

In addition to want of books, libraries also lacked good current periodicals in their collections. The Committee also made a special note of the low academic standards in many colleges and universities and the "unhealthy competition for candidates between neighbouring universities".

This report, however, did not offer any comprehensive, detailed, and realistic solutions to the problems. In 1935, Ministry of Education was formed in each province, as per the provisions of the dyarchy in the Montague-Chelmsford Reforms of 1919, supplemented by those of the new Government of India Act of 1935.

The Ministry of Education in India requested the Central Advisory Board of Education in 1944 to survey the educational conditions in the country. The Board's report, known as the Sargeant Report, after its Chairman, Sir Sargeant, the Educational Advisor to the Government of India, came up with a master-plan for the development of education in the post-World War II India. Its terms of reference covered education at all levels-primary, secondary, and higher.

The Indian universities, as they existed then, despite many admirable features, did not fully satisfy the requirements of a national system of education. During the British rule, several committees and commissions set up periodically, paved way for the foundation of several colleges and the establishment of many universities and in many cases the libraries were also established along with them.

It is also true that as compared to the first two decades the development of university libraries after 1924 did make better progress but the college libraries were still neglected and were struggling to get their recognition.

There were only 12 universities in India in 1924 and their number swelled to 18 by the time India got freedom in 1947. In fact, the academic libraries during the British rule had no significance in the academic life of the institutions of higher education and the pivotal role that can be played by the academic libraries in the life of the institutions could very well be seen in the policy statement of higher education of the free India and the fact was also proven when at the time of national reconstruction, the importance of libraries in teaching and research was recognized, and libraries received the early attention of the Government of India.

Academic Libraries in India after Independence

The actual process for the development of university libraries in India can be said to have been set in motion with the appointment of the University Education Commission presided over by Dr. S. Radhakrishnan and its recommendations, such as, annual grants, open access system, working hours, organization of the library, staff, steps to make students book conscious and the need to give grants to teachers to buy books.

The section on libraries of the report opens with a powerful statement on the importance of libraries in university education and states, "teaching is a cooperative enterprise. Teachers must have the necessary tools for teaching purposes in the shape of libraries and laboratories as also the right type of students."

The Commission in the course of its study of the academic libraries, found that "libraries were hopelessly inadequate to serve the curricular needs of a modern university. They were ill-housed, illstocked, and ill-staffed and were totally lacking in standard literary and scientific journals. Service was in the hands of personnel that had hardly any notion of the objectives of university education. The annual appropriation for book purchase seldom exceeded the ten thousand mark."

In addition, the annual grant for these libraries were not sufficient. Therefore, the Commission recommended that at least six per cent of the total budget of each academic institution should be set aside for the library.

It added that if institutions were not willing to allocate six per cent of their budget to libraries, they should spend Rs. 40 per student enrolled. The Commission also suggested that greater attention should be paid to improve the reference services in the university libraries. Documentation and biblio-graphical services must be developed in order to promote research among the faculty and students, make libraries proper centres for research activities, and to raise the standards of services.

As far as the library staff is concerned, the Commission was of the view that it is very important to have well-qualified staff, including the Director, in order to provide excellent service in any library. The Director's qualifications must include Ph.D. in Library Science and he must have the rank and salary of a professor, capabilities of organization and management, and should have full powers of an administrator to run the library effectively.

University Education Commission. There is no doubt that the recommendations of the Commission "were based on the needs of the modern library services in universities for the promotion of research and creative learning." It was for the first time that such detailed attention was paid to the library matters by a commission on university education in India.

Ranganathan Committee (1957)

The most comprehensive and significant document on the university and college libraries is the Report of the UGC library committee, chaired by Ranganathan. The Report was published by the University Grants Commission in 1959 entitled 'University and College Libraries.' It was perhaps the first attempt by any Library Committee in India to systematically survey the academic libraries on a national basis, and it was also the first time that the government of India had decided to seek advice from a professional librarian regarding academic libraries. The committee was to advice the UGC on the standards of libraries, building, pay scales, and library training.

After the survey the library committee invited all academic librarians to a seminar on "Work flow in university and college libraries," at Delhi from March 4 to 7, 1959 to keep them informed about the progress the committee had made surveying the academic libraries. It wanted to discuss its recommendations with them. Some of the recommendations of the Committee included the provision that the UGC and the State Government should help the college and the university libraries in the collection development of both books and periodicals.

The formula suggested by the committee was that funds be given "at the rate of Rs. 15 per enrolled student and Rs. 200 per teacher and research fellow. There should also be special initial library grants in the case of a new university and of a new department in an existing university, a similar scale should be followed for the college libraries. In order to promote co-operation among libraries, a Union Catalogue of books and a Union List of periodicals to be prepared.

The Committee strongly recommended that an open access system be introduced in every academic library. Committee also stressed "that reference service is the essential human process of establishing contact between the right reader and the right book by personal service. Reference service is vital in promotion of reading habit in student each library should provide an adequate number of reference librarians to function as library hosts and human converters."

Other recommendations included building up a microfilm collection, copying facilities for microfilms and book material, appointment of a committee to look into the standards of teaching, examination and research in the library schools, and appointment of full-time teaching faculty members rather than asking librarians to teach part time in the library schools.

The Committee added that "the status and the salary of the library staff should be the same as that of the teaching and research staff', *i.e.*, Professor, Reader, and Lecturer etc." The recommendations of the committee had a farreaching effect on the development of the university libraries later.

They had not only provided a framework to the UGC to implement its grants-in-aid programmes but also given to the university authorities important guidelines. Particular mention, in this connection, may be made of the recommendations concerning the library finances which had helped libraries to secure enough finances by way of annual grants from the universities themselves and of development grants from the UGC.

The recommendations on the library personnel and staff strength have given to the library staff status and salaries equivalent to the academic staff and ensure provision for adequate staff for various library operations. The Committee submitted its report to the UGC with the hope that it will provide a blueprint for the systematic development of university libraries in the country.

Hence, inspite of many hurdles like education being a state subject in the Indian Constitution, considerable development in the university libraries has taken place and as such the condition of these libraries in 1953 was much better than in the 1940's and even the early 1950's.

Kothari Commission

The Education Commission under the chairmanship of Dr. D. S. Kothari marked another important stage in the history of university libraries in India.

The Commission devoted considerable attention to the development of the university libraries and made suitable recommendations on the following points:

* Norms for financial support;
* Long range planning for library development;
* The need for the establishment of a well equipped library before the starting of a university, college, or department;
* Suitable phasing over of the library grants;
* Encouraging the students in the use of books;
* Interdisciplinary communication; and
* Documentation service in libraries etc.

The Education Commission had also addressed itself to the role of libraries in adult education and recommended establishment of a network of public libraries. It wanted the school libraries to be integrated with public libraries for purposes of the adult education programmes. The Report, submitted by Dr. D. S. Kothari, on June 29, 1966, emphatically pointed out that "nothing can be more damaging than to ignore its library and to give it a low priority. No new college, university or department should be opened unless adequate number of books in the library are provided."

The Commission was shocked to note that the recommendations of the Radhakrishnan Commission had not been fully implemented, for only four universities in India has spent five per cent or more of their budget on books and periodicals acquisitions, though the 1948's Commission has suggested that six per cent of the total budget be spent on libraries. Other universities had spent less than five per cent of their budget on libraries, "Surprisingly enough there are five universities which spent even less than one per cent of the total budget on the libraries."

It was clear proof that the university libraries in India were not functioning properly to fulfil the needs of higher education. The Kothari Commission recommended that a long range plan for library development should be drawn up for each academic institution taking into consideration anticipated increase in enrollment, introduction of new subjects and research needs etc., and documentation service be encouraged in libraries, and documentation experts be appointed to help researchers and do indexing and abstracting. It was further recommended that "the book selection should be oriented towards supporting instruction and research." The library should "provide resources necessary for research in fields of special interest to the university; provide library facilities and services necessary for the success of all formal programmes of instruction."

Monetary guidelines were also suggested by the Commission. "As a norm, a university should spend each year about Rs. 25 per student registered and Rs. 300 per teacher depending on the stage of development of each university library." It was also suggested that "the foreign exchange needed for university and college libraries should be allowed separately to the UGC."

The Wheat Loan Programme

During the 1950's and early 1960's the Indian academic libraries received huge grants from the UGC amounting up to Rs. 100,000 for books, buildings, equipment and even for additional staff. At the same time many libraries got additional grants from a special US fund called the 'Wheat Loan Programme.' The American Congress passed a special Act, in 1951 known as the 'Public Law 480' to loan India $ 19,000,000 to buy much needed wheat from the US. Under the agreement of the loan, India had to buy American books, periodicals and scientific equipment worth $ 50,000 to be used for research purposes in the Indian libraries.

This, money India had to pay as interest on the loan. Part of the money was to be spent on the exchange of scholars, including librarians, between the two countries. The United States authorities bought some educational material and equipment from India for research purposes and higher education in the American Universities.

During 1951-1961 Indian libraries spent US $ 1,400,000 of the purchase of American books, US dollar 160,000 on libraries, US $ 40,000 on the travel and study grants for thirty three Indian librarians to visit the United States and US $ 75,000 on the travel and study grants of the five Americans.

College Libraries

The College libraries in India have a significant role to play in higher education. Majority of the undergraduate students, *i.e.*, 88.5 per cent and graduate students, *i.e.*, 53 per cent, attend these colleges. When India attained Independence many among the 533 affiliated colleges did not have their own libraries, but at present, every college in the country has a library.

Majority of the college libraries do not have proper facilities to meet the needs of their users. Their collections are not up-to-date, budgets are their very inadequate and limited, and a large number of them are single libraries. In many colleges, there is neither a library hall nor a sufficient big room, not to think of a separate building for the library.

Any unused room, quite often somewhere out of sight, would be considered adequate to house a few shelves of books. And in most college libraries there is complete darkness even during the day time, as the windows are closed out of a fear that the books may be stolen.. Different studies, conducted by scholars and Srivastva have explicitly established that the condition of the college libraries in India are far from satisfactory.

The college libraries are open only six to eight hours a day. Many do not have any qualified librarian on their staff and have closed stacks only. The several commissions and committees, like the Radhakrishnan Commission of 1948, did not stress the importance of the college libraries in their reports. However, the University Grants Commission gives more importance to the college libraries.

As the quality of higher education and research, especially at the graduate level, depends upon, among other things, the standard of the college libraries and their services. Therefore, the UGC has played a significant role in the growth and development of college libraries since 1953 by giving grants for books, equipment, staff and library buildings and has done a remarkable job in salary improvement of the college librarians.

The UGC's contribution to the college libraries is at the rate of Rs. 15 per student with a maximum of Rs. 10,000 with some additional and special grants for text books, when a new subject is introduced in the Curriculum.

On the other hand, the colleges and the state governments have failed to provide their equal share. The total Expenditure on the college libraries according to the recommendation of the Education Commission should be 6.25 per cent of the total budgets of the colleges, but in most cases it has remained between 1.5 per cent and 2.3 per cent.

Sardana Collection development of the college libraries are done without taking into consideration the actual needs of the faculty and the students of the colleges as sixty per cent of them consist of text books and 20 per cent cover fiction.

Even this small inadequate collection, in depth and content, is not used effectively due to the closed stacks system and lack of staff and facilities for instruction concerning their use. The net result is that the utility factor of the college libraries comes practically to nothing.

In most college libraries, books are neither properly classified nor catalogued. In several libraries no systematic classification is followed for collection arrangements. The only service the college library renders to its clientele is book-lending. There are colleges where students are not even allowed inside the library.

The UGC is aware of the slow progress of the college libraries. In addition to providing financial help for development, it has also from time to time organized seminars to keep the college librarians aware of the new developments in the field. But these seminars have made only a limited effect on the progress of the college libraries. The condition of the college libraries in the country should be a cause for alarm among the academic community.

In the interests of the development of higher education in the country along proper lines, it is important to make a detailed study of the style of functioning of the college libraries and of the utilization of the library resources and facilities by the students and teachers. This will help in the preparation of more realistic and operational policies and programmes for ensuring the proper functioning, utilization and development of the college libraries. The college library has to be made the intellectual hub of the institution, serving equally, both the students and teachers.

This is all the more necessary because about 90 per cent of the students in higher education in India pursue their studies in colleges and they have only very small and substandard college library resources to fall back upon. Although, owing to various efforts of the UGC as well as other forces, the traditional concept that the college library is a custodian of books has changed, yet there is evidence enough to show that the condition of the college libraries is generally poor, their development is rather slow and that the position of the college libraries and their librarians in India, with a few exceptions, is pitiable.

University Libraries

University libraries all over the world have their own place of importance in the scheme of higher learning. Libraries are not only repositories of knowledge but also dispensers of such knowledge. There is no doubt that where libraries of universities and institutions of higher learning are ignored or not given due recognition, the country as a whole suffers because the standards of study, teaching and research very heavily depend upon the qualitative and quantitative service rendered by the university libraries.

The Radhakrishnan Commission expressed that "the library is the heart of all the university's work, directly so, as regards its research work and indirectly as regards its educational work, which derives its life from research. Scientific research needs the library as well as its laboratories while for humanistic research the library is both library and the laboratory in one. Both for humanistic and scientific studies, a first class library is essential in a university."

The growth of university libraries since Independence can be seen in respect of the initiatives taken by the Central Government considering the vital importance of higher education and role of libraries in the educational development, commitment to fulfill the demand of higher education, and the foundation of the UGC in 1953 by an Act of Parliament. The Radhakrishnan Commission recognized the value and importance of a well equipped and organized library system and its role in higher education.

It had found many drawbacks and pitfalls in the university libraries and had made many recommendations for the improvement of library facilities. The Ranganathan Committee, appointed by the UGC in 1957, made some outstanding recommendations, which included standards for library building, collection development, staff and services and furniture etc. These recommendations were accepted by the UGC and forwarded for implementation.

The Kothari Commission also made valuable recommendations for this purpose, but the role of the University Grants Commission deserves special mention, because it has played a vital role by "regularly providing appropriate grants and funds to all universities for development of libraries, to purchase books and journals. . . ., construction of new library buildings and for library equipment and furniture."

Dr. D. S. Kothari, the Chairman of University Grants Commission, said, "Libraries play a vital role in the development of institutions of higher learning. The University Grants Commission attaches great importance to the strengthening of library facilities in the universities and colleges and their efficient administration. The commission has also been giving grants to institutions for books and journals construction of library building and appointment of library staff."

One of the most remarkable and identifiable development in the history of higher education and libraries was the foundation of the INFLIBNET in 1991. Information and Library Network Centre is an autonomous Inter-University Centre of the UGC of India. It is a major National Programme initiated by the UGC in 1991 with its Head Quarters at Gujarat University Campus, Ahmedabad. Initially started as a project under the IUCAA, it became an independent Inter-University Centre in 1966.

Its objectives are:

* To promote and establish communication facilities to improve capability in information transfer and access, that provides support to scholarship, learning, research and academic pursuit through cooperation and involvement of agencies concerned.
* *To establish Inflibnet*: Information and Library Network a computer communication network for linking libraries and information centres in universities, deemed to be universities, colleges, UGC information centres, institutions of national importance and R&D institutions, etc. avoiding duplication of efforts.

Inflibnet performs following major activities:

* Provides grants to universities to automate the libraries, establishing the network facilities and create an information technology environment.
* Developed and distributed Software for University

Libraries (Soul) which is an integrated userfriendly library management software. The latest version of the software is 2.0 which is competent to operate with the latest technologies and international standards such as MARC21, Unicode based and NCIP 2.0 based protocols for electronic surveillance and control.

* Indian Catalogue of University Libraries in India (IndCat) is Online Library Catalogue of books, theses and journals available in major university libraries in India which provides bibliographic description, location of the material in all subjects available in more than 112 university libraries. Thus, IndCat has over 10 million bibliographical records of books from more than 113 universities. In addition, the database of theses, expert databases, project databases and Sewakoffline database access facilities are also extended to the libraries of higher learning institutions.
* To enhance the skills of university library staff for implementation of Inflibnet programme, it conducts training programme for library staff, onsite training for member library staff, training on SOUL software, holding Caliber convention every year and workshops for senior level staff of the university libraries are conducted.
* It has brought out a document entitled 'Inflibnet Standards and Guideline for Data Capturing' prepared by a task force of experts based on Common Communication Format (CCF).

Another very important and significant landmark in the history of higher education and development of libraries in India is the establishment of "Ugcinfonet Digial Library Consortium" by the UGC on the concluding day of its Golden jubilee celebrations by his Excellency the then President of India, Dr. A.P.J Abdul Kalam at Vigyan Bhawan on 28th December 2003. UGC-Infonet is an innovative project launched by UGC to facilitate scholarly e-resources to Indian academies through joint partnership of UGC, Inflibnet and Ernet.

This includes interlinking of universities and colleges in the country electronically with a view to achieve maximum efficiency through Internet enabled teaching, learning and governance. The UGC-Infonet is overlaid on Ernet infrastructure in a manner so as to provide assured quality of service and optimum utilization of bandwidth resources. The network will be run and managed by Ernet India.

The project is funded by UGC with 100 per cent capital investment and up to 90 per cent of recurring costs. UGC and Ernet India have signed the necessary MoU for this purpose. A joint technical and tariff committee, has been setup to guide and monitor the design, implementation and operations of Ugcinfonet. Information for Library Network (Inflibnet) an autonomous Inter-University Centre of UGC, is the nodal agency for coordination and facilitation of the linkage between Ernet and the Universities.

Under this programme, information and communication technologies (ICT) and internet will be used to transform learning environment from a monodimensional one to a multidimensional one. This was created to help and benefit more than 310 universities and about 14,000 colleges affiliated with these universities and approximately 10 million students with the e-journals, thus, is a boon to higher education system in many ways.

The UGC-Infonet digital Library consortium has the following objectives: Bhatt,

* To subscribe electronic resources for the members of the consortium at highly discounted rates of subscription and with the best terms and conditions.
* Promote the rational use of funds.
* Guarantee local storage of the information acquired for continuous use by present and future users.
* To impart training to the users, librarians, research scholars and faculty members of the institutions on the electronic resources with an aim to optimize the usage of the electronic resources.
* To have more interaction amongst the member libraries.
* To increase the research productivity of the institutions in terms of quality and quantity of publications

* Strategic alliance with institutions that have common interests resulting reduced information cost and improved resource sharing.

National Knowledge Commission

The National Knowledge Commission was set up by the Government of India on 13th June 2005 with a time-frame of three years, from 2nd October 2005 to 2nd October 2008. As a high-level advisory body to the Prime Minister of India, the National Knowledge Commission was given a mandate to guide policy and direct reforms, focusing on certain key areas such as education, science and technology, agriculture, industry, e-governance etc. Easy access to knowledge, creation and preservation of knowledge systems, dissemination of knowledge and better knowledge services are core concerns of the Commission.

The Commission envisaged the future road map for the growth and development of academic libraries by imbibing core issues such as, set up a national commission on libraries, prepare a national census of all libraries, revamp LIS education, training and research facilities, re-assess staffing of libraries, set up a central library fund, modernize library management, encourage greater community participation in library management, promote information communication technology applications in all libraries, facilitate donation and maintenance of private collections, and encourage public private partnerships in LIS development, etc.

SARASWATHI MAHAL LIBRARY

Saraswathi Mahal Library is located in Thanjavur, Tamil Nadu, India. It is one of the oldest libraries in Asia, and has on display a rare collection of Palm leaf manuscripts and paper written in Tamil, Hindi, English, Telugu, Marathi, and a few other languages indigenous to India.

The collection comprises well over 60,000 volumes, though only a tiny fraction of these are on display. The library has a complete catalogue of holdings, which is being made available online. Some rare holdings can be viewed on site by prior arrangement.

HISTORY

The Saraswathi Mahal library started as a Royal Library for the private pleasure of the Nayak Kings of Thanjavur who ruled AD 1535-1675. The Maratha rulers who captured Thanjavur in 1675 patronised local culture and further developed the Royal Palace Library until 1855. Most notable among the Maratha Kings was Serfoji II, who was an eminent scholar in many branches of learning and the arts.

In his early age Serfoji studied under the influence of the Dutch Reverend Schwartz, and learned many languages including English, French, Italian and Latin. He enthusiastically took special interest in the enrichment of the Library, employing many Pandits to collect, buy and copy a vast number of works from all renowned Centres of Sanskrit learning in Northern India and other far-flung areas.

Since 1918 the Saraswathi Mahal Library has been a possession of the state of Tamil Nadu. Its official name of the Library was changed to "The Thanjavur Maharaja Serfoji's Sarasvati Mahal Library" in honour of the great royal Marathan patron.

EFFORTS

The library is open to the public; it also supports efforts to publish rare manuscripts from the collection, as well as ensuring all volumes are preserved on microfilm. The Library has installed computers in 1998 for the Computerisation of Library activities. As a first phase, the Library catalogues are being stored in the Computer for easy information retrieval. It is also proposed to digitalise the manuscripts of this Library shortly.

THE COLLECTION

The bulk of the manuscripts (39,300) are in Sanskrit, written in scripts such as Grantha, Devanagari, Nandinagari, Telugu. Tamil manuscripts number over 3500, comprising titles in literature, music and medicine. The Library has a collection of 3076 Marathi manuscripts from the South Indian Maharastrian of the 17th, 18th, and 19th centuries; this includes the hierarchy of the Saints of Maharashtra belonging to Sri Ramadasi and Dattatreya Mutts. The Marathi manuscripts are mostly on paper but a few were written in Telugu script on palm-leaf. There are 846 Telugu manuscripts in the holdings, mostly on palm leaf. There are 22 Persian and Urdu manuscripts mostly of 19th century also within the collection.

Apart from these manuscripts there are 1342 bundles of Maratha Raj records available at the Library. The Raj records were written in the Modi script of the Marathi language. These records encompass the information of the political, cultural and social administration of the Maratha kings of Thanjavur.

SOME OF THE RARE BOOKS AND MANUSCRIPTS

* Dr. Samuel Johnson's dictionary published in 1784
* The pictorial Bible printed in Amsterdam in the year 1791
* The Madras Alamnac printed in 1807
* Lavoisier's *Traité Élémentaire de Chimie* ("Elements of Chemistry")
* The notes of Bishop Heber on Raja Serfoji II
* The correspondence letters of William Torin of London who purchased a lot of books for Raja Serfoji II and the Saraswathi Mahal Library
* The Globe used by the raja.
* Ancient maps of the world
* Town planning documents of Thanjavur including the underground drainage system, the fresh water supply ducting system
* Pictorial charts of the theory of evolution of man as evinced by Charles Le Brun

LIBRARY MUSEUM

A Museum is located in the Library building to reveal the importance of the Library to the Public. This Museum is small but organised into sections highlighting ancient Manuscripts, Illustrated Manuscripts, Printed copies of the Original Drawings, Atlases, Thanjavur-style Paper Paintings, Canvass Paintings, Wooden Paintings, Glass paintings, Portraits of the Thanjavur

Maratha kings, and the Physiognomy charts of Charles Le-Brun. These materials give an idea of the total variety in the vast collection within the Library.

The Saraswati Library is situated within the campus of the Thanjavur Palace. Visitors can have a glimpse of preserved books and can sit and read in the library premises. Better preservation of books and facilities like air-conditioning with dehumidifiers, redesigning of space for comfortable reading, online catalogue facility should be taken up to preserve this internationally renowned treasure trove of books and palm-leaf manuscripts!

Efforts were made to microfilm and catalogue the contents way back in 1965 when Indira Gandhi was Information and Broadcasting Minister, Government of India who sanctioned the fund for the library's development. Since then no efforts were made to scan the documents and computerise the same using present day technology. It is also a designated 'Manuscript Conservation Centre' (MCC) under the National Mission for Manuscripts established in 2003.

KHUDA BAKHSH ORIENTAL LIBRARY

Khuda Bakhsh Oriental Library is one of the national libraries of India. It was opened to public in October, 1891 by Khan Bahadur Khuda Bakhsh with 4,000 manuscripts, of which he inherited 1,400 from his father Maulvi Mohammed Bakhsh.

It is an autonomous organization under Ministry of Culture, Government of India, and is governed by a Board with the Governor of Bihar as its ex-officio Chairman. known for its rare collection of Persian and Arabic manuscripts. It also hosts paintings made during the Rajput and Mughal eras of India. It is also a designated 'Manuscript Conservation Centre' (MCC) under the National Mission for Manuscripts.

HISTORY

The library finds its origin in private collection of a bibliophile Mohammad Bakhsh and expanded by his son Khuda Bakhsh, who inherited 1,400 manuscripts and continued to add to the collection and eventually converted it into a private library by 1880. The library was opened to public upon its inauguration by Sir Charles Elliot, Governor of Bengal on 5th October, 1891.

In 1969 through a Federal Legislation, an Act of Parliament, namely 'Khuda Bakhsh Oriental Public Library Act (1969), the Government of India declared Khuda Bakhsh Oriental Public Library a centre of national importance and government took over the funding, maintenance and development of the library. Today it continues to attract scholars from all over the world.

Past directors of the library have been Dr. Abid Reza Bedar, who after remaining with the Raza Library, came as Director to the institution in 1972, and did some important work towards reviving the library along with his successor Habibur Rehman Chighani, at present the Director of the library is the Dr. Imtiaz Ahmad, since February, 2004.

COLLECTION

Some of the notable manuscripts are *Timur Nama* (*Khandan—Timuria*), *Shah Nama, Padshah Nama, Diwan-e-Hafiz* and *Safinatul Auliya*, carrying the autograph of Mughal Emperors and princes and the book of Military Accounts of Maharaja Ranjit Singh. Apart of it the library also has specimens of Mughal paintings, calligraphy and book decoration and Arabic and Urdu manu-scripts, including a page of Quran written on deer skin.

BHANDARKAR ORIENTAL RESEARCH INSTITUTE

The Bhandarkar Oriental Research Institute (BORI) is located in Pune, Maharashtra, India. It was founded on July 6, 1917 to honour the life and work of Dr. Ramakrishna Gopal Bhandarkar (1837–1925), long regarded as the founder of Indology (Orientalism) in India. The institute is well known for its collection of old Sanskrit and Prakrit manuscripts.

THE INSTITUTE

This institute is of a public trust registered under Act XXI of 1860. Initially, the institute received an annual grant of 3000 Rupees from the Government of Bombay. Presently, it is partially supported by annual grants from the Government of Maharashtra. The Institute also receives grants from the Government of India and the University Grants Commission for specific research projects.

The institute has one of the largest collections of rare books and manuscripts in South Asia, consisting of over 1,25,000 books and 29,510 manuscripts. The institute publishes a journal, *Annals of the Bhandarkar Oriental Research Institute* four times a year. The Institute also hosts the Manuscripts Resource and Conservation Centre under the auspices of the National Mission for Manuscripts, a project of the Ministry of Culture, Government of India. In 2007, the Rigveda manuscripts preserved at the Institute were included in UNESCO's Memory of the World Register.

THE MANUSCRIPT COLLECTION

The Government of Bombay, in 1866, started a pan Indian Manuscript Collection project. Noted scholars like George Bühler, F. Kielhorn, Peter Peterson, Ramkrishna Gopal Bhandarkar, S. R. Bhandarkar, Kathavate and Ghate collected more than 17,000 important manuscripts under this project. This collection was first deposited at Elphinstone College in Bombay.

Then it was transferred to Deccan College (Pune) for better preservation. After the Bhandarkar Oriental Research Institute was founded in 1917, the BORI founders proposed to offer even better preservation and research.

Hence Lord Willingdon, the then Governor of the Bombay Presidency and the first president of BORI, transferred the valuable Government collection of manuscripts to the BORI on April 1, 1918. The first curator, P.K. Gode took active initiatives to enhance this collection. Presently, the Institute has over 29,000 manuscripts.

The largest part of the collection (17,877 Manuscripts) is part of the "Government Manuscript Library", while there is an additional collection of 11,633 manuscripts also. The most prized collections include a paper manuscript of the Cikitsâsâra-sangraha dated 1320 and a palmleaf manuscript of the Upamiti-bhavaprapañcakathâ dated 906. Among the several scholars referring to the works at BORI, the most well-known person arguably is the Bharat Ratna awardee, Pt. Pandurang Vaman Kane.

THE CRITICAL EDITION OF THE MAHABHARATA

A long term project under the auspices of BORI, started on

April 1, 1919, was the preparation of a Critical Edition of the Mahabharata. V.S. Sukhtankar was appointed general editor of the project on August 1, 1925 and he continued until his death on January 21, 1943.

After his death, S.K. Belvalkar was appointed general editor on April 1, 1943. On April 1, 1961 P. L. Vaidya appointed as General Editor of the project on the retirement of S. K. Belvalkar. R. N. Dandekar appointed as the joint general editor on July 6, 1957. To widespread acclaim, the completion for publication was announced on September 22, 1966, by Dr. Sarvapalli Radhakrishnan, then President of India, at a special function held at the institute.

The Critical Edition was collated from 1,259 manuscripts. This edition in 19 volumes (more than 15000 demi-quarto size pages) comprised the critically constituted text of the 18 *Parvas* of the Mahabharata consisting of more than 89000 verses, an elaborate Critical Apparatus and a Prolegomena on the material and methodology.

Further work since the initial publication has produced a Critical Edition of the Harivamsa, a Pratika Index, a Bibliography of ancillary materials, and a Cultural Index. The project of preparing a critical edition of the Harivamsa was inaugurated by the President of India, Rajendra Prasad on November 19, 1954. The publication was completed in November, 1971.

The critical edition in two volumes consists the 4 *Parvan*s of the Harivamsa. The Pratika Index in 6 volumes consists 360000 verse quarters with appendices. Two volumes of the Cultural Index have been published so far. The constituted text of the critical edition has also been made available on the CD-ROM.

VANDALISM IN 2003

The institute was vandalized in December 2003 by a mob made up of members of an extremist self styled Maratha youth squad, calling themselves the Sambhaji Brigade, named after Shivaji's elder son. They claimed to be angered by the help provided by the institute's staff (in translating manuscripts) to a Western writer, Dr. James Laine, who discussed the telling and retelling of stories about Shivaji's parentage and life in his book on narrations of the Shivaji story.

The mob also damaged thousands of manuscripts and attacked Shrikant Bahulkar, a Sanskrit scholar who had only explained some Sanskrit references to Laine. The incident provoked widespread reaction and historian Gajanan Mehendale to destroy parts of his in-progress biography of Shivaji.

The vandalism and a ban on the book were denounced by historians who put their signatures to the statement include R.S. Sharma, R.C. Thakran, Suraj Bhan, Irfan Habib, D.N. Jha, Shireen Moosvi and K. M. Shrimali. Oxford University Press-publisher of James Laine's, 'Shivaji: Hindu king in Islamic India', withdrew the book after protests from Ninad Bedekar and other right-wing politicians as it contained allegedly objectionable statements about Shivaji.

ASIATIC SOCIETY LIBRARY

At present, the library of the Asiatic Society has a collection of about 1,17,000 books and 79,000 journals printed in almost all the major languages of the world. It has also a collection of 293 maps, microfische of 48,000 works, microfilm of 387,003 pages, 182 paintings, 2500 pamphlets and 2150 photographs.

The earliest printed book preserved in this library is Juli Firmici's *Astronomicorum Libri* published in 1499. It has in its possession a large number of books printed in India in the late 18th and early 19th centuries. The library also possesses many rare and scarcely available books. The library has a rich collection of about 47,000 manuscripts in 26 scripts. The most notable amongst them are an illustrated manuscript of the *Qur'an*, a manuscript of the *Gulistan* text, and a manuscript of *Padshah Nama* bearing the signature of Emperor Shahjahan. The number of journals in thepossession of the library is about 80,000 at present.

The early collection of this library was enriched by the contributions it received from its members. On March 25, 1784 the library received seven Persian manuscripts from Henri Richardson. The next contribution came from William Marsden, who donated his book, *History of Island of Sumatra* (1783) on November 10, 1784. Robert Home, the first Library-in-Charge (1804) donated his small but valuable collection of works on art.

The first accession of importance was a gift from the

Seringapatam Committee on February 3, 1808 consisting of a collection from the Palace Library of Tipu Sultan. The library received the Surveyor-General Colonel Mackenzie's collection of manuscripts and drawings in December 1822.

MANUSCRIPT COLLECTION

Manuscript Collection of the society is varied and rich, and covers most of the Indian languages and scripts and even several Asian ones, *e.g.*, Assamese, Bengali, Gujarati, Gurumukhi, Kanarese, Urdu, Marathi, Modi, Nagari, Newari, Oriya, Rajasthani, Sarada, Armenian, Sinhalese, Arabic, Persian, Pushto, Javanese, Turki, Burmese, Chinese, Siamese, Tibetan etc. The materials used for the manuscripts are also varied: palm and palmyra leaves, barks of different trees, papers of various grades.

Sanskritic Manuscripts

The manuscripts cover the period from 7th c. A.D. down to the 19th century. These are useful source materials to illustrate the development of the Indian scripts (especially Bengali, Nagari etc.). The colophons and post-colophons contain information relating to socio-economic conditions of the people.

Besides, they help us to fix the chronology of the Royal dynasties of India. Where the inscriptions fail to ascertain dates and chronology, the manuscripts may throw some light, provided a thorough critical study of these and their colophons and postcolophons were made.

Some of the rare Sanskrit manuscripts may be mentioned here:

* Brihati,
* Amrita Vindu,
* Kiranavali,
* Charucharya,
* Nartaka Nirnaya,
* Parasika-prakasa,
* Sanskrita-ratnakara,
* Lalitavistara,
* Horoscope of a Muslim of the Mughal Court (A.D. 1640) A Deed of Mortgage (1639),

* Ramayana (Bengali) of Ramananda Yati,
* Vajrayana text (11th c.),
* A text on Buddhist Nyaya,
* Rigveda Padapatha,
* Laghu-Kalachakra-tika,
* Kalachakravetara,
* Kuttanimatam,
* Vajravalinama mannadalopayika,
* Ramacharita of Sandhyakar Nandi,
* Bhattikavyatika of Srinivasa, and
* Paragali Mahabharata.

The manuscript of Kubjikamatam is of the 7th Century A.D. The manuscript of Rigveda Padapatha, copied in A.D. 1362, is perhaps "the oldest manuscript of the Rigveda."

Islamic Section

Of the many Islamic Manuscripts there are some which are extremely rare and unique.

Of these only a few may be mentioned:

* Tahdhib Sharh As-Sab' at Mullaqat (early 12th c. Arabic),
* Qalaid al-Iquian wa Mahasin al-Ayan (12th c.),
* Kharidat al-Qasr (12th c.),
* Al-Jam Baynas as-Sahihin abridged version with autograph, (13th c.),
* A-Madkhul(13th c.),
* Tafsir-i-Quran (Persian, 13th c., important also for calligraphy),
* Tuhfat al-Ahbar fi usul at Hadith wa'l Akhbar (15th c.),
* Kitab al-I'lan (18th c.),
* Saha' if-i-Shara' if or Duraral Mansur (Persian, 19th c., an autographed copy), and
* Adab-i-Alamgiri (18th c.).

There are large numbers of illuminated and illustrated manuscripts of different schools, many of which are unique for their calligraphy, delicacy of their lines, and elegance of composition and charming colour schemes. These miniatures still afford glimpses of India's past achievements, of these unique manuscripts (earliest belonging to the 10th Century A.D.) mention may be made of a few:

* Astasahasrika Prajnaparamita,
* Aparimitayurnama Mahayana sutra,
* Pancharaksha,
* Paramarthanama Sangati,
* Devimahatmya,
* Viveka Panchamrita,
* Bhagavatgita,
* Shahnama,
* Kullayat-i-Saadi,
* Suwaru'l aqalim,
* Farang-i-Aurang Shahi,
* Ain-i-Akbari,
* Diwan-i-Makhfi,
* Qissa-i-Nush-Afarin,
* Jamiut-Twarikh,
* Amir nama Tutinama,
* Iyar-i-Danesh,
* Bihar-i-Danesh,
* Tarjuma Mahabharata,
* Tafribul-Imarah (by Silchand, dedicated to J. H. Lushington), and
* Imaratut-Akbar (by Chitarmal for James Duncan).

Many scholars are using the collection for editing their texts and for translation in modern languages.

English Manuscripts

In the Library there are preserved a large number of old letters some of which date back to1784, just after the Society was founded. These letters were received by the Society from persons belonging to different walks of life, requesting information on such subjects as old and rare manuscripts, ancient monuments, coins etc.

Some among the writers of these letters were persons well known for their literary, scientific and other cultural accomplishments. These old files constitute important documents relating to the history of the Society, as also of many other scientific and humanistic organisations that were established in India either in the 19th or in the 20th century.

Urdu Manuscripts

The Society has a fine collection of about 234 Urdu manuscripts many of which were received as a gift from the Fort William College.

Sino-Tibetan and Burmese Manuscripts

The Society has a complete set of Kanjur and Tanjur texts of the Buddhist scriptures and some extra-canonical works. These were collected by B. H. Hodgson and A. Csoma de koros. A section of the collection has been catalogued. There are over one hundred titles of Chinese books, some of which are rare and valuable for Chinese studies.

These cover almost all the subjects relating to Chinese Culture, Civilization and Science and Buddhism. Subjects covered include Classical Literature, Language. History, Geography, Topography, Philosophy, Religion, manners and customs, biography of scholars, sciences (Botanical, Astronimical, Zoological).

The Society has a valuable collection of about 162 Burmese manuscript written on parabaikes and palm leaf. The manuscripts deal with Buddhistic texts, Religion, History of the world and also of Burmja and Arakan, works on Gramour (including that of kaccayana) and Rhetoric, Buddhist cosmography, Astrology, Medicine etc.

Bengali Manuscripts

Other than Sanskrit, a few Bengali manuscripts have been found written by Bengali Brahmins residing in Varanasi. Parageli Mahabharat, Chuti Khan's Asvamedha Parva, and many other important manuscripts were purchased. Mss. donated by Justice Ramaprosad Mukherjee and Sri A Roy enriched the collection. The society has 703 Bengali and 12 Assamese manuscripts in the collection. It comprises Asiatic Society's own collection, Government collection, Indian Museum collection and donors' collection.

At present, the collection of Bengali manuscripts in the possession of Asiatic Society is rich in respect of number and rarity. The Society has manuscripts on Ramayana, Mahabharata,

Srimadbhagavat, Mangala Kavyas, treatises on Vaisnava faith and its allied subjects. Folk literature, erotic verses and Vaisnaba Sahajiya Cult etc.

Rajasthani Manuscripts

The Society possesses very rare, valuable and important Rajasthani Manuscripts which date the pre-middle and middle years. The Society prepared and brought out a descriptive catalogue of Rajasthani manuscripts comprising 636 manuscripts.

RARE BOOK DIVISION

In 1978 the Council decided to open a Rare Book Division. The preliminarhy screening of the collection has since been started.

Among the earliest printed books mention may be made of the following:

* Julii Firmici Astronomicorum libri octo integri (Venice 1499),
* Kitabal-Qanum (Arabic/Romae 1595),
* Kripar Sstrer Arthabhed (Bengali in Roman Character, Kisbon 1743);
* S. Purchas's Purchas: His Pilgrimage (London, 1 61 4),
* N. Halhed's Grammar of the Bengal Language, (Hooghly, 1778),
* Malabar and English Dictionary, (Madras, 1779),
* Rasamanjari (Sanskrit, Banaras, 1791),
* Ram Ram Bose's Lipimala (Bengali, Serampore, 1802),
* The Ramayana 3 vols, (Bengali, Serampore, 1803),
* Hitopadesa (Sanskrit, Serampore, 1804),
* Colebrooke's Grammar of the Sanskrit language vol. 1 (Serampore, 1805).

3

Information and Information Science

INFORMATION

Information, in its most restricted technical sense, is a sequence of symbols that can be interpreted as a message. Information can be recorded as signs, or transmitted as signals. Information is any kind of event that affects the state of a dynamic system.

Conceptually, information is the message being conveyed. This concept has numerous other meanings in different contexts. Moreover, the concept of information is closely related to notions of constraint, communication, control, data, form, instruction, knowledge, meaning, mental stimulus, pattern, perception, representation, and especially entropy.

ETYMOLOGY

The English word was apparently derived from the Latin stem (*information-*) of the nominative (*informatio*): this noun is in its turn derived from the verb "informare" (to inform) in the sense of "to give form to the mind", "to discipline", "instruct", "teach": "Men so wise should go and inform their kings." *Inform* itself comes from the Latin verb *informare,* to give form, to form an idea of.

Furthermore, Latin itself already contained the word *information* meaning concept or idea, but the extent to which this may have influenced the development of the word *information* in English is not clear. The ancient Greek word for *form* was (morph) and also (*eidos*) "kind, idea, shape, set", the latter word was famously used in a technical philosophical sense by Plato (and later Aristotle) to denote the ideal identity or essence of something. "Eidos" can also be associated with thought, proposition or even concept.

INFORMATION THEORY APPROACH

From the stance of information theory, *information* is taken as a sequence of symbols from an alphabet, say an input alphabet χ, and an output alphabet Υ. Information processing consists of an input-output function that maps any input sequence from χ into an output sequence from Υ. The mapping may be probabilistic or determinate. It may have memory or be memoryless.

AS SENSORY INPUT

Often information is viewed as a type of input to an organism or system. Inputs are of two kinds. Some inputs are important to the function of the organism or system by themselves. In his book *Sensory Ecology,* Dusenbery called these causal inputs. Other inputs are important only because they are associated with causal inputs and can be used to predict the occurrence of a causal input at a later time. Some information is important because of association with other information but eventually there must be a connection to a causal input.

In practice, information is usually carried by weak stimuli that must be detected by specialized sensory systems and amplified by energy inputs before they can be functional to the organism or system. For example, light is often a causal input to plants but provides information to animals.

The coloured light reflected from a flower is too weak to do much photosynthetic work but the visual system of the bee detects it and the bee's nervous system uses the information to guide the bee to the flower, where the bee often finds nectar or pollen, which are causal inputs, serving a nutritional function.

AS REPRESENTATION AND COMPLEXITY

The cognitive scientist and applied mathematician

Ronaldo Vigo argues that information is a relative concept that involves at least two related entities in order to make quantitative sense.

These are: any dimensionally-defined category of objects S, and any of its subsets R. R, in essence, is a representation of S, or, in other words, carries or conveys representational information about S. Vigo then defines the amount of information that R conveys about S as the rate of change in the complexity of S whenever the objects in R are removed from S. Under "Vigo information", pattern, invariance, complexity, representation, and information—five fundamental constructs of universal science—are unified under a novel mathematical framework. Among other things, the framework aims to overcome the limitations of Shannon-Weaver information when attempting to characterize and measure subjective information.

AS AN INFLUENCE WHICH LEADS TO A TRANSFORMATION

Information is any type of pattern that influences the formation or transformation of other patterns. In this sense, there is no need for a conscious mind to perceive, much less appreciate, the pattern. Consider, for example, DNA. The sequence of nucleotides is a pattern that influences the formation and development of an organism without any need for a conscious mind.

Systems theory at times seems to refer to information in this sense, assuming information does not necessarily involve any conscious mind, and patterns circulating in the system can be called information. In other words, it can be said that information in this sense is something potentially perceived as representation, though not created or presented for that purpose. For example, Gregory Bateson defines "information" as a "difference that makes a difference".

If, however, the premise of "influence" implies that information has been perceived by a conscious mind and also interpreted by it, the specific context associated with this interpretation may cause the transformation of the information into knowledge. Complex definitions of both "information" and "knowledge" make such semantic and logical analysis difficult, but the condition of "transformation" is an important point in the study of information as it relates to knowledge, especially in the business discipline of knowledge management.

In this practice, tools and processes are used to assist a knowledge worker in performing research and making decisions, including steps such as:

* Reviewing information in order to effectively derive value and meaning
* Referencing metadata if any is available
* Establishing a relevant context, often selecting from many possible contexts
* Deriving new knowledge from the information
* Making decisions or recommendations from the resulting knowledge.

Stewart argues that the transformation of information into knowledge is a critical one, lying at the core of value creation and competitive advantage for the modern enterprise. The Danish Dictionary of Information Terms argues that information only provides an answer to a posed question. Whether the answer provides knowledge depends on the informed person.

So a generalized definition of the concept should be:

"Information" = An answer to a specific question"

When Marshall McLuhan speaks of media and their effects on human cultures, he refers to the structure of artifacts that in turn shape our behaviours and mindsets. Also, pheromones are often said to be "information" in this sense.

AS A PROPERTY IN PHYSICS

In 2003 J. D. Bekenstein claimed there is a growing trend in physics to define the physical world as being made of information itself. Information has a well-defined meaning in physics. Examples of this include the phenomenon of quantum entanglement where particles can interact without reference to their separation or the speed of light.

Information itself cannot travel faster than light even if the information is transmitted indirectly. This could lead to the fact that all attempts at physically observing a particle with an "entangled" relationship to another are slowed down, even though the particles are not connected in any other way other than by the information they carry.

Another link is demonstrated by the Maxwell's demon thought experiment. In this experiment, a direct relationship between information and another physical property, entropy, is demonstrated. A consequence is that it is impossible to destroy information without increasing the entropy of a system; in practical terms this often means generating heat.

Another, more philosophical outcome is that information could be thought of as interchangeable with energy. Thus, in the study of logic gates, the theoretical lower bound of thermal energy released by an *AND gate* is higher than for the *NOT gate*. Physical information is of particular importance in the theory of quantum computers.

TECHNOLOGICALLY MEDIATED INFORMATION

It is estimated that the world's technological capacity to store information grew from 2.6 exabytes in 1986, which is the informational equivalent to less than one 730-MB CD-ROM per person in 1986 to 295 exabytes in 2007. This is the informational equivalent of almost 61 CD-ROM per person in 2007.

The world's combined technological capacity to receive information through one-way broadcast networks was the informational equivalent of 174 newspapers per person per day in 2007. The world's combined effective capacity to exchange information through two-way telecommunication networks was the informational equivalent of 6 newspapers per person per day in 2007.

AS RECORDS

Records are a specialized form of information. Essentially, records are information produced consciously or as by-products of business activities or transactions and retained because of their value. Primarily their value is as evidence of the activities of the organization but they may also be retained for their informational value. Sound records management ensures that the integrity of records is preserved for as long as they are required.

The international standard on records management, ISO 15489, defines records as "information created, received, and maintained as evidence and information by an organization or person, in pursuance of legal obligations or in the transaction of business".

The *International Committee on Archives* (ICA) Committee on electronic records defined a record as, "a specific piece of recorded information generated, collected or received in the initiation, conduct or completion of an activity and that comprises sufficient content, context and structure to provide proof or evidence of that activity".

Records may be maintained to retain corporate memory of the organization or to meet legal, fiscal or accountability requirements imposed on the organization. Willis expressed the view that sound management of business records and information delivered "...six key requirements for good corporate governance...transparency; accountability; due process; compliance; meeting statutory and common law requirements; and security of personal and corporate information."

INFORMATION AND SEMIOTICS

Beynon-Davies explains the multi-faceted concept of information in terms of signs and signal-sign systems. Signs themselves can be considered in terms of four inter-dependent levels, layers or branches of semiotics: pragmatics, semantics, syntax, and empirics. These four layers serve to connect the social world on the one hand with the physical or technical world on the other...

Pragmatics is concerned with the purpose of communication. Pragmatics links the issue of signs with the context within which signs are used. The focus of pragmatics is on the intentions of living agents underlying communicative behaviour. In other words, pragmatics link language to action.

Semantics is concerned with the meaning of a message conveyed in a communicative act. Semantics considers the content of communication. Semantics is the study of the meaning of signs-the association between signs and behaviour. Semantics can be considered as the study of the link between symbols and their referents or concepts; particularly the way in which signs relate to human behaviour.

Syntax is concerned with the formalism used to represent a message. Syntax as an area studies the form of communication in terms of the logic and grammar of sign systems. Syntax is devoted to the study of the form rather than the content of signs and sign-systems.

Empirics is the study of the signals used to carry a message; the physical characteristics of the medium of communication. Empirics is devoted to the study of communication channels and their characteristics, *e.g.*, sound, light, electronic transmission etc..

Nielsen discusses the relationship between semiotics and information in relation to dictionaries. The concept of lexicographic information costs is introduced and refers to the efforts users of dictionaries need to make in order to, first, find the data sought and, secondly, understand the data so that they can generate information.

Communication normally exists within the context of some social situation. The social situation sets the context for the intentions conveyed and the form in which communication takes place. In a communicative situation intentions are expressed through messages which comprise collections of inter-related signs taken from a language which is mutually understood by the agents involved in the communication.

Mutual understanding implies that agents involved understand the chosen language in terms of its agreed syntax and semantics. The sender codes the message in the language and sends the message as signals along some communication channel. The chosen communication channel will have inherent properties which determine outcomes such as the speed with which communication can take place and over what distance. More recently Shu-Kun Lin proposed a simple definition of information: Information is the amount of the data after data compression.

CHARACTERISTICS OF INFORMATION

A central theme in books and articles within different areas of the field of business administration is that the world is changing at a faster and faster pace. The reasons given for this is globalization, investments in ITtechnology and the rapid pace of technological change in combination with escalating costs of research and development. Therefore, companies are believed to need information about environmental events. Information is important since it is believed to be a cornerstone for long-term company survival.

Information can reduce uncertainty, risks in decision-making are an important input in the process of strategy formulation, serve as a base for competence development and so on. But the process of gathering information is not trouble free. A theme stressed in the literature is the paradoxical situation that, although there is an abundance of information available, it is often difficult to obtain useful, relevant information when it is needed. Useful, relevant and needed are the keywords here.

By consulting the literature, a tentative conclusion may be that companies do not necessarily need more information; what they need is useful and relevant information in time. This fact has been noticed by researchers within different academic disciplines, not to mention the variety of consulting firms within this area. But the area is blurred, we feel.

The reason for this is that there are a lot of different terms used to describe how useful and relevant information might be collected, interpreted, analysed, distributed and so forth. Some of the more popular terms used are Business intelligence, Information management, Marketing research, and Environ-mental scanning. These terms or approaches have a lot in common, but also there are significant differences.

Purpose

Thus, the purpose of this paper is to identify similarities and differences in these terms, relate them to and compare them with each other, but also to identify their underlying concepts and the course of events they represent. The intent with this paper is not to present a complete list of references on the subject, but rather to study some of the literature at hand as a first step towards a mapping of the characteristics stressed in the different terms/approaches.

Terms, Concepts and Course of Events

It is important to look behind terms to discover their meaning. Carl Hempel made this point clear; it is very important to make a distinction between terms and concepts. By looking behind the terms we mean trying to locate the domain(s) they are supposed to reflect, but also to try to identify the concept(s) underlying the terms.

A term is believed to represent a certain object or a course of events. The object or course of events is contained in a certain concept; the term means this concept. In this paper, Marketing research is an example of a term. The term is represented by the Marketing research process, which is a course of events or a domain.

Marketing research may be defined as "the function that links the consumer, customer, and public to the marketer through information", which is the concept that the term Marketing research means. The purpose with this distinction is basically to facilitate communication and exchange of meaning. This idea is shown visually in figure.

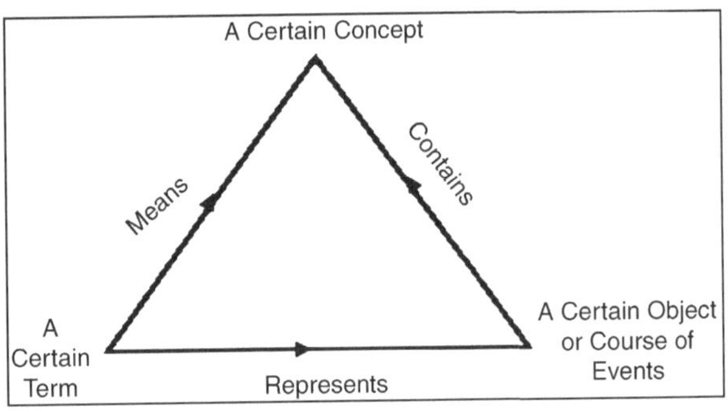

Fig 3.1. The Difference between Terms, Concepts and Course of Events.

Information Processing Approaches

The terms or approaches Environmental scanning, Business, Competitive, Competitor, Market, and Political intelligence, Marketing research, and Information management will be described. The information system approach is described together with the term Information management. Our intent was originally also to include *Management information systems* (MIS) as an approach here.

This proved very difficult since there seems to be no consensus with regard to how the term is used. Lee and Gosain claim that the MIS discipline is "a fragmented adhocracy characterized by research that is rather personal, weakly coordinated in the field as a whole, with weak entry barriers from one fragment to the other and common sense language dominating". Based on our limited knowledge of the field, we agree with these authors and therefore choose to exclude the term/approach MIS in this paper.

Environmental Scanning

Augilar, Environmental scanning is defined as "the activity of acquiring information". Hamrefors has a somewhat complementary view and claims, "by scanning I mean the behaviour of attending to the events and phenomena in the environment". Under the term scanning Augilar includes not only purposeful search but also undirected viewing.

Aguilar maintains that the importance of scanning derives from the importance of the decisions involved. He further argues that information is useful for making decisions about strategy and long-range plans. The dependence of decision-making on scanning becomes apparent as soon as one examines the various steps of the decision-making process.

The most important type of information received through Environmental scanning is external strategic information, and information is classified as such when it refers to information about events or relationships in the firms outside environment that unveil opportunities to exploit the firms strengths, accentuate the firms weaknesses, or highlight potential threats facing the firm.

Before proceeding, what is actually being scanned? How can "environment" be defined? Stewart, and Sweo most research definitions of organizational or business environment has been based on the work of Duncan. Duncan defines the environment as all of the relevant factors outside an organization's boundary that are incorporated into its decision-making.

Further, the environment could be anything material or social in the surroundings, close or distant to an individual. Considering these relevant factors, the environment can be divided into two distinct strata named task and general environment.

The task environment involves sectors in which there is direct interaction with other organizations, suppliers, customers, and competitors being good examples. The general environment includes sectors with indirect interaction with the organization such as government, economic conditions, and socio-cultural factors. Environmental scanning is a quite new phenomenon on the organizational scene.

Only in the latest 15 years has this topic started to be of importance on the agenda of many organizations, even if it is by no means a new phenomenon. When consulting the literature, we can see that from the 1960s onwards a lot has been written using the term Environmental scanning in such prominent magazines as ASQ, Management Science, Academy of Management Journal, and the Strategic Management Journal. Issues that were addressed among others were environmental uncertainty environmental characteristics, scanning behaviour of executives and scanning behaviour in relation to competence development.

Business, Competitive, Competitor, Market and Political Intelligence

The question of Environmental scanning has been raised in several contexts. One is the need to identify changes in the organizational environment that the management thinks is important for the organization. This kind of Environmental scanning is often labeled *Business intelligence* (BI), a wording that reflects that it is often inspired by Military intelligence. Business intelligence could be broadly defined as systematized Information management aimed at generating insight into the future developments that are assumed to have an impact on the organization as decision support in organizations.

Usually, the term intelligence is used for indicating that it is an organized activity and an interpretation of the environmental events, rather than sheer information about them. To put it another way, intelligence is actionable, processed, and organized information. Another characteristic of intelligence is that it is future oriented.

By using organized intelligence activities one tries to forecast how relevant parts of the environment will develop in the future. In the literature the term intelligence is often used to capture the process and organization of transforming information into something that makes sense and that could be used in decision-making. Almost all major corporations have Business intelligence units today. The purpose of BI is proactively to support information to decision-makers for their actions.

Often a distinction is made between tactical and strategic intelligence, which originates from the military intelligence tradition that the authors of BI often come from. Furthermore, the proactivity of BI often distinguishes between the ability of finding critical information, without the decision-makers having to ask for it, and the proactivity to anticipate future questions from the management.

Methodologically, the BI operations are based on the intelligence cycle. This cycle has been described by many authors all having their own version of the same basic cycle. The cycle used here is adopted from Ashton and Stacey.

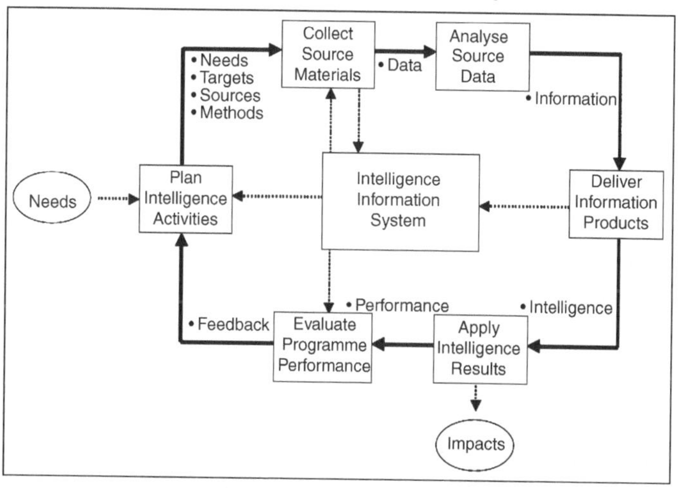

Fig 3.2. The S&T Intellegence Process.

The first step includes planning the intelligence activities. Effective intelligence is based on clear identification of user or customer needs to be served by the intelligence activity and careful forethought about information gathering and analysis. The second step is to collect source materials.

Sources of information can be internal or external, formal or informal, personal or electronic. The secret lies primarily in narrowing down what information are relevant, identifying where to find it, and knowing how to analyse it in order to support decision-making. The third step involves analysis of the materials and sources to interpret their meaning in the light of intelligence objectives or user needs.

This includes, for example, interpreting the meaning of information, to develop results, and to assess implications. The fourth step is to deliver the information products. This can be done through formal presentation, through e-mail, or by other means. Once developed and disseminated, intelligence results are applied or used in some way to affect organizational decisions or actions. Typically, the findings are either used as the basis for specific action or simply stored for possible later use in actions.

Finally, in step 6, the intelligence process and results should be evaluated with regard to whether they serve user needs and ultimately have beneficial impacts on the organization. The purpose of the evaluation is to improve future operations by making them more responsive to company needs, to further clarify those needs and to adjust practices accordingly. By looking at the model, it is easy to get the impression that the activities are sequential, starting with the planning of intelligence activities. It should be emphasized though that the intelligence cycle describes a continuous activity; a never-ending process oscillating between search and decision.

Marketing Research

Effective decision-making depends on the quality of the information input, and Marketing research plays an essential role in providing accurate and useful information. Marketing research is the firm's formal communication link with the environment. It is the means by which the firm generates, transmits, and interprets information from the environment about or relating to the success of the firms marketing plans. Marketing research is broadly concerned with the application of theories, problem-solving methods and techniques to the identification and solution of problems in marketing. Marketing research may be defined as "the function which links the consumer, customer, and public to the marketer through information Finformation used to identify and define marketing opportunities and problems; generate, refine, and evaluate marketing actions; monitor marketing performance; and improve our understanding of marketing as a process".

Marketing research links the organization with its market environment. It involves the specification, gathering, analysis, and interpretation of information to help management understand that particular market environment, to identify its problems and opportunities, and to develop and evaluate courses of marketing action.

As with the Business intelligence cycle, the Marketing research process has been described by several authors, for example, Churchill, Kumar. Except some minor differences, the process seems to be quite similar, independent of the author. Step 1 in the research process, agree on research process, comprises a shared understanding between the manager and the researcher of problems or opportunities to be studied, decision alternatives to be evaluated and users of the research results.

Then, the research objectives are established. The research objective is a statement, in as precise terminology as possible, of what information is needed. A research objective has three components. The first is the research question. It specifies the information the decision-maker needs.

The second and third elements help the researcher make the research question as specific and precise as possible. After establishing objectives, it is necessary to have an estimate of the value of the informationFthat is, the value of obtaining answers to the research questions.

Such an estimate will help determine how much if anything should be spent on research. The research is then designed, the data collected, the data analysed, and the results are reported together with recommendations.

Over the last ten years, research within the area of Marketing research has been concerned with advertising and media research, brand evaluation and choice, brand management, buyer and consumer behaviour, channels of distribution, new product research, pricing research, and other marketing-related activities.

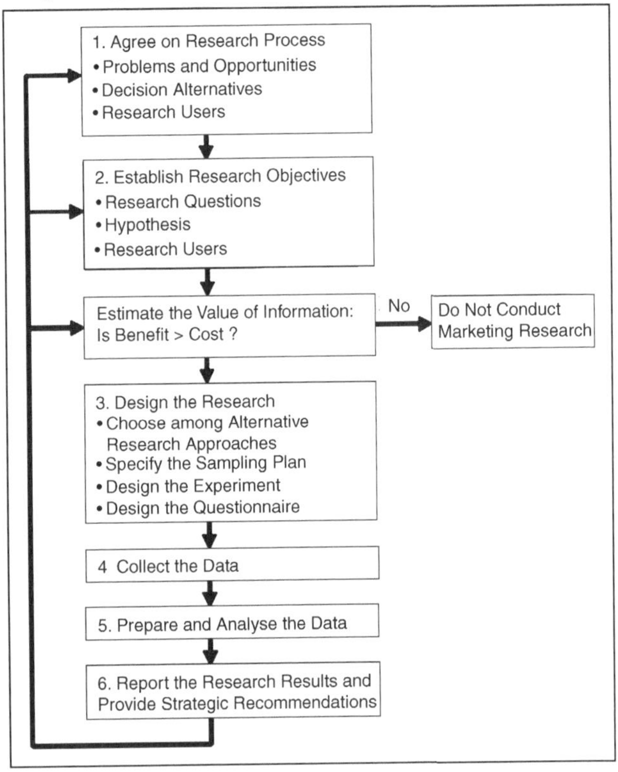

Fig 3.3. The Marketing Research Process.

Information Management and Information Systems

Information management has emerged as the most common brief name for the management of the use of information technology in an organization. In this context, information technology refers to the hardware and software of computing and telecom, and associated resources. A central theme in

Information management, independent of perspective, is information processing. Information processing might be viewed as doing something to information to make it into something else, *e.g.* subjective knowledge, differently arranged information or summary information.

In general terms, Information management can be viewed as a response to, and a search for new and improved means of controlling the information explosion and the resultant increasing complexity of decision-making by improving the flow, the control, the analysis and the synthesis of information for decision-makers.

The following definition of Information management may be used:

* "The aim of Information management is to promote organizational effectiveness by enhancing the capabilities of the organization to cope with the demands of its internal and external environment in dynamic as well as stable conditions. Information management includes organizational wide information policy planning, the development and maintenance of integrated systems and services, the optimization of information flows and the harnessing of leading edge technologies to the functional requirements of end-users, whatever their status in the parent organization. Information management has two dimensions, the management of the information process and the management of data resources".

Rowley has also suggested a framework for Information management, with the intention of presenting a structure of the knowledge, research and practice within the area of IM. This framework can be found below.

The framework shows the different levels at which Information management can be studied. Outside the circles we find the information environmentF the environment that surrounds information contexts; it consists of political, legal, regulatory, societal, economic and technological forces. In the same way business or marketing systems exist in a wider environment, so the contexts in which Information management occurs can be placed in a wider context.

The outer circle Finformation contextFis the context in which information systems are encountered. The context influences system design, and encompasses the user. Organizations and businesses are an important category of context, but other contexts are also possible, including education, home and community.

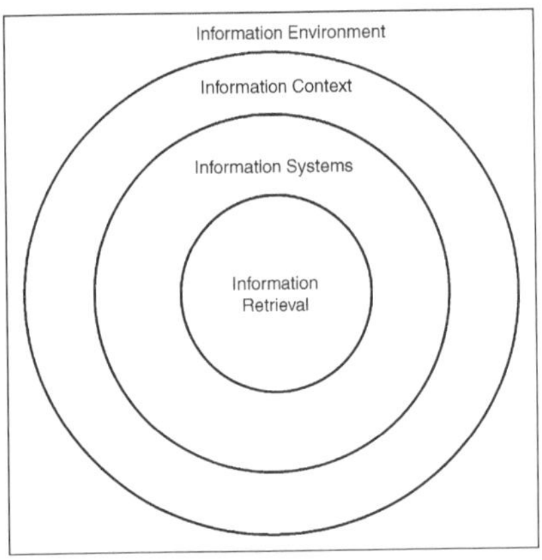

Fig 3.4. A Framework for Information Management Environments.

Information contexts are the contexts in which information processing and management take place. As can be read in the definition of IM, part of Information management is information systems, a point also made by Cronin and Davenport. These systems are used in many organizations for daily operations.

An information system may be defined as an organized combination of people, hardware, software, communication networks, and data resources that collects, transforms, and disseminates information in an organization. Information systems are the systems designed to enter information, store it and facilitate effective retrieval. Facilities to support efficient and accurate data entry must be coupled with adequate physical storage capacity and appropriate logical database structures.

Systems include hardware and software, and data, and in some models, users. Information systems should be the invisible tools that support the information processing of individuals or organizations.

The impact of such systems on information processing and developments in information processing in recent years have been so significant that it is appropriate to consider this level in the framework explicitly. An alternative perspective might actually be that the entire framework is concerned with information systems, since either an organization or an individual can be regarded as an information system.

The key issues in IS from IS-managers perspectives are:

* Improving the links between information systems strategy and business strategy,
* Developing and implementing information infrastructure,
* Implementation of knowledge management systems, and
* Reducing IT projects completion time and budget deviations.

Recent academic research has centered on IS development, studies of decision support systems, IS evaluation, IS implementation, and studies of expert systems/artificial intelligence. Finally, the inner circleFthe information retrieval circleFis concerned with the individual interfacing with a system or range of systems or sources with a view to meet specific conscious or unconscious information requirements.

It concerns the actions, methods, and procedures for recovering information from stored data. Information retrieval commences with an individual's explicit or implicit need for information. Typically, the individual will then select one or more sources which on the basis of previous experience might expect to offer access to the required information. Once an appropriate source has been selected the user interacts with that source.

Comparison of the Different Approaches

After describing the different terms/approaches used to describe how information might be collected, interpreted, analysed, distributed and so forth, it is now time to compare these approaches with the characteristics mentioned in each approach. As will be soon evident, there are a lot of similarities between these approaches even if the terms used seem to differ a lot at first glance. The comparison of the different approaches and their characteristics are summarized in figure.

Table3.1. Comparison of the Different Information Processing Approaches

	Characteristics					
	Future Orientation	Focus	Methodology	Ennobled (Value-added)	Ties to Decision-making	Scope
Environmental Scanning	Yes	Acquire general info. of events or phenomena in the environment	Scanning process	Yes and No	Strong	Broad, contains BI
Business Intelligence	Yes	Interpretation of information of changes in environment	Intelligence cycle	Yes	Strong	Part of Env. Scanning, contains all other intelligence terms
Competitive Intelligence	Yes	Interpretation of information about competitive position	Intelligence Cycle	Yes	Strong	Part of BI
Competitor Intelligence	Yes	Interpretation of information about competitors	Intelligence Cycle	Yes	Strong	Part of BI

Market Intelligence	Yes	Interpretation of information with focus on customers	Intelligence Cycle	Yes	Strong	Part of BI
Political Intelligence	Yes	Interpretation of information about political factors	Intelligence Cycle	Yes	Strong	Part of BI
Marketing Research	Yes	Information from environment about firms marketing plans	Marketing Research Process	Yes	Strong	Narrow, but touches on other approaches
Information Management	Yes (to some extent)	Prime focus on management of IT but also info policy planning, info systems, info flows	N/A	Yes and No	Strong	Broad, contains information systems

First, as suggested, claim that all the approaches are future oriented in the sense that they aim at generating insight into future developments. Augilar claimed that the most important type of information received through Environmental scanning is information that let the firm exploit its strengths, accentuate weaknesses, or highlight potential threats.

This information can be used for making decisions about strategy and long-range plans, something that appears in a close or remote future. Svensson-Kling claims that one characteristic of Business intelligence is that it is future oriented. By using organized intelligence activities a company tries to forecast how relevant parts of the environment will develop in the future.

This should not be surprising, since BI is viewed as a part of the broader area named Environmental scanning. Further, the purpose of the evaluation step in the intelligence cycle is to improve future operations by making them more responsive.

Since Market, Competitor, Technological, and Political intelligence are viewed as subgroups to the approach Business intelligence, they too are future oriented, trying to generate insights from various areas. And so is the approach Marketing research. Marketing research may help a decision-maker to understand a particular marketing environment in order to evaluate courses of action for the future that might concern new product research or consumer behaviour, for example.

The approach Information management is also future oriented, at least to some extent, although this is not explicitly stated in the preceding description. Although a lot of emphasis is put on IT-technology and infrastructure, the aim is to support decisionmaking, aiming at better future decisions. Information management has its prime focus on the management of the use of information technology in organizations.

Here, information technology refers to hardware and software of computing and telecom, and associated resources. Information management also focuses on information policy planning, information systems and optimization of information flows. Here, the issue is not what kind of information that is at stake; the issue is, for example, how information is distributed to end-usersFby which means.

Some of the approaches but not all are based around a certain methodology, *i.e.* how the activities are carried out. Environmental scanning is, according to Augilar based around the scanning process. This process is comprehensive and extensive, looks like an enormous blueprint, and is not contained in this report. Business intelligence, and its subgroups Competitive, Competitor, Market, and Political intelligence all seem to be based around the intelligence cycle, described by Ashton and Stacey, Collins and Lagerstam among others.

The cycle may vary from author to author, but the basic idea remains the same. Marketing research is based on the Marketing research process. It is worth to note that the Marketing research process can be cyclical; provided results and recommendations may trigger new problems or opportunities, thus starting the process all over again. But the process may also be carried out just on a one-time basis.

In contrast, the intelligence cycle describes a continuous activity; a never-ending process oscillating between search and decision. Information management is not, based on our limited research, based on a certain common methodology. This might be due to the fact that the IM approach is focused more on infrastructure, and that the IM approach is more diverse than for example Marketing research.

Moreover, most of the approaches appear not to be able to avoid the consideration of the processing of information in one way or the other, *i.e.* making information ennobled. In the Environmental scanning approach, the issue of information processing is not addressed explicitly.

However, Augilar talks about purposeful search for information, which can be interpreted as separating important information from less important. In the different intelligence approaches, ennobling of information is central. Intelligence usually indicates an interpretation of environmental events, rather than sheer information. Intelligence is actionable, processed and organized information.

When information is transferred into something that makes sense it is often called intelligence. Marketing research, too, is concerned with ennobling of information. It involves, among other things, interpretation of information and so is Information management, to some extent.

Information processing is considered a central theme, and is viewed as doing something to information to make it into something else. Further, all approaches have strong ties to decision-making. The dependence of decisionmaking becomes apparent as soon as one examines the various steps of the decision-making process, according to Augilar.

The tie to decision-making is also apparent in Duncan's definition of environment. Business intelligence, as well as the other intelligence approaches, is tied to decision-making too. The aim of BI is to generate insight into future developments as decision support in organizations or as Hamrefors puts it, the purpose of BI is to proactively support information to decision-makers for their actions.

Ashton and Stacey has similar thoughts and thinks that once developed and disseminated, intelligence results are applied or used in some way to affect organizational decisions or actions. This is not surprising since adequate information is a prerequisite for rational decision-making.

The Marketing research approach is also strongly tied to decision-making. Churchill claims, for example, that effective decision-making depends on the quality of the information input, and that Marketing research plays an essential role in providing accurate and useful information.

Finally, Information management is concerned with decision-making too. Rowley claims, for example, that IM is a means for controlling the information explosion and the resultant increasing complexity of decision-making by improving the flow, the control, the analysis and the synthesis of information for decision-makers.

Finally, each approach has a distinct scope, marking the boundaries or frame of the approach. Environmental scanning has a broad scope, and contains the approach of Business intelligence within its scope. The approach of Business intelligence, in turn, contains all the other intelligence terms or approaches within its scope. The scope of Information management can also be said to be broad, and contains within its boundaries the term information systems.

With regard to some issues, for example the purpose of making information ennobled and future orientation, these two approaches touches on each other in terms of scope. Marketing research might also be related to these two in terms of scope, since there might be similarities with, for example, Marketing intelligence and Information management in terms on ties to decisionmaking.

NATURE OF INFORMATION

Information as a resource has been a topic of discussion of academics and practitioners in various subject fields-especially in the field of economics. Economists such as Machlup, Porat and Bell pioneered the ideas of information economy with information as the transforming resource for postindustrial society.

Authors such as Horton pioneered the view of information as a corporate resource, which like other resources such as people, money, raw materials, equipment and energy, should be managed to give a competitive edge. These authors helped develop both the idea of information as a resource and the idea of information-resources management.

In the wake of information and communication technologies, Hawkins confirmed that information has become a commodity. Yet requirements for economic enhancement are not necessarily requirements for development in rural communities when it comes to the basic survival of people.

This immediately raises the question of what prerequisites a resource should comply with in order to be useful for development purposes. Of course, many other resources are needed for developing people in rural communities with which information as a resource should favourably compare-for example, farming practices in rural communities will require input resources, farming implements (tractors, ploughs), credit, markets, infrastructure, and natural resources (soil, water, climatic conditions).

At first glance, when comparing information with these resources, it seems that most of them are tangible in nature, while information is not. And yet, many view information as one of the most important resources needed for rural development. Although information is recognised as an important, yet still under-utilised, development resource, one needs to look critically at the attributes of information to determine whether they could aggravate the problem of under-utilisation.

Attributes of Information

While investigating the validity of information as a resource, the natural approach would be to compare attributes of information with those of other resources, in order to find some commonality. A comparison of this nature necessitates a closer look at the attributes of the different resources.

To this end, Burk and Horton give eight basic similarities between information and other traditional resources to fit into a resource-management framework, namely:

* Information is acquired at a definite, measurable cost.
* Information has a definite value, which may be quantified and treated as an accountable asset.
* Information consumption can be quantified.
* Cost-accounting techniques can be applied to help control the costs of information.
* *Information has a Clear Life Cycle:* Definition of requirements, collection, transmission, processing, storage, dissemination, use, and disposal.
* Information may be processed and refined, so that raw materials (*e.g.*, databases) are converted into finished products (*e.g.*, published directories).
* Substitutes for any specific item or collection of information are available, and may be quantified as more expensive, or less expensive.
* Choices are available to management in making trade-offs between different grades, types and costs of information.

From this it is clear that Burk and Horton felt that information should be seen as something tangible, physical and concrete, while viewpoints from within the information profession emphasise the intangibility of information. Counter-arguments from authors such as Vickers, White, Cleveland,

Boulding, Repo, Cronin and Gudrim show that information differs from tangible things generally thought of as valuable resources.

In classifying resources needed for development, Boon distinguishes between material resources and know-how resources. Information, together with data and knowledge, is listed as a know-how resource. There is also the viewpoint of Boulding that information should be seen as a dynamic force, which constantly alters and extends a store of knowledge. Shannon was probably the first to state that information can alleviate uncertainty-another intangible attribute.

In trying to identify those attributes of information that focus on its intangibility, Eaton and Bawden combine the viewpoints of various authors to come to the following key distinctions:

* *Value of Information*: Unlike other tangible resources, information is not readily quantifiable-that is, it is impossible to predict the ultimate value of information to its users. Also, over time, there is no predictable change in the value of information.
* *Multiplicative Quality of Information*: The results produced by the use of information differ greatly from those produced by the use of other resources-for instance, information is not lost when given to others, and does not decrease when 'consumed': sharing information will almost always cause it to increase-that is, information has a self-multiplicative quality.
* *Dynamics of Information*: Information cannot be regarded as a static resource to be accumulated and stored within the confines of a static system. It is a dynamic force for change to the system within which it operates. It adds value to an organisation through encouraging innovation and change without being tangible.
* *Life Cycle of Information*: Information seems to have an unpredictable life cycle. Ideas come into, go out of, and finally come back into, fashion.
* *Individuality of Information*: Information comes in many different forms, and is expressed in many different ways. Information can take on any value in the context

of an individual situation. This proves that, as a resource, information is different from most other resources. The very fact that information is characterised as a dynamic force, 'constantly altering and extending a store of knowledge', corresponds with situations in development in which outside information is offered to focus groups to alter their understanding of certain practices, which in turn can help them solve problems.

Apart from the attributes identified by Eaton and Bawden, the following, also containing elements of intangibility, may be added to the list:

* *Alleviation of Uncertainty:* Mark and Pierce, Shannon, as long ago as 1948, defined information as the resolution of uncertainty. This is perhaps one of the intangible attributes best known among a variety of researchers.
* *Interdependency*: Information almost always forms part of technology-it is the "soft" part. Without its information component, technology has little value as a resource for potential users who are not familiar with its workings or its background. With regard to developing rural communities, one should bear in mind that it is not necessarily new technology that brings about these achievements. All outside technology applied for the first time could be viewed as *new* to the user group or that particular situation, and could have similar effects.
* *Enhancement of Economic Growth*: A frequent complaint is that information is often denied its role as a resource. Yet, when looking at the effect of information in development situations, there seems to be an underlying awareness of its importance. Kaimowitz refer to the impact of new technology in agriculture on the basis of such aspects as increased farm income, reduced risk, resource conservation, improved health, better (food) security, and overall economic growth.
* *Extension of the Knowledge Base*: From a development

point of view, there is more emphasis, first, on improving peoples' lives socially, and only secondly on economic improvement. In development, outside technology is often introduced with the help of education, training and visual demonstrations. Rogers states that training helps people in rural communities to expand horizons, increase perceptions, enhance competencies, enlarge sense of perspective, and enhance self-esteem.

The above seem to emphasise the impact of the dynamic force of information, where the 'extension or altering of people's stores of knowledge' positively affected their social well-being.

Thus, although information is an intangible entity, it has the ability to bring about change for the better; which is the ultimate goal of development:

* *Context Dependency*: The value of information as a resource in rural development depends largely on situation-specific issues: for example, one could argue that agriculture-related information is mostly technical in nature. However, people with little exposure to modern society have many related issues they need to know about. Ozowa, for example, identified certain types of basic information needed for the development of crop production by traditional farmers; *inter alia,* information about agricultural input (seeds, fertilizer, etc.), extension, technology (farming equipment, etc.), implementation techniques (ploughing, sowing, pest and weed control), soil, water and climatic conditions, conservation, credit, marketing and infrastructure.
* *Culture Dependency*: Another attribute of information that can influence its usefulness as a development resource is that it is culture dependent-involving conceptual and cognitive differentiation. Pickering is of the opinion that because information is culture specific, it is incommunicable unless acculturated-that is, adapted for the cultural environment or the cultural mind-set of the recipient group. Here, Shields and Servaes also point out that information is not totally value-

free, but is socially conditioned and shaped by the social structures that apply it. This aspect has serious implications for developers' efforts to transfer information to the rural communities of developing countries.

* *Medium Dependency*: Information is not only culture dependent, but also medium dependent. Once information is concretised outside the human memory it should be packaged in some or other format to be communicated to someone else. Unless receivers know how to use that particular format, the information will remain inaccessible and rendered useless; for example, an electronic medium directed at users who are unfamiliar with such facilities can impede access to available information.

Thus, medium dependency of information can have serious implications for quite a number of rural people who are dependent on oral communication, owing to their oral tradition and the fact that many of them are not literate.

This attribute could cause information to be a less useful resource when compared with other resources needed for development purposes:

Conversion Dependency: It is a well-known fact that information is not used in the original form offered by its creator alone-.often, it needs to be adapted to suit a particular situation or specific circumstances. It can also happen that only a small chunk of the original information is used together with other chunks of information to form a new information package needed for a particular situation. In this way, more value can be added to the appropriateness of information. Particularly in a situation where outside information from the industrialised world is used to improve a practice in rural development, the information content needs to be adapted to bring it to the level of understanding of potential recipients.

Suitability of Attributes

It is evident that information differs phenomenally from

other resources needed for development-especially because it is intangible in nature. Although some of its attributes make it a suitable development resource (such as its ability to act as a dynamic force), others render it less suitable (such as its inaccessibility owing to its dependency on culture and media). As far as the requirements for rural development are concerned, it seems that the attributes can be divided into two categories, those suitable for development, and those less suitable for development:

A comparison of the attributes of information:

* Attributes suitable for development:
* Dynamic force
* Extends the knowledge base
* Increases perceptions
* Enhances competencies
* Enhances self-esteem
* Enhances growth
* Multiplicative
* Versatile
* Attributes less suitable for development:
* Intangible
* Interdependent
* Culture dependent
* Medium dependent
* Content dependent
* Conversion dependent

INFORMATION SCIENCE

Information science (or information studies) is an interdisciplinary field primarily concerned with the analysis, collection, classification, manipulation, storage, retrieval and dissemination of information. Practitioners within the field study the application and usage of knowledge in organizations, along with the interaction between people, organizations and any existing information systems, with the aim of creating, replacing, improving or understanding information systems.

Information science is often (mistakenly) considered a branch of computer science. However, it is actually a broad, interdisciplinary field, incorporating not only aspects of computer science, but often diverse fields such as archival science, cognitive science, commerce, communications, law, library science, museology, management, mathematics, philosophy, public policy, and the social sciences.

Information science should not be confused with information theory, the study of a particular mathematical concept of information, or with library science, a field related to libraries which uses some of the principles of information science.

SCOPE AND APPROACH

Information science focuses on understanding problems from the perspective of the stakeholders involved and then applying information and other technologies as needed. In other words, it tackles systemic problems first rather than individual pieces of technology within that system.

In this respect, information science can be seen as a response to technological determinism, the belief that technology "develops by its own laws, that it realises its own potential, limited only by the material resources available and the creativity of its developers. It must therefore be regarded as an autonomous system controlling and ultimately permeating all other subsystems of society."

Many universities have entire colleges, departments or schools devoted to the study of information science, while numerous information science scholars can be found in disciplines such as communication, computer science, law, library science, and sociology. Several institutions have formed an I-School Caucus but there are numerous others besides these with comprehensive information foci.

Within information science, attention has been given in recent years to human–computer interaction, groupware, the semantic web, value sensitive design, iterative design processes and to the ways people generate, use and find information.

DEFINITIONS OF INFORMATION SCIENCE

An early definition of Information science is:

* "Information science is that discipline that investigates

the properties and behaviour of information, the forces governing the flow of information, and the means of processing information for optimum accessibility and usability.

* It is concerned with that body of knowledge relating to the origination, collection, organization, storage, retrieval, interpretation, transmission, transformation, and utilization of information. This includes the investigation of information representations in both natural and artificial systems, the use of codes for efficient message transmission, and the study of information processing devices and techniques such as computers and their programming systems. It is an interdisciplinary science derived from and related to such fields as mathematics, logic, linguistics, psychology, computer technology, operations research, the graphic arts, communications, library science, management, and other similar fields. It has both a pure science component, which enquires into the subject without regard to its application, and an applied science component, which develops

Some authors treat informatics as a synonym for *information science*, especially related to the concept developed by A.I. Mikhailov and other Soviet authors in the mid sixties, which suggested that informatics is a discipline related to the study of Scientific Information. Because of the rapidly evolving, interdisciplinary nature of informatics, a precise meaning of the term "informatics" is presently difficult to pin down.

Regional differences and international terminology complicate the problem. Some people note that much of what is called "Informatics" today was once called "Information Science" at least in fields such as Medical Informatics.

For example, when library scientists began also to use the phrase "Information Science" to refer to their work, the term informatics emerged:

* In the United States as a response by computer scientists to distinguish their work from that of library science, and

* In Britain as a term for a science of information that studies natural, as well as artificial or engineered, information-processing systems.

There is considerably differences between what is considered a subfield of information science and what is not (or what belongs to one information science and what belongs to another. If we take *information systems* as an example, Vickery is a book written by a leading information scientist and that book places information systems within IS. Ellis, Allen, and Wilson is, on the other hand a bibliometric investigation describing the relation between two different fields: "Information science" and "information systems".

A Multitude of Information Sciences

Michael Buckland wrote an article *What Kind of Science Can Information Science Be?* from the perspective of Library and information science: "other important fields have also used the name "information science." One is computer science, concerned with the theory and application of algorithms. Another, concerned with entropy, probability, Shannon-Weaver information theory, physical patterns, and related topics, is sometimes referred to as the "physics of information."

Also, the word information is, of course, used in information technology, but largely restricted in practice to the use of electronics for communication and computation. These other areas are not considered here. Instead, we are concerned with those areas generally understood as being within the scope of *library and information science* (LIS) and the interests of the American Society for Information Science and Technology."

PHILOSOPHY OF INFORMATION

Philosophy of information (PI) studies conceptual issues arising at the intersection of computer science, information technology, and philosophy. It includes the investigation of the conceptual nature and basic principles of information, including its dynamics, utilisation and sciences, as well as the elaboration and application of information-theoretic and computational methodologies to its philosophical problems.

ONTOLOGY

In computer science and information science, an ontology formally represents knowledge as a set of concepts within a domain, and the relationships between those concepts. It can be used to reason about the entities within that domain and may be used to describe the domain.

More specifically, an ontology is a model for describing the world that consists of a set of types, properties, and relationship types. Exactly what is provided around these varies, but they are the essentials of an ontology. There is also generally an expectation that there be a close resemblance between the real world and the features of the model in an ontology.

In theory, an ontology is a "formal, explicit specification of a shared conceptualisation". An ontology renders shared vocabulary and taxonomy which models a domain with the definition of objects and/or concepts and their properties and relations.

Ontologies are the structural frameworks for organizing information and are used in artificial intelligence, the Semantic Web, systems engineering, software engineering, biomedical informatics, library science, enterprise bookmarking, and information architecture as a form of knowledge representation about the world or some part of it. The creation of domain ontologies is also fundamental to the definition and use of an enterprise architecture framework.

HISTORY OF INFORMATION SCIENCE

Early Beginnings

Information science, in studying the collection, classification, manipulation, storage, retrieval and dissemination of information has origins in the common stock of human knowledge. Information analysis has been carried out by scholars at least as early as the time of the Abyssinian Empire with the emergence of cultural depositories, what is today known as libraries and archives.

Institutionally, information science emerged in the 19th century along with many other social science disciplines. As a science, however, it finds its institutional roots in the history of science, beginning with publication of the first issues of *Philosophical Transactions,* generally considered the first scientific journal, in 1665 by the Royal Society.

The institutionalization of science occurred throughout the 18th Century. In 1731, Benjamin Franklin established the Library Company of Philadelphia, the first library owned by a group of public citizens, which quickly expanded beyond the realm of books and became a center of scientific experiment, and which hosted public exhibitions of scientific experiments.

Benjamin Franklin did invest a town in Massachusetts with a collection of books that the town voted to make available to all free of charge, which formed the first Public Library. Academie de Chirurgia (Paris) published *Memoires pour les Chirurgiens,* generally considered to be the first medical journal, in 1736.

The American Philosophical Society, patterned on the Royal Society (London), was founded in Philadelphia in 1743. As numerous other scientific journals and societies are founded, Alois Senefelder develops the concept of lithography for use in mass printing work in Germany in 1796.

19th Century

By the 19th Century the first signs of information science emerged as separate and distinct from other sciences and social sciences but in conjunction with communication and computation. In 1801, Joseph Marie Jacquard invented a punched card system to control operations of the cloth weaving loom in France. It was the first use of "memory storage of patterns" system.

As chemistry journals emerged throughout the 1820s and 1830s, Charles Babbage developed his "difference engine," the first step towards the modern computer, in 1822 and his "analytical engine" by 1834. By 1843 Richard Hoe developed the rotary press, and in 1844 Samuel Morse sent the first public telegraph message. By 1848 William F. Poole begins the *Index to Periodical Literature,* the first general periodical literature index in the US.

In 1854 George Boole published *An Investigation into Laws of Thought...,* which lays the foundations for Boolean algebra, which is later used in information retrieval. In 1860 a congress was held at Karlsruhe Technische Hochschule to discuss the feasibility of establishing a systematic and rational nomenclature for chemistry.

The congress did not reach any conclusive results, but several key participants returned home with Stanislao Cannizzaro's outline (1858), which ultimately convinces them of the validity of his scheme for calculating atomic weights.

By 1865, the Smithsonian Institution began a catalog of current scientific papers, which became the *International Catalogue of Scientific Papers* in 1902. The following year the Royal Society began publication of its *Catalogue of Papers* in London. In 1868, Christopher Sholes, Carlos Glidden, and S. W. Soule produced the first practical typewriter.

By 1872 Lord Kelvin devised an analogue computer to predict the tides, and by 1875 Frank Stephen Baldwin was granted the first US patent for a practical calculating machine that performs four arithmetic functions.

Alexander Graham Bell and Thomas Edison invented the telephone and phonograph in 1876 and 1877 respectively, and the American Library Association was founded in Philadelphia. In 1879 *Index Medicus* was first issued by the Library of the Surgeon General, U.S. Army, with John Shaw Billings as librarian, and later the library issues *Index Catalogue,* which achieved an international reputation as the most complete catalog of medical literature.

European Documentation

The discipline of *documentation science,* which marks the earliest theoretical foundations of modern information science, emerged in the late part of the 19th Century in Europe together with several more scientific indexes whose purpose was to organize scholarly literature. Many information science historians cite Paul Otlet and Henri La Fontaine as the fathers of information science with the founding of the *International Institute of Bibliography* (IIB) in 1895.

A second generation of European Documentalists emerged after the Second World War, most notably Suzanne Briet.

However, "information science" as a term is not popularly used in academia until sometime in the latter part of the 20th Century.

Documentalists emphasized the utilitarian integration of technology and technique towards specific social goals. Ronald Day, "As an organized system of techniques and technologies, documentation was understood as a player in the historical development of global organization in modernity–indeed, a major player inasmuch as that organization was dependent on the organization and transmission of information."

Otlet and Lafontaine (who won the Nobel Prize in 1913) not only envisioned later technical innovations but also projected a global vision for information and information technologies that speaks directly to postwar visions of a global "information society."

Otlet and Lafontaine established numerous organizations dedicated to standardization, bibliography, international associations, and consequently, international cooperation. These organizations were fundamental for ensuring international production in commerce, information, communication and modern economic development, and they later found their global form in such institutions as the League of Nations and the United Nations. Otlet designed the Universal Decimal Classification, based on Melville Dewey's decimal classification system.

Although he lived decades before computers and networks emerged, what he discussed prefigured what ultimately became the World Wide Web. His vision of a great network of knowledge focused on documents and included the notions of hyperlinks, search engines, remote access, and social networks.

Otlet not only imagined that all the world's knowledge should be interlinked and made available remotely to anyone, but he also proceeded to build a structured document collection. This collection involved standardized paper sheets and cards filed in custom-designed cabinets according to a hierarchical index (which culled information worldwide from diverse sources) and a commercial information retrieval service (which answered written requests by copying relevant information from index cards).

Users of this service were even warned if their query was likely to produce more than 50 results per search. By 1937 documentation had formally been institutionalized, as evidenced by the founding of the American Documentation Institute (ADI), later called the American Society for Information Science and Technology.

Transition to Modern Information Science

With the 1950s came increasing awareness of the potential of automatic devices for literature searching and information storage and retrieval. As these concepts grew in magnitude and potential, so did the variety of information science interests. By the 1960s and 70s, there was a move from batch processing to online modes, from mainframe to mini and microcomputers.

Additionally, traditional boundaries among disciplines began to fade and many information science scholars joined with library programmes. They further made themselves multi-disciplinary by incorporating disciplines in the sciences, humanities and social sciences, as well as other professional programmes, such as law and medicine in their curriculum. By the 1980s, large databases, such as Grateful Med at the National Library of Medicine, and user-oriented services such as Dialog and Compuserve, were for the first time accessible by individuals from their personal computers.

The 1980s also saw the emergence of numerous special interest groups to respond to the changes. By the end of the decade, special interest groups were available involving non-print media, social sciences, energy and the environment, and community information systems. Today, information science largely examines technical bases, social consequences, and theoretical understanding of online databases, widespread use of databases in government, industry, and education, and the development of the Internet and World Wide Web.

4

Dr. S.R. Ranganathan

BIRTH AND PARENTAGE

Ranganathan was born in Shiyali in Tanjavoor District of Tamil Nadu (then part of Madras Presidency) in his maternal grandfather's house in North Rampart Street, (Vadakku Madavilaga Theruvu) around 9.30 A.M. on 9th August 1892. It was a Gayathri Japam day in the month of *Adi* of the year *Nandana.* On that day and at that time, South Indian Brahmins recite Manthram to Gayathri to redeem them from the sins committed by them thus far.

His Janmanakshatra was *Danishta* and Lagna *Kanya.* He was the first child of his parents and the first grandchild of the grandparents both paternal and maternal. His father, Ramamrita Ayyar, belonged to the village of Ubhayavedanthapuram in the Nannilam Taluk at Tanjavoor District.

He was a landlord holding a medium-sized property of wet land, growing paddy, the principal food crop of the Cauvery delta. He was a learned and cultured man, used to giving *Ramayana Pravachanam* to small audiences was influential and was held in high esteem by the people of the neighbourhood and by visiting officials. The parents had three sons and a daughter—one of the sons died in its early age and the daughter was born a posthumous child.

Ramamrita Ayyar died (on 13 January 1898) rather suddenly after a bout of illness at the age of 30, when Ranganathan was only six years old. Ranganathan's mother survived this loss for nearly 55 years and died at Delhi due to a fire accident at the home in January 1953. Ranganathan's another brother Nateshan died in 1964 at Madras and his sister is alive.

FAMILY LIFE

Ranganathan married when he was fifteen years old in 1907. Rukmini was his wife's name. She was very devoted to Ranganathan and an able house keeper. But she died in an accident on 13 November 1928 at the Parthasarathy Koil Tank, Triplicane, Madras where she had gone for a bath. The couple had no children. Ranganathan married again in 1929 to Sarada in December 1929; she was also devoted to Ranganathan and helped him to work ceaselessly for the cause of the library profession.

She even persuaded him to donate large sums of money for the Chair of Library Science in Madras University and to the Endowment. She died at the age of 78 years on 30 July 1985 in Bangalore. Ranganathan was blessed with only one son, Shri R. Yogeswar, born in 1932.

He is an Engineer by profession and is an international consultant on machine tool design and development. He has two sons and a daughter. All of them are living in Luxembourg. Ranganathan had a simple taste for food. He would not unnecessarily waste money and energy. He was sympathetic to good people; encouraged intelligent students and guided them towards better goal and achievements.

EDUCATION

Ranganathan's education was initiated on Vijayadasami day in October, 1897 with *Aksharabyasam* at Ubhayavedanthapuram near Shiyali. After this, Ranganathan was admitted to a school in Shiyali, and was handed to the care of Subba Ayyar, a brother of his maternal grandfather and a primary school teacher.

During his school days, Ranganathan came under the influence of two of his teachers who shaped his mind - R. Antharama Ayyar and Thiruvenkatachariar, the Sanskrit teacher. From them Ranganathan learnt about the life teachings of nayanars (*Shaivaite Bhaktas*) and *Alwars* (*Vaishnavaite Bhaktas*).

Depth of scholarship and essence of life were ingrained in Ranganathan which kept in good stead in his later life to make decisions at crucial junctures. Ranganathan attended the

S.M. Hindu High School at Shiyali and passed Matriculation examination in 1908/1909.

Ranganathan passed the examination in First Class, in spite of sickness such as anaemia, piles, and stammering. In his high school career he came under the influence of P.A. Subramanya Ayyar, a scholar on Sri Aurobindo. Ranganathan joined the junior intermediate class at the Madras Christian College in March 1909. Even in those days, there were paucity of college seats. Ranganathan was picked up for his excellent marks in all the subjects and the principal.

Prof. Skinner spotted him in a crowd of students and admitted him into the course. Ranganathan passed B.A. with a first class in March/April 1913. In June, same year, he joined the M.A. class in Mathematics with Professor Edward B. Ross as his teacher. Being a favourite student of Prof. Ross, Ranganathan had an excellent Guru-Shishya relationship.

More than class room discussions, corridor and staircase discussions were taken recourse to. Ranganathan ingrained this trait into his own discipline later on. Ranganathan did his Master's degree in 1916 and he wanted to be a teacher in Mathematics. He also took a course in teaching technique and gained L T degree from a teachers' college.

During his college days, Ranganathan cultivated intimacy with his teachers, Professors Moffat and J.P. Manickam of Physics, Prof. Sabhesan of Botany, Prof. Chinnathambi Pillai and L.N. Subramanyam of Mathematics. But Prof. Ross remained his favourite Guru throughout his life.

TEACHING CAREER

In 1917 Ranganathan was appointed to the Subordinate Education Service and worked as Assistant Lecturer in the Government College in Mangalore and Coimbatore between 1917 and 1921. In July 1921, he joined the Presidency College, Madras as Assistant Professor of Mathematics.

At Mangalore and Coimbatore, Ranganathan taught Physics and Mathematics and at the Presidency College, he taught Algebra, Trigonometry and Statistics. He was a follower of the individual method of teaching putting discussion method into active use. The classes used to be lively, learning-active, and teaching-purposive. Ranganathan earned an epithet *born teacher*. He would interpose his teaching with many anecdotes and examples from life which would keep his students engaged and attentive.

Each hour of his class used to be punctuated by applauses. He also adopted the technique of assigning students with new topics, to gather data from books, and learning from discussions among themselves and amidst teachers. He organised several seminars and colloquia for students. He continued the same methods with greater vigour while teaching Library Science to students. Ranganathan was also active in extracurricular activities. From 1921 to 1923, he was Secretary of the Mathematics and Science Section of the Madras Teacher's Guild. He roused public awareness by lectures.

He introduced some uniformity and standardization in compiling the question papers for various examinations. He obtained pension facilities for private school teachers through his writings in papers and association journals. He augmented the finances of the Indian Mathematical Society.

He was a popular figure in the mathematical circles and was regarded as an efficient organiser of meetings. His friends have quoted Ranganathan's attitude to work, thus: Our right is only to do the work falling to our share, never to the fruits of our work. Flirt not with fruits.

TOWARDS LIBRARIANSHIP

Ranganathan left Presidency College in January 1924 to take appointment as the first librarian of Madras University. It was natural for Ranganathan-who was a lively teacher and had thrilling intellectual experiences with students and faculties of the Presidency College-not to opt for the post of librarian, even though it carried a handsome salary.

Ranganathan quite often narrated to us that he never wished to be a librarian. He said that Providence had made him one, for which he never regretted in his later life. In spite of his diffidence and lack of interest, his colleagues and supervisors-being keen on using his innate abilities—saw to his appointment as the Librarian of the Madras University in 1924.

He took charge of the University Library at 4.00 P.M. on Thursday, 4th January 1924. But Ranganathan was back within a week at Presidency College to plead with the Principal, *I have come with a specific request. I can't bear the solitary imprisonment day-after-day. No human being, except the staff. How different from the life in the college.*

The principal, Mr. Duncan, had to pacify him by saying: "If you feel bored even after you return from England, I shall certainly take you. I shall see that your place in the college is not permanently filled up till you come back from your travel and training abroad." Ranganathan left for England in September 1924 and returned in July 1925, after 9 months of study-cum-observation tour. In England, Ranganathan came in close contact with W.C. Berwick Sayers, Chief Librarian of Croydon Public Library and a lecturer in the University School of Librarianship, London.

Under his guidance, Ranganathan visited a large number of libraries. He witnessed how the libraries there had become community reading centres. He also found how the libraries rendered service to various strata of the society: to children, to the working class and to women, besides other groups. This made a lasting impression on his mind; it considerably changed his outlook and he discovered a social mission in his mind; thus he discovered a social mission for the library profession and for himself.

The impact of these experiences was expressively stated in 1931 by Sir P.S. Sivaswamy Aiyar, one of the enlightened statesmen of Madras Presidency at that time: He has brought to his task extensive knowledge of literature on the subject of libraries, personal acquaintance with methods of management of libraries in Britain, trained analytical intellect and a fervid but enlightened enthusiasm for the library movement. He has been the pioneer of the library movement in the Madras Presidency and has been carrying on an energetic propaganda to spread it. He knows how to rouse and sustain the interest of the reader.

ACTIVITIES AT MADRAS

After returning to Madras, Ranganathan began a mission for librarianship. He began to reorganise the University Library. His first concern was to attract more readers to the library and provide facilities for them. He took it upon himself to educate the public on the benefits of reading to one's society and to oneself. He charged the library with a mission of self-education for every one.

He used mass media to make the library hub of activity. The University Library soon acquired a niche in the world of the enlightened public of Madras. The Government of Madras took a keen interest in this and offered a handsome annual grant on a statutory basis. Within the library, Ranganathan initiated behind the scene work in several aspects of ab initio.

Here emerged the Five Laws of Library Science, the Colon Classification, the Classified Catalogue Code. and the Principles of Library Management. Active reference service began to blossom. He introduced open shelved system and provided open access. This gave impetus for readers to come quite often. The atmosphere throbbed with human activity and intellectual atmosphere. Ranganathan designed a functional library building near Madras Beach.

All these changes did not happen in a piecemeal but were developed in a holistic manner, inspired by his Five Laws of Library Science:

* Books are for use;
* Every reader, his book-,
* Every book, its reader,
* Save the time of the reader; and
* A library is a growing organism.

Outside the library, Ranganathan, launched an endless and eternal mission. He gathered the enlightened persons of the area and formed the Madras Library Association, which became the living symbol of the library movement. Ranganathan worked as the Founder Secretary from 1928 until he left Madras in 1945.

He pushed the library movement to all the comers of the Madras Presidency, which at that time covered almost two-thirds of South India. Looking at his efforts today, after nearly 60 years, we see that the public library network is quite widespread in South India.

The seed sown by Ranganathan has been cultivated for nearly 60 years, and it is currently yielding fruits. A school of library science was also initiated by Ranganathan in 1929, first under the auspices of the Madras Library Association and later taken over by Madras University.

Ranganathan was the director of the school for nearly 15 years. Later in 1957, during centenary celebrations of the University, he donated his life's savings of one lakh rupees to the University to endow a chair known as Sarada Ranganathan Professorship in Library Science. The students of this school have taken leading parts at all levels of activity-local, national, and international.

ACTIVITIES AT BANARAS

Having performed active library service for 21 years, Ranganathan sought voluntary retirement in 1945 and wanted to engage himself in active research. But he received an invitation to develop the library system of the Banaras Hindu University, by the then Vice-Chancellor Sir. S. Radhakrishnan. At Banaras, Ranganathan found the library in a chaotic condition. He reorganized the entire collection single-handedly, classified and catalogued about 100,000 books with a missionary zeal during 1945-47. He also conducted the Diploma Course in Library Science during the same period.

ACTIVITIES AT DELHI

Ranganathan moved over to Delhi University in 1947 on an invitation from Sir. Maurice Gwyer. He did not take the responsibility of organising the library. He confined himself to teaching and research in library science. Prof. S. Das Gupta, one of Ranganathan's brilliant students, became the librarian of Delhi University.

Delhi began courses in Bachelor of Library Science and Master of Library Science between 1947 and 1950. It was probably for the first time in the whole of the Commonwealth, Study Circle and Research Circle meetings were organized.

The Research Circle met every Sunday at his residence. Many new ideas and innovations began to emerge. Team research began to develop. Ranganathan was also elected the President of the Indian Library Association (ILA) and Shri S. Das

Gupta was elected as its Secretary. The Association was activated and as part of its programme a confluence of three journals, *viz*.. Annals, Bulletin, and Granthalaya were founded.

An acronym ABGILA was given to this composite, three-in-one periodical. The Annals contained research papers of the Delhi Research Circle and soon gained international acclaim. While Ranganathan was in Delhi, his international contacts began to grow. He had a close liaison with Donker-Duyvis, the then dynamic Secretary-General of FID.

Ranganathan was the Chairman of the Classification Research Group of the International Federation for Documentation (FID) between 1950-62, when he produced 12 research reports for FID and from 1962 he was the Honourary Chairman of FID/CR till his death in 1972. While he was in Delhi, Ranganathan drafted a comprehensive 30 year plan for the development of library system for India as a whole.

He was intimately involved in the founding of the Documentation Committee of the Indian Standards Institution of which he was the Chairman till 1967. In 1950, the Indian National Scientific Documentation Centre (INSDOC, Delhi) was founded. During this period, he also promoted the Madras Public Library Act. He also initiated the Classification Research Group at London. He visited USA in 1950 under Rockfeller Foundation and wrote the book *Classification and Communication.*

TOWARDS ZURICH

In order to gain first hand knowledge of Industrial documentation and to meet his international commitments Ranganathan moved over to Zurich. He wrote the second edition *of Prolegomena to Library Classification* (Published by the Library Association, London). He also regularly contributed to the Annals of Library Science published by the INSDOC.

ACTIVITIES AT BANGALORE

In 1957, Ranganathan moved over to Bangalore. He did not plan for any institutional organization of documentation activities. But it happened that Bangalore began to be industrialized and was in its ascendancy towards metropolis.

Ranganathan was helping as an adviser, the INSDOC, the Planning Commission, and the University Grants Commission. However, soon Ranganathan's solitude ended. Many young librarians of Bangalore began to gather around him. Informal discussions and research investigations were carried out to publish books and other research papers.

The crowning point of Ranganathan's activity was in the founding of *the Documentation Research and Training Centre, Bangalore* under the auspices of the Indian Statistical Institute in 1962. The main functions of this Centre are centred around research and teaching activities in library and information science. Ranganathan was the Honourary Professor of this Centre during 1962-72. He directe'' the institutional activities with great efficiency and created an atmosphere of academic excellence and simplicity. It was like a Gurukula.

Around Ranganathan were his young students eager to learn from him and Ranganathan was equally eager to get the new ideas from them. In 1965, Ranganathan was recognised by the Government of India and made him the National Research Professor in Library Science.

This was also an honour to library science and librarianship. At that time, only four other National Research Professors were there. They were Dr. C.V. Raman (Physics), S.N. Bose (Physics), P.V. Kane (Law), S.K. Chatterjee (Literature and Linguistics). Ranganathan was honoured by Delhi University and Pittsburgh University by awarding Doctor of Letters degrees in 1948 and 1964. Ranganathan received these awards and honours in simple and humble stride and advised his students to do hard work saying that reward would come in appropriate time.

He used to say "God has chosen me as an instrument, the honour done to me should act as an incentive to the younger generation to devote their lives wholeheartedly to library science and service." Most of his salary as National Research Professor and the royalties on his books were donated to the Sarada Ranganathan Endowment for Library Science (1961).

During the last five years, Ranganathan abstained from travelling and did deep thinking and intensive writing. He wrote many books and articles. He postulated *Absolute Syntax* for indexing language. He kept on working on Colon Classification and proved that the design and development a scheme for classification is a life time activity.

Until the end of his life, to the very last day, Ranganathan kept on working. He died on 27 September 1972 after a fruitful 80 years of his life. While he himself contributed to the field of library service, science and profession, he catalysed a human movement whose manifestation is witnessed even today. He wrote sixty books and 2000 articles. His life was a symbol of immortality.

The integral nature of Ranganathan's theory emerged from occasional intuition; and his intellect strove to make it more explicit to the rational mind of the scientific worker. His contributions sometimes bordered on a poetic beauty and sometimes on uncouth prose-but his life and work in the field of library science modelled an ever-enquiring mind, well-entrenched in the philosophy of *Bhagavad Gita* (Chapter 18, Verse 20).

5

Types of Libraries

PUBLIC LIBRARY

A public library is a library that is accessible by the public and is generally funded from public sources and operated by civil servants. There are five fundamental characteristics shared by public libraries. The first is that they are supported by taxes; they are governed by a board to serve the public interest; they are open to all and every community member can access the collection; they are entirely voluntary in that no one is ever forced to use the services provided; and public libraries provide basic services without charge.

Public libraries exist in many countries across the world and are often considered an essential part of having an educated and literate population. Public libraries are distinct from research libraries, school libraries, and other special libraries in that their mandate is to serve the general public's information needs.

Public libraries also provide free services such as preschool story times to encourage early literacy, quiet study and work areas for students and professionals, or book clubs to encourage appreciation of literature in adults. Public libraries typically allow users to take books and other materials off the premises temporarily; they also have non-circulating reference collections and provide computer and Internet access to patrons.

SERVICES OFFERED

In addition to print books and periodicals, most public libraries today have a wide array of other media including audiobooks, e-books, CDs, cassettes, videotapes, DVDs, and video games, as well as facilities to access the Internet and inter-library loans. Readers' advisory is a fundamental public library service that involves suggesting fiction and nonfiction titles.

Public libraries may also provide other services, such as community meeting rooms, storytelling sessions for infants, toddlers, preschool children, or after-school programmes, all with an intention of developing early literacy skills and a love of books. In person and on-line programmes for reader development, language learning, homework help, free lectures and cultural performances, and other community service programmes are common offerings.

One of the most popular programmes offered in public libraries are summer reading programmes for children, families, and adults. In rural areas, the local public library may have, in addition to its main branch, a mobile library service, consisting of one or more buses furnished as a small public library, serving the countryside according to a regular schedule.

Public libraries also provide materials for children, often housed in a special section. Child–oriented websites with on-line educational games and programmes specifically designed for younger library users are becoming increasingly popular. Services may be provided for other groups, such as large print or Braille materials, Books on tape, young adult literature and other materials for teenagers, or materials in other than the national language.

California and Nevada now offer a new service called Link+. This new programme links county libraries across the two states, allowing patrons access to books their library may not have in their collection.

Librarians at most public libraries provide reference and research help to the general public, usually at a reference desk but can often be done by telephone interview. As online discussion and social networking allow for remote access, reference is becoming available virtually through the use of the Internet and e-mail.

Depending on the size of the library, there may be more than one desk; at some smaller libraries all transactions may occur at one desk, while large urban public libraries may employ subject-specialist librarians with the ability to staff multiple reference or information desks to answer queries about particular topics at any time during regular operating hours. Often the children's section in a public library has its own reference desk.

Public libraries are also increasingly making use of web 2.0 services, including the use of online social networks by libraries. Public libraries in some countries pay authors when their books are borrowed from libraries. These are known as Public Lending Right programme.

DIGITAL DIVIDE

As more commercial and governmental services are being provided online, public libraries increasingly provide Internet access for users who otherwise would not be able to connect to these services.

Part of the public library mission has become attempting to help bridge the digital divide. A study conducted in 2006 found that "72.5 per cent of library branches report that they are the only provider of free public computer and Internet access in their communities". A 2008 study found that "100 per cent of rural, high poverty outlets provide public Internet access, a significant increase from 85.7 per cent last year".

The *American Library Association* (ALA), addresses this role of libraries as part of "access to information" and "equity of access"; part of the profession's ethical commitment that "no one should be denied information because he or she cannot afford the cost of a book or periodical, have access to the internet or information in any of its various formats."

In addition to access, many public libraries offer training and support to computer users. Once access has been achieved, there still remains a large gap in people's online abilities and skills. For many communities, the public library is the only agency offering free computer classes and information technology learning.

As of 2008, 73.4 per cent of public libraries offered information technology training of some form, including information literacy skills and homework assignment help. A significant service provided by public libraries is assisting people with e-government access and use of federal, state and local government information, forms and services.

Internationally, public libraries offer *information and communication technology* (ICT) services, giving "access to information and knowledge" the "highest priority." While different countries and areas of the world have their own requirements, general services offered include free connection to the Internet, training in using the Internet, and relevant content in appropriate languages. In addition to typical public library financing, *non-governmental organizations* (NGOs) and business fund services that assist public libraries in combating the digital divide.

ORIGINS AS A SOCIAL INSTITUTION

The culmination of centuries of advances in the printing press, moveable type, paper, ink, publishing, and distribution, combined with an ever growing middle class, increased commercial activity and consumption, new radical ideas, massive population growth and higher literacy rates forged the public library into the form that it is today. Public libraries are not a new idea; Romans made scrolls in dry rooms available to patrons of the baths, and tried with some success to establish libraries within the empire.

Naturally, only those few that could afford an education would be able to use the library, where those less than rich or without control of money; women, children and slaves could not. In the middle of the 19th century, the push for truly public libraries, paid for by taxes and run by the state gained force after numerous depressions, droughts, wars and revolutions in Europe, felt mostly by the working class.

Matthew Battles states that:

> "It was in these years of class conflict and economic terror that the public library movement swept through Britain, as the nation's progressive elite recognized that the light of cultural and intellectual energy was lacking in the lives of commoners."

Libraries had often been started with a donation, an endowment or were bequeathed to various, parishes, churches, schools or towns, and these social and institutional libraries formed the base of many academic and public library collections of today.

Andrew Carnegie had the biggest influence in financing libraries in the United States of America, from the east to west coast. From just 1900 to 1917, almost 1,700 libraries were constructed by Carnegie's foundation, insisting that local communities first guarantee tax support of each library built.

The establishment of circulating libraries by booksellers and publishers provided a means of gaining profit and creating social centers within the community. The circulating libraries not only provided a place to sell books, but also a place to lend books for a price. These circulating libraries provided a variety of materials including the increasingly popular novels.

Although the circulating libraries filled an important role in society, members of the middle and upper classes often looked down upon these libraries that regularly sold material from their collections and provided materials that were less sophisticated. Circulating libraries also charged a subscription fee, however the fees were set to entice their patrons, providing subscriptions on a yearly, quarterly or monthly basis, without expecting the subscribers to purchase a share in the circulating library.

Circulating libraries were not exclusively lending institutions and often provided a place for other forms of commercial activity, which may or may not be related to print. This was necessary because the circulating libraries did not generate enough funds through subscription fees collected from its borrowers. As a commerce venture, it was important to consider the contributing factors such as other goods or services available to the subscribers.

Many claims have been made for the title of "first public library" for various libraries in various countries, with at least some of the confusion arising from differing interpretations of what should be considered a true "public library". Difficulties in establishing what policies were in effect at different times in the history of particular libraries also add to the confusion.

The first libraries open to the public were the collections of Greek and Latin scrolls which were available in the dry sections of the many buildings that made up the huge Roman baths of the Roman empire. However, they were not lending libraries.

The "halls of science" run by different Islamic sects in many cities of North Africa and the Middle East in the 9th century were open to the public. Some of them had written lending policies, but they were very restrictive. Most patrons were expected to consult the books on site. The later European university libraries were not open to the general public, but accessible by scholars.

PUBLIC LIBRARIES IN INDIA

Public library is largely regarded as the People's University. It has tremendous developments in India from the early period to till date at various stages. Most of the Indian states now have free public library services to develop the people of India at different levels.

ANCIENT PERIOD

> "The history of the development of the public library may be said to be as old as that of education in India". During Vedic times, the pupils stayed in the *guru-gruha* for several years for education. Since ancient times, India is being very much pertinent in search of knowledge and wisdom. Oral communication was the best means amongst the people of India and writing was not available. "The earliest written and recorded materials found in India are the inscriptions on stone pillars of King Asoka; these inscriptions could be called the first outside open libraries". Later, *Ashrams* came into existence in India and students study under the supervision of well-known teachers. They kept many manuscripts for use of the teachers and students as well as for the visitors. Many students joined ashrams and such big ashrams were known as *vidyapeeth,* where numbers of teachers are engaged to teach the students. These educational institutions collected many different manuscripts and other materials which can help in their teaching and daily routine. They kept and preserved carefully. "The

reading materials, of course, related to many subjects formed the source material for transmitting knowledge in different streams of education and culture. The collections might be likened to modern libraries since they were carefully maintained and extensively used by students and teachers alike". Such *ashrams* or *vidyapeeths,* where manuscripts and other reading materials were reserved, may be regarded as a kind of library as they serve information and knowledge to the students and community in different ways. Pandey S K Sharma stated that; "In India, since the ancient times libraries have been functioning as light houses for those who wanted to read and to extend the boundaries of various disciplines. References are available to prove that Nalanda University had its own multistoried library in AD 600 with massive collection of manuscripts. The collection of the library was housed in three buildings, each having nine floors and three hundred rooms. This library was opened by the then Emperor of India, King Davapal. The library was open for any body that was known scholar and took interest in reading, interpreting and even copying the documents kept in the library. Chinese traveller Whuen Sang is known to have consulted this library in the seventh century and to have taken from here hundreds of treatises to China and Japan. This library was completely destroyed by Bakhtiar Khilaji, who invaded India in AD 1205. And burnt the library. The library kept on burning for about six months".

Libraries in ancient India also developed at other famous centers of learning, such as *Vikramshila* and *Odantapuri.* Universities of ancient India, like Taxila and Vikramshala also have valuable collection on *tantras* and manuscripts in their libraries.

MEDIEVAL PERIOD

Muslims mostly rule the Medieval Period of India. Historically, it is also known as Mughal Period. There were great changes not only in social and political, but also on education and library system during this period. The Muslim rulers made great contributions to Indian culture and libraries played a significant role in the sociocultural development of the nation. "The period of Mughal is considered as the golden period of Indian history for its educational, literary, and library activities". Babur, king of Kabul invaded India and annexed Delhi to his kingdom. "He established the first Mughal Imperial Library in 1526".

Babur inherited manuscripts from his father and kept in his library and also collected books from different sources of his kingdom. Babur died in 1530 and was succeeded by his son Humayun. Humayun much lived in Agra and established library in his palace. He set up a library at Agra Fort, which was managed by Lal Beg.

In his library, he kept books, gilded pen cases, portfolios, picture books and beautiful works of calligraphy. After the death of Humayun, his son, Akbar, succeeded him in 1356. Akbar is regarded as one of the greatest Mughal king. Akbar improved the management of library with some technical works. He appointed Sheik Faizi to manage and control library services.

Akbar was very interest in manuscripts and appointed calligraphers to copy good manuscripts. He established a separate library for women at Fatehpur Sikri and made great improvement to the library. At the time of his death in 1605, the Imperial Library has twenty-four thousand books.

Jahangir, another rule of Mughal period, made a law that when a wealthy man died heirless, the property should be used for building and repairing schools, monasteries, libraries, and other institutions. Some wealthy and scholars, like Abdul Rahim Khan-i-Khanan, Shaik Faizi, Gulbadan Begum and ruler of Mysore and Jaipur also have their private libraries.

Some Hindu learning centers also have libraries. "The libraries of these centers contain huge collections of manuscripts on religion and philosophy as well as other subjects like medicine, science and history". Christian missionaries have also contributed for the libraries since the coming of Vasco da Gama in India.

During the Mughal period, library technical works, *viz.* Accessioning, Classification and Cataloguing were also carried out in some ways. The head librarian was known as *"Nizam"* and the assistant librarian *as "Muhatin"* or *"Darogha"*. Other staff of libraries during Mughal period is Scribes, Book Illustrators, Calligraphers, Copyists, Translators, Bookbinders and Gilders.

THE BRITISH PERIOD

The Britishers came to India primarily to establish trade and commerce. Some of them were very interested for the upliftment of rich cultural heritage of India. "A number of Academic institutions were established during the British period by the East India Company and by the Christian missionaries".

The University of Calcutta was established in 1857 and its library was opened in 1873. Other Universities, University of Bombay and University of Madras were established in 1879 and 1907 respectively. There were only nineteen Universities in India before 1947. Universities were equipped with libraries in accordance with the Indian University Act of 1904.

The Bengal Royal Asiatic Society set up library in 1784, Bombay Royal Asiatic Society in 1804 and Calcutta Public Library in 1835. Establishment of these libraries enlightened the community and may be regarded as the foundation of the concept of public libraries to the Indian people.

Some of the important libraries set up in 19th. Century in India are Andrews Library, Surat in 1850, Gaya Public Library, Gaya in 1855, Long Library, Rajkot in 1856, Connemara Public Library, Madras in 1860, Government Library, Janagarh in 1867, Adyar Library, Adyar in 1886 and Dahi Laxmi Library, Nadiad in 1892.

Apart from these, other libraries, like Gujarat Vernacular Society along with a library, in Ahmedabad 1848 and Barton Library, Bhavnagar in 1882 were also established. Some of the Indian states also established public libraries.

Such as Baroda established Baroda State Library in Baroda in 1877, Cochin established Public Library and Reading Room in Trichur in 1873, Dhar established Victoria General Library in Dhar in 1856, Indore established General Library in Indore in

1852, Jaipur established Maharajah's Public Library in Jaipur in 1899. Others states also established such kind of libraries, *viz.* Jammu and Kashmir in 1879, Kahtiawar, in 1886, Kolhapur in 1850, Nizam's Dominion in 1891 and Travancore in 1829.

The first significant date in the development of public libraries in India is 1808 when the Bombay Government initiated a proposal to register libraries, which were to be given copies of books published from the 'Funds for the Encouragement of Literature'.

The contributions of His Highness the Maharaja Sayajirao III, Gaekwar of Baroda towards library movement in India cannot be overlooked. He is remembered today as the Father of Library Movement in India. At the age of 18, in 1881, he was entrusted with full power of the government of Baroda in the Gujarat speaking region of the Bombay Presidency and the Peninsula of Kathiawar.

Baroda's population was predominantly rural, the main occupation was agriculture. The people in general were economically poor and socially backward. Education was the foundation to reconstruct a new social and economic life and education should be the right of the humblest villager.

He introduced free and compulsory education in his princely states. Baroda became the first territory not only among the native states but also in British India to have compulsory free primary education. He opined that primary education was to be the very base and decided to preserve it by means of libraries, which were the only agencies for perpetual universal self-education.

He decided to establish library as an experiment in one of the towns of a *taluka* and in order to implement his idea immediately; he issued orders to his ministers. "In conformity to his ruler's instructions, the Minister of Education prepared a detailed plan to open Circulating Libraries in the State, which was approved in March, 1907. Every public library instituted through the State's financial assistance was to be named as Circulating Library".

In 1906, he went to America as "an observer, a student desirous of acquiring all the knowledge and experience that could enable him to make his own State a model one in India". He was very much impressed by the library services of America for the development of the people in their social, economic and educational life. He then invited an American, William Alanson Borden, a pupil-assistant of Charles A Cutter, who is working as Librarian of the Young Men's Institute, New Haven, Connecticut to come and established library services in India.

In response to his invitation, Borden reached Baroda on November 6, 1910, and became the Director of State Libraries. It can be traced back that public library movement started since 1910 in India. Borden makes a survey of libraries in Baroda and concludes that there were over 241 libraries, holding a little over 100000 volumes. But he did not find any of those libraries adequately housed, nor did he find them shelved in such a manner as to make them most attractive to readers or convenient to those in charge.

He then make proposal for the best services of libraries in the State as:

* Should Your Highness feel disposed to grant me the necessary authority, I propose to organize a Department of Public Libraries, to rank with the other Departments of Your State, with the necessary equipments of officers and clerks, etc. and to bring all the libraries under its control and management;
* To unify all the collections of books in Baroda City into one Central library;
* To add to this Central library, general and technical books;
* To erect a suitable library building of fireproof construction, with reading grooms, study rooms, Women's Library, Children's library, Lecture hall, Library school, and executive offices;
* To make that library to be Free Public Library of Baroda City, and also the main storehouse for all the valuable historical documents and papers now in private hands in the State, but which the owners would probably be glad to have stored in a safe place;
* To make it also the center from which traveling libraries should start and from which the books, new

and old, could be distributed to the various branch libraries in the different towns, cities, and villages of the State.

The Maharaja apparently accepted Borden's proposals, and ordered that the whole scheme might be implemented in parts. The Library Department was created under Order No.9/19, January 30, 1911, for organizing libraries in Baroda.

As the Director of state libraries, he planned a network of free public libraries consisting a state central library, four district or divisional libraries, forty-five town libraries, and more than a thousand village libraries-all integrated into one chain system.

Borden played a leading role for the establishment, management and organization of public libraries in India. As a result of system, within two decades 85% of the Baroda urban and rural population had access to libraries.. Borden developed library classification scheme to suit Indian libraries.

Another great contribution of Borden was the establishment of the first library school in India, in which he trained his own assistants and successors. Borden conducted the first formal library-training programme in India at Baroda in 1911. He was instrumental in the foundation of the Baroda Library Club and its journal, "Library Miscellany", published quarterly in three languages between 1912 and 1919.

University of Madras created the post of University Librarian in 1923 and Dr. S R Ranganathan joined the post on 4 January 1924. Ranganathan published his Five Laws of Library Science in 1931, Colon Classification in 1933 and Classified Catalog Code in 1934.

He also prepared Model Public Library Bill and drives to legislate library bill in Indian states. He made a tremendous contribution for the development of libraries in India. Scholars, educationists and people of library bent of mind founded Calcutta Public Library in 1835 and the same was opened on 21 March 1836 for the public.

In 1944, Calcutta Public Library was shifted to a new and spacious building, constructed in honour of the Governor-General of India, Lord Metcalf. Indian War of Independence broke out in 1857 resulted in to Europeans of Calcutta withdrew their support for the library management in 1899. Consequently, the management and establishment of the library were gradually waning and by the end of the century, the activities of the library came into standstill.

Lord Curzon, the then Viceroy and Governor-General of India visited Calcutta in 1899 and found a miserable condition of Calcutta Public Library. He bought the rights of the Library from the proprietors and later merged it with the Official imperial Library consisting of government departmental libraries of the East India Company. He then declared open of a new Imperial Library of India on 30 January 1903 in the Metcalf Hall. In 1948, one year after the independence of India, Imperial Library was transformed into National library of India and was housed to the Viceroy's Palace in Calcutta, namely, the Belvedere Palace.

POST-INDEPENDENCE PERIOD

Public libraries in India made a tremendous growth after the independence of India in 1947. The central and the state governments took a number of steps forward for the development of the nation from the point of education and considered library as essential part of it.

The programmes executed by provincial and central governments since 1910 for the social and adult education of the populace paved the way for the enactment of library laws and rules for grants-in-aid in the country. Hence public library became part of the education budget.

To enhance the level of literacy of 16% in 1941, the government undertook some programmes such as extension services, continuing education, social education, non-formal education and adult education. The government further initiated steps for the development of community and organized some projects in this regard. Libraries were considered to be an essential part of the Community Development Project that was launched during the first plan period.

In order to accelerate the pace of socioeconomic development, the government considered public libraries to be an integral part of development projects.. The Connemara Public Library in Madras became the State Central Library in 1950 under the provision of Madras Public Libraries Act 1948, and became one of the three depository libraries in 1955.

Delhi Public Library was established in 1951 as the first UNESCO Public Library Pilot Project under the joint auspices of UNESCO and Government of India to adopt "Modern Techniques to Indian Conditions" and to serve as a model public library for Asia.. In 1954, the Delivery of Book Act was passed to include newspaper.

The act obligated every publisher in India to deposit one copy each of its publications to the National Library in Calcutta, the Asiatic Society Library in Bombay, Connemara Public Library in Madras, and Delhi Public Library in New Delhi The Advisory Committee for Libraries as constituted in 1957 by the Government of India, with K P Sinha as the Chairman.

The Committee submitted its report in 1959 with a drafted Model Library Bill. The Planning Commission constituted a Working Group on Public Libraries in 1964 and the Commission submitted its report in 1965 with a Model Public Libraries Act. The model bill was sent to all the states/UTs, which do not have Public Libraries Act.

In 1972, the Government of India, Planning Commission constituted Working Group on Development of Public Libraries to make recommendations for library development. Raja Rammohun Roy Library Foundation, an autonomous body under the Department of Culture, Ministry of Education, was established in 1972.

The main objective of the Foundation was to assist state library services in developmental works. In 1979, a library section was established in the Department of Culture under the Ministry of Education, which section was under the charge of an Under Secretary. The objective was to promote the development of public libraries in India.

A Working Group on Modernization of Library Services and Informatics was appointed by the Planning Commission in 1983 and submitted its report in 1984 with the formulation of National Policy on Library Services and Informatics. Delhi Public Library became a copyright library in 1982.

National Literacy Mission was adopted in 1986, which

emphasized education for women and also establishment of rural libraries. Library networks and systems were strengthened at the national level institutions in the development of literature in neoliterates. Fourteen states namely, Tamil Nadu, Andhra Pradesh, Karnataka, Maharashtra, West Bengal, Manipur, Kerala, Haryana, Mizoram, Goa, Orissa, Gujarat, Uttaranchal and Rajasthan have enacted Public Libraries Bills during 1948 to 2006.

The Government of India, Department of Culture, appointed a Committee on National Policy on Library and Information System in 1985. The National Policy on Education, 1986 states that a nationwide movement for improvement of existing libraries and the establishment of new ones will be taken up, provision will be made in all educational institutions for library facilities, and the status of librarianship improved.

The National Book Policy, 1986 also had an impact on libraries, as:

* Provision of reading material for children by all the agencies involved;
* That 10 per cent of the annual education budget of the governments be used to purchase books for libraries.

These goals are to be achieved by using formal, non-formal, and open channels of learning.. Rural libraries should become the focal point for postliteracy and continuing educational programmes. Publishers, voluntary organizations, and school library programmes undertaken as part of the "Operation Blackboard Scheme" of the National Education Policy on Education, 1986 were given assistance. The following five libraries were regarded as national importance and may be stated in a very brief manner.

National Library, Kolkata

National Library, Kolkata was established in 1836 in the name of Calcutta Public Library. It was not a Government institution running on a proprietary basis. The then Governor General, Lord Metcalf transferred 4,675 volumes from the library of the College of Fort William to the Calcutta Public Library.

This and donations of books from individuals formed the nucleus of the library. Prince Dwarkanath Tagore was the first proprietor of the Calcutta Public Library. Both the Indian and foreign books, especially from Britain, were purchased for the library. In the report of 1850 we find that the library started collecting books in Gujarati, Marathi, Pali, Ceylonese and Punjabi.

The Government of Bengal and North Western Provinces regularly made by individuals as well as donations. The Calcutta Public Library had a unique position as the first public library in this part of the country. Such a well-organized and efficiently run library was rare even in Europe during the first half of the 19th century. Because of the efforts of the Calcutta Public Library, the National Library has developed rare books and journals in its collection.

The Imperial Library was formed in 1891 by combining a number of Secretariat libraries. Of these, the most important and interesting was the library of the Home Department, which contained many books formerly belonging to the library of East India College, Fort William and the library of the East India Board in London.

But the use of the library was restricted to the superior officers of the Government. Lord Curzon, the then Governor General of India, was the person who conceived the idea of opening a library for the use of the public. He noticed both the libraries, Imperial Library and Calcutta Public Library, were under-utilized for the want of facilities or restrictions. So, he decided to amalgamate the rich collection of both of these libraries.

He was successful in effecting the amalgamation of Calcutta Public Library with the then Imperial Library under certain terms. The library, called Imperial Library, was formally opened to the public on 30th January 1903 at Metcalf Hall, Kolkata.

The aims and objectives of the Imperial Library, well defined in a Notification in the 'Gazette of India' *as ' It is intended* that it should be a library of reference, a working place for students and a repository of material for the future historians of India, in which, so far as possible, every work written about India, at any time, can be seen and read.

Librarian of the British Museum, London, was appointed as the first Librarian of the Imperial Library. After his death, the famous scholar and linguist Harinath De took over the charge of the library. After his death J. A. Chapman became the librarian. Mr. Chapman showed keen interest in the affairs of the library and worked hard to improve its status. After his retirement, Khan Bahadur M.A. Asadulla was appointed as the librarian and he continued as the librarian till July 1947.

The policy of acquisition broadly adhered to by the Imperial Library was enunciated by Lord Curzon in his speech at the opening ceremony of the library, "The general idea of the whole Library is that it should contain all the books that have been written about India in popular tongues, with such additions as are required to make it a good all-round library of standard works of reference."

After the independence the Government of India changed the name of the Imperial Library as the National Library, with an enactment of the Imperial Library Act 1948 and the collection was shifted from the Esplanade to the present Belvedere Estate. On 1st February 1953 the National Library was opened to the public, inaugurated by Maulana Abul Kalam Azad. Sri B.S. Kesavan was appointed as the first librarian of the National Library.

The reviewing Committee in its report of 1969 suggested that the following should be the basic features of the National Library; Acquisition and conservation of all significant printed materials produced in the country to the exclusion of ephemera:

* Collection of printed materials concerning the country wherever published and also acquisition of photographic record of such materials that are not available within the country;
* Acquisition and conservation of manuscripts having national importance;
* Planned acquisition of foreign materials required by the country;
* Rendering of bibliographical and documentation service of retrospective materials, both general and specialized;
* Acting as a referral centre purveying full and accurate knowledge of all sources of bibliographical activities;
* Provision of photocopying and reprographic services; and

* Acting as the centre for international book exchange and international loan..

Khuda Bakhsh Oriental Public Library, Patna

Khuda Bakhsh Oriental Public Library, Patna was open for the public in October 1891 with 4000 Oriental manuscripts. Maulvi Khuda Bakhsh donated his entire collection to the nation by a deed of trust.

Acknowledging the immense historical and intellectual value of its rich and valued collection, the Government of India declared the Library as Institution of National Importance by an act of Parliament in 1969. The Library is now fully funded by the Ministry of Culture. This autonomous institution is being governed by a Board with the Governor of Bihar as its ex-officio Chairman and Director is carrying the responsibility of dayto-day management of Library affairs.

Rampur Raza Library, Rampur

Rampur Raza Library, Rampur was founded by Nawab Faizullah Khan in AD 1774. It was brought under the management of a Trust till the Government of India took over the library on 1 July 1975 under the Act of Parliament, which declared it as an institution of National importance.

It contains very rare and valuable collection of manuscripts, historical documents, specimens of Islamic calligraphy, miniature paintings, astronomical instruments and rare illustrated works in Arabic and Persian languages besides 80,000 printed books. Nawab Faizullah Khan who ruled the state of Rampur, from 1774 to 1794, established the library with his personal modest collection kept in the Tosha Khana of his Palace.

Now the Library occupies the position of an autonomous institution of national importance under Department of Culture, Government of India and is fully funded by Central Government. The Library has now attained an International status of higher studies.

Thanjavur Maharaja Serfoji's Sarasvati Mahal Library, Thanjavur

Thanjavur Maharaja Serfoji's Sarasvati Mahal Library,

Thanjavur is one among a few medieval libraries existing in the world. It contains very rare and valuable collections of manuscripts, books, maps and paintings on all aspects of Art, Culture and Literature.

The *Encyclopaedia Britannica* in its survey of the Libraries of the world mentions this as "the most remarkable Library in India". The Library houses a rich and rare collection of manuscripts on art, culture and literature. Conceived and christened as the Royal Palace Library by the Nayak Kings of Thanjavur. And the Maratha rulers nourished it for intellectual enrichment.

In 1918 this library was made as a public library. A body constituted by the Government and financed by the Central and State Governments now administers the library. During the reign of Nayaks of Thanjavur, "Sarasvati Bhandar" was formed and developed. The Maratha rulers who captured Thanjavur in 1675 A.D. patronized the culture of Thanjavur and developed the Royal Palace Library till A.D. 1855.

The Sarasvati Bhandar was situated within the Palace campus and the Manuscripts used for the purpose of reading by the Royal personages. Among the Maratha Kings, King Serfoji II, was an eminent scholar in many branches of learning and with great enthusiasm he took special steps for the enrichment of the Library.

It is a fitting tribute to the great collector Serfoji that the Library is named after him. Till the survival of the last Maratha Queen, the Library was the Palace property. After that, the Library together with the Palace properties formed the subject of litigation in Civil Courts.

The Royal Family members voluntarily came forward to delete this Library from the suit properties formed an Endowment and dedicated this Library to the public with one lakh rupees for its maintenance and upkeep. The Government of Madras in their G.O. Ms. No.1306 Home dated 5th October 1918, took possession of the Library under the Charitable Endowment Act and framed scheme for the Library management.

In 1983, the Library was declared as an Institution of National Importance. The Government of Tamil Nadu abolished the Five Member Committee of administration and made it as a

Registered Society as per G.O. 209 (EST) dated 1-2-83. The Society was constituted and got registration on 9-7-1986 under the Tamil Nadu Registered Societies Act of 1975.

The Society consists of ex-officio members of Central and State Governments, nominated Scholars, Member from the Royal family and the Director of the Library. The Hon'ble Education Minister of the Government of Tamil Nadu is the ex-officio Chairman of this society.

Harekrushna Mahtab State Library, Bhubaneswar

Harekrushna Mahtab State Library, Bhubaneswar was conceived during 1st Five-year Plan under the advice of Government of India and was completed in 1959, enshrined within a beautiful land of 3 acres in a prime location of Capital City of Bhubaneswar.

In 1967, it was named as Gandhi Bhawan commemorating birth centenary of Mahatma Gandhi, the father of the nation. In 1987 it was renovated and entire space of the four storied building was utilized for the functioning of two Libraries *i.e.* State Library for the entire State of Orissa and another Public Library for Bhubaneswar City.

In 1987, Government decided to rename the State Library and the Public Library as Harekrushna Mahtab State Library and the Bhubaneswar Public Library respectively. The former is a Reference Library and lending of books is not permitted whereas the latter is a Lending Library for the public of Bhubaneswar City. These two Libraries have managed to function over the limited space. Total readers seats available are about 350 against the present demands of 600-700 readers per day.

LIBRARY LEGISLATION IN INDIA

Since the beginning, the public libraries served as the local information centers making the source of knowledge readily available to the public. The local community from the local fund or individual munificence could not achieve the services of a public library. Public leaders, scholars and learned societies have realised that the only way to establish and develop a public library system is through legislation.

The UNESCO Public Library Manifesto, 1972 stated that, "The public library should be established under the clear mandate of law", which is substantiated by the IFLA/UNESCO Public Library Manifesto 1994 as;

> "The public library shall in principle be free of charge. The public library is the responsibility of local and national authorities. It must be supported by specific legislation and financed by national and local government. It has to be an essential component of any long-term strategy for culture, information provision, literacy and education".

Libraries are recorded under the Article 246 of Indian Constitution, Seventh Schedule List II of State List No.12 and the Indian Constitution Act, 1956, "Libraries, museums and other similar institutions controlled or financed by the State; ancient and historical monuments and records other than those to be of national importance.

Provision of public library service is the responsibility of the State Government as the subject matter of libraries is relatable to entry 12 of the State List in the Seventh Schedule to the Constitution of India.

Dr. S R Ranganathan regarded as the pioneer of library legislation in India. "The concept of legislation for libraries is a contribution of S R Ranganathan to Indian public libraries". He made library legislation obligatory for the implementation of the second law of library science, "Every reader his/her book". Ranganathan the second law can be properly carried out only by legislation.

Dr. S R Ranganathan strived a lot for library legislation and prepared different library bills for the Indian Union and constituent states; such as;

* Model Library Act for constituent states of India;
* Bengal;
* Bombay;
* Central Province and Berar;
* Old Madras state which later became Act in 1948;
* United Province;
* Cochin;
* Travancore;

* Union Government;
* Madhya Pradesh;
* Union and Constituent States;
* Constituent States;
* Union;
* West Bengal;
* Kerala;
* Uttar Pradesh;
* Mysore which became Act in 1965;
* Assam;
* Gujarat and Model Library Bill.

Public libraries also considered as community information centers providing access at local level to a wide range of knowledge and information for the benefit of the individual and society as a whole. To ensure sustained development and information network services public libraries should be based on legislation.

Public library legislation may be in various forms depending upon the government structure. It can be simple, allowing the establishment of public libraries but leaving standards of service to the level of government directly responsible for the library, or more complex, with specific detail on what services should be provided and to what standard.

But no British Government passed library Act for creation of public library system in Indian states.. There have been different efforts to work out library legislation models in India. In the pre-independent and post-independent of India, there have been five models of public library bills suggested by experts and national level professional associations and organizations.

MODEL PUBLIC LIBRARIES ACT OF DR. S R RANGANATHAN

The first Model Public Libraries Acts was prepared by Dr. S R Ranganathan in 1930 and revised in 1957 and 1972. It was discussed at the First All Asia Educational Conference held at Banaras during 26-30 December 1930. It was introduced in West Bengal Legislature in 1931 and in Madras Legislature in 1933. The Bill could not be passed due to financial clauses on library grant, library cess etc.

Salient features of final version are:

* Establishment of public libraries in city, rural and other areas;
* Constitution of State Library Authority *i.e.* Minister of Education;
* Constitution of State Library Committee as an advisory body of the State Library Authority;
* Constitution of Local Library Authority for each city and one for each district;
* State Library Authority, Government and Local Library Authority may determine library rate in such a manner and may determine collection of library cess from time to time.

MODEL PUBLIC LIBRARIES BILL OF MINISTRY OF EDUCATION

The Government of India, Ministry of Education appointed an Advisory Committee for Libraries in 1957, under the Chairmanship of Shri K P Sinha, former Director of Public Instruction, Bihar. This committee recommended the need for library legislation for each state. As a follow-up action of the Advisory Committee, the Ministry of Education, Government of India appointed a committee under the Chairmanship of Dr. M D Sen. The Committee drafted Model Public Libraries Bill in the year 1963.

The salient components of this Bill are:

* Constitution of State Library Authority as an apex body to advise the Government in the matter of library developments;
* Constitution of State Library Directorate for direction and controlling of library services;
* Constitution of District Library Committee in each district;
* Treatment of employees as government servant;
* Collection of library cess at the rate of 6 paise per rupee on house tax and property tax.

MODEL PUBLIC LIBRARIES BILL OF THE PLANNING COMMISSION

The Planning Commission, Government of India,

constituted a 'Working Group on Libraries' in 1964 to plan and advice on the development of Libraries during the Fourth Five Year Plan. The Working Group recommended a Library Development Scheme to be implemented during the Fourth Plan period with a financial commitment of Rs.309 million, which was appended by Model Public Libraries Bill and submitted its report in 1965. Bill was not considered even by a single state.

The Bill included the following features:

* Establish, maintain, develop and integrated adequate public library service in the state;
* Constitution of Committee of Experts to prescribe the standards of service;
* Constitution of State Library Council to advise the government for the promotion and development of library service;
* Establishment of State Library Directorate to control, direct and supervise library system in the state;
* Establishment of State Central Library, State Regional Libraries and District Libraries;
* Treatment of employees in the system of State Government Servants
* Government shall be the financial source and shall maintain the public library system in the state.

MODEL PUBLIC LIBRARIES BILL OF INDIAN LIBRARY ASSOCIATION

The Indian Library Association (ILA) formed in 1933, has keen interest in library legislation. The ILA discussed library legislation at its various seminars organized in 1964, 1978 and 1981. Consequently, ILA Council at its meeting held on 23 June 1989, keeping in view of the developments and experiences gain from the existing Acts, resolved to prepare a Model Library Bill.

Accordingly, as asked by ILA, Dr. Velaga Venkatappaiah, Chairman, Central Sectional Committee on Public Libraries of the ILA prepared a Model Public Library Bill. ILA accepted the draft Bill with minor changes at its National Seminar on Public Library Legislation in 1990 at the final product of the Model Public Libraries Bill was published in 1991.

The Bill was circulated to all the states and union territories but few states reacted favourably to the Bill. This Model Bill was again discussed in a National Seminar on Library Legislation and revised as the Model State Public Library and Information Service Act in 1995. In view of emergence of Information Technology at all levels, the model act was again revised in 2000.

The important components of this Bill are:

* State Library and Information Service, based on a State Policy;
* Constitution of State Library Authority at the apex level with Minister of Libraries as Chairman as policy making and executive body;
* Establishment of Directorate of Public Libraries for directing, controlling and supervising;
* Constitution of City, District Library Authority for rendering service from district to village level;
* Provision for network of Public Library and Information Services from state to village level;
* Constitution of State Library and Information Service;
* Collection of Library cess on house tax and property tax, entertainment tax, professional tax, vehicle tax, etc.;
* Constitution of State Boards for education, book production, co-ordination, etc.;
* Accountability of public expenditure and services.

MODEL UNION LIBRARY ACT

The Government of India appointed a committee to explore the possibilities to establish a National Central Library at New Delhi in 1948. Dr. S R Ranganathan, a member of the committee drafted a Library Development plan in 1950 with a 30-year programme and a draft Library Bill for the states and Union Public Library Act.

This was revised in 1959 and again in 1972. However, libraries falls under the state list of the constitution and it may not be possible to pass Bill as a Union Act, unless and until the constitution is suitably amended for this purpose.

The main features of this model Act are:

* Constitution of a National Library Authority;
* Establishment of national central libraries;
* Constitution of National Library Committee as an advisory body to the National library Authority;
* Constitution of National library fund;
* Amendment to the delivery of Books and Newspaper Act, 1954.

The IFLA/UNESCO Public Library Manifesto 1994 reads that, "The public library is the local center of information, making all kinds of knowledge and information readily available to its users". Public libraries, to become an enthusiastic source of information and knowledge for the local community, needs certain forms of developments in terms of infrastructure, collection and the trinity of library as well. It cannot survive by the local contributions and dedication alone, but through the support of government.

"The pubic library, as a democratic institution operated by the people for the people, should be established and maintained under the clear authority of law; supported wholly or mainly from public funds; open for free use on equal terms to all members of the community regardless of occupation, creed, class or race". Efforts have been going on well under the initiatives of professional associations and learned societies in this context. "In India, the post independence era was favourable to the establishment of public libraries based on legal basis"..

STATES WITH LIBRARY LEGISLATION

During the last six decades, 14 Public Library Bills were enacted in different states of India, such as:

* Tamil Nadu: The Tamil Nadu Public Libraries Act 1948;
* *Andhra Pradesh*: The Andhra Pradesh Public Libraries Act 1960;
* *Karnataka:* The Karnataka Public Libraries Act 1965;
* *Maharashtra*: The Maharastra Public Libraries Act 1967;
* *West Bengal:* The West Bengal Public Libraries Act 1979;

* *Manipur:* The Manipur Public Libraries Act 1988;
* *Kerala*: The Kerala Public Libraries Act 1989;
* *Haryana:* The Haryana Public Libraries Act 1989;
* *Mizoram:* The Mizoram Public Libraries Act 1993;
* *Goa:* The Goa Public Libraries Act 1993;
* *Orissa*: Orissa Public Libraries Act, 2001;
* *Gujarat:* Gujarat Public Libraries Act, 2001;
* *Uttaranchal:* Uttaranchal Public Libraries Act, 2005.
* *Rajasthan:* Rajasthan Public Libraries Act, 2006

Tamil Nadu

Tamil Nadu is the first state that enacted Public Libraries Act in independent India. It came into force with effect from 1 April 1950. The objectives of the Act are contained in its Preamble as, 'An act to provide for the establishment of public libraries in the province of Tamil Nadu and the organization of comprehensive rural and urban Library Service therein". It has 19 sections.

The salient features of this Act are given below:

* This Act facilitates establishment of Public Libraries in the State.
* Constitution of State Library Committee for the purpose of advising the government on such matters relating to libraries.
* Provision for appointment of Director of Public Libraries to control, direct and supervise public libraries.
* Constitution of Local Library Authorities, one for the City of Madras and one for each district.
* Every Local Library Authority shall levy in the area a library cess in the form of a surcharge on property tax or house tax at the rate of six paise per rupee.
* The Government shall contribute Library Fund to each of the Local Library Authority, except the City of Madras, to the amount of library cess collected.
* The Act amended Sec.9 of the Press and Registration of Books Act, 1867, Central Act XXV of 1867 to the effect that every printer shall deliver five copies of each

book to the State Government out of which four will be deposited in the State Central Library, Madras.

Tamil Nadu was very rich in public libraries. The Connemara Public Library was opened for the public in 1896 and became the State Central Library from 1 April 1950. There is a tremendous growth and development of public libraries since an enactment of Tamil Nadu Public Libraries Act 1948 being the first state in India with Library Legislation.

As on March 1998, the state has public library service units, as–1 State Central Library, 29 District Central Libraries, 1548 Branch Libraries, 506 Village Libraries, 649 Part-time Libraries, and 8 Mobile Libraries. The Department of Public Libraries has been offering extension services, like–Mobile Library Service, Home Delivery Service, Library Service for Children, Library Service for Police Personnel, Library Service for state workers and remote settlers in the hills, Hospital Library Service, Rural Library Service, Part-time Library Service, Library Service for Students, Library Service for research scholars and Library Service for competitions for various civil services.

Andhra Pradesh

The state of Andhra Pradesh was formed in 1956, comprising Andhra areas of composite Madras state and Telengana area of Hyderabad area, whereas Madras Public Libraries Act in force in Andhra area. To solve administrative problems on two acts in operational in one state; both the acts were amalgamated, modified and up-to-date as Andhra Pradesh Public Libraries Act 1960.

It received the Governor assent on 18th. February 1960. Andhra Pradesh is the second state that has enacted Public Libraries Act in independent India. Its Preamble reads that, "*An Act to* consolidate and amend the laws relating to the establishment and maintenance of Public Libraries in the State of Andhra Pradesh and matters connected therewith".

It has seven chapters. Important features of this Act are as below:

* Constitution of 'The Andhra Pradesh Granthalaya Parishad', as a corporate body, having perpetual succession and power to the provisions of this Act.

* Constitution of Directorate of Public Libraries to direct, supervise and control Public Library System.
* Constitution of Zilla Granthalaya Samastha, one for the City of Hyderabad, one for the district of Hyderabad and one for each districts.
* Provision to collect library cess by every Zilla Granthalaya Samstha in its area as surcharge on property tax or house tax up to eight paise per rupee.
* The accounts of Zilla Granthalaya Samstha shall be open to inspection.
* Provision of Government Grant-in-aid to private libraries.
* Provision for constitution of a Library Service for the Zilla Granthalaya Samstha for the appointment of Librarians.

Andhra Pradesh is one of the leading states in India for the promotion of library services in India. It is the second in India with Public Libraries Act in 1960.

The structure of public library services can be classified into three categories consisting of:

* *Government Libraries:* 1 State Central Library, 6 Regional Libraries, and 1 Mobile Library,
* *Zila Grandhalaya Samstha Libraries:* 23 District/City Central Libraries, 1448 Branch Libraries, 355 Village Libraries, 3 Mobile Libraries, and 576 Book Deposit Centers,
* *Aided Libraries:* 1238 Gram Panchayat Libraries, 37 Cooperative Society Libraries, and 680 Private Libraries.

Karnataka

Karnataka is the third state in an independent India that have enacted Public Libraries Act. The objective of this Act can be seen in its Preamble that reads, '*An* Act to provide for the establishment and maintenance of Public Libraries and the organization of a comprehensive rural and urban library service in the State of Karnataka '.

Important features of this Act are given below:

* Constitution of State Library Authority to meet twice

in a year, Minister of Public Libraries as its Chairman and State Librarian as *ex-officio* Secretary.

* Provision for creation of an independent Department of Public Libraries with a profession as its head, to supervise, direct and control library services.
* Provision for the establishment of State Library as apex of public library system in the state.
* Constitution of Local Library Authority, City Library Authority and District Library Authority.
* Provision for setting up of Advisory Library Committee for Branch and Village Library Services.
* Collection of library cess on tax on lands and buildings.
* Additional sections in State Central Library
* State Bureau of Copyright Collection
* State Library for the Blind
* State Bureau of Inter Library Loan
* State Bibliographical Bureau
* State Bureau of Technical Service.

Karnataka is the third state in India that enacted Public Library Bill in 1965. The Belgaum Native General Library, established in 1848 by M.J.D. Invararity, was regarded as the first library started in Karnataka state. There were other seven libraries or reading rooms in Belgaum, namely, Library at Chikkodi established in 1886, Nippani Library in 1875, Gokak Library in 1865, Athani Library in 1865, Sampagaon Library in 1866, Khanapur Library in 1868, and Saundatti Library in 1870.

The existing public libraries in Karnataka are-1 State Central Library, 1 Indira Priyadarshini Chidren's Library, 1 Public Technical Library, 27 District Central Library, 19 City Central Library, 14 Mobile Libraries, 490 Branch Libraries, 107 Service Stations, 31 Reading Rooms, 5766 Gram Panchayat Libraries, 21 Aided Libraries, 200 Slum Libraries and 600 Reading Rooms in Slum Areas.

Maharashtra

Consequent upon the constitution of Maharashtra state, The Maharashtra Public Libraries Act, 1967 succeed Kolhapur Public

Libraries Act 1945. The fourth state in an independent India that has enacted Public Libraries Act is Maharashtra state. Preamble of the Act read that, "To provide for the establishment, maintenance, organization and development of public libraries in the state of Maharashtra".

Important features of this Act are:

* Constitution of State Library Council. Minister for Education shall be the ex-officio President of the Council. The Council will advise the State Government on all matters connected with the administration of this Act.
* Constitution of a separate department of Libraries and the appointment of a professional Director;
* Establishment of Maharashtra State Library Service;
* Establishment of State Central library and a Divisional Library for each Division;
* Constitution of District Library Committee in each of the district. Chairman of the Education Committee of a Zilla Parishad in the district shall be ex-officio President of the Committee.
* Constitution of Library Fund by the State Government for carrying out the purpose of this Act. The State Government will contribute not less than a sum of twenty-five lakhs to the Library Fund every year.

The Birtishers started public libraries in Maharashtra after defeating Marathas in 1818 but no Indians were allowed membership of these libraries till 1830. Pioneer libraries established by Indian in Maharashtra were at Ahmednagar in 1838, Bombay in 1845, and Poona in 1848. In 1939, the government constituted a Library Development Committee to prepare a plan for public library development in the state of Bombay.

The report was implemented from 1955 to 1967. After an enactment of Maharashtra Public Libraries Act 1967, public library system was developed through voluntary organizations with grants from the government. As on 1998, Maharashtra has different categories of public libraries as–1 State Central Library, 6 Divisional Libraries, 31 District Libraries, 63 Taluka Grade A Libraries, 144 Taluka Grade B Libraries, 58 Taluka Grade C Libraries, and 3842 Recognized Libraries.

West Bengal

The West Bengal Legislature passed this Act and assent of the President was first published in the Calcutta Gazette, Extraordinary on the 7th January 1980. West Bengal enacted the Public Libraries Act in 1979 to become the fifth state of India with library legislation. Its preamble stated that, *"An Act to provide for the* establishment of Public libraries in the State of West Bengal and to regulate, guide, central, supervise and to grant recognition to the existing libraries in the State as also to provide for a comprehensive rural and urban library service in the State of *west Bengal".*

Some of the important salient features of this Act are:

* Constitution of State Library Council for the purpose of advising the Government on the matters of public library services. Minister-in-Charge of Library Services shall be the Chairman of the Council;
* Constitution of the Department of Libraries to supervise and direct the maintenance of Public Libraries;
* Constitution of Local Library Authority for each district. The District Magistrate shall be the Chairman of the Local Library Authority. Provision for constitution of Executive Committee for Local Library Authority;
* The Government is empowered to appoint District Library Officers and District Librarians in districts. The Government, in consultation with the Local Library Authority may place a person in charge of a District Library to be called as District Librarian;
* Financial management of local libraries rests upon the Local Library Authority. Means of augmenting funds are:
* Contributions, gifts and income form endowments;
* Grants from the government
* Collection of Local Library Authority under the Act.

In 1780, Mr. John Andrews run a commercial library in Fort William and the first public library; Calcutta Public Library was established during the British period in 1836, which is now known as National Library. By 1900, there were 50 public libraries in Bengal.

The state government took up a seven tier library development scheme, which envisaged setting up of public libraries at different levels-State Central Library; District Library; Sub-Division/Area Library; Rural Library; Village Library; and Delivery Stations/Book Deposit Centers. By 1996, West Bengal has one State Central Library, 22 District Libraries, 120 Sub-Divisional/Town Libraries, and 2276 Rural/Area/Primary Unit Libraries. There are also around 3000 non-governmental/non-sponsored public libraries. West Bengal is the fifth state in India with Library Legislation in 1979.

Manipur

Manipur is the sixth state in an independent India that has enacted Public Libraries Act in 1988. The preamble stated the objectives of this Acts as, "An Act to provide the establishment and maintenance of Public Libraries in the State of Manipur and matters connected therewith".

Salient features of this Act are given hereunder:

* Constitution of a State Library Committee, to advise the State Government on all matters arising under this Act and to exercise and perform such other powers and duties as may be prescribed.
* Constitution of a separate Department of Public Libraries under the Director, as its head.
* Constitution of District Library Authority for each district to supervise library services in the area of its jurisdiction.
* Provision to constitute Executive Committee and Sub-Committees of District Library Authority to enquire into and report or advice on any matters, which it may refer to them.
* Constitution of Library fund formed mainly with the contribution of the State Government.

Manipur is the sixth state in India with Public Library Acts in 1988. Manipur Club established in 1927 was changed over into Manipur Book Club/Manipur Club Library and again changed into Jubabati Memorial Library in 1933. But the library had a setback during the Second World War.

Imphal Public Library, also known as Khwai Public Library was established in 1938 but was functioning till 1960 and later it was demolished in 1994. District Library and Children's Library-cum-Museun were merged on 26 August 1970 and came to be known as State Central library.. There are 9 District Libraries, 1 State Central Library, and 215 Libraries organized by Voluntary Organizations..

Kerala

Kerala Public Libraries Act, 1989 is also known as Kerala Granthasala Sanghom, 1989. Kerala enacted its pubic Libraries Act in 1989 to become the seventh state in India with library legislation. Preamble of this Act stated its objectives as, *"An Act* to consolidate and unify the library laws in the State and to provide for the recognition in the entire library system in the State of Kerala with a view to the development and maintenance of comprehensive rural and urban library service and for matters connected therewith or incidental hereto".

Important features of the Act are:

* Constitution of Kerala State Library Council with Executive Committee to advise the government on all matters connected with this Act and to supervise and direct all maters relating to library service in the state;
* Secretary of the State Library Council shall be the Chief Executive Authority of the State Library Council;
* Constitution of District Library Council to supervise, co-ordinate and control the Library service under its jurisdiction and to promote co-operation between libraries and cultural and educational institutions in the country;
* Constitution of Taluk Library Union, with the power to supervise, coordinate and control the library services in the Taluk and to give directions and advise to affiliated libraries in regard to their day to day function and management;
* The Government may make every year a grant to the State library council with a maximum of one per cent

of the education budget of the State.

* The State Library Council shall maintain a fund called State Library fund. Library cess collected and grants of State and Central Government will be credited to the State Library fund.
* Transfer of Kerala Granthaala Sangham with its staff, assets, and liabilities to the State Library Council.
* Collection of Library Cess in the form of a surcharge on the building tax or the property tax at the rate of 5 paise for the whole rupee.

Christian missionaries started libraries in Kerala during the 19th century. The history of public library movement in Kerala started in 1829 with the establishment of Trivandrum Public Library. There are more than 5000 public libraries in Kerala now, one in every 8 square kilometers.

Public libraries can be grouped into four categories, as– Libraries directly run by the Government, Libraries run by the local bodies, Grant-in-Aid libraries affiliated to the Kerala Grandhasala Sangham, and Libraries run by the Local Library Authorities.

The Kerala Grandhasala Sangham was established in 1947 and was registered under Section 9 of the Travancore Company Act, 1939 and in 1948 the Government approved it as the Central Agency of the Libraries. It plays an incredible role for the promotion, development and encouraging the people of the state through library services. Kerala enacted Public Library Bill in 1989 to become the seventh state in India with Library Legislation.

Haryana

Haryana is the eighth state in India with library legislation. The preamble stated its objectives as, "An Act to provide for the establishment, maintenance and development of Public Libraries in the State of Haryana and for matters ancillary *thereto.*"

Some of the important features of this Act are:

* Constitution of State Library Authority to advise the Government on all matters for the promotion of library services in the State. Minister-in-charge of libraries will be the Chairman;

* Establishment of State Library Directorate to execute the programmes approved by the State Library Authority;
* Establishment of State Central library;
* Constitution of District Library in each district and Municipal/City/Town library; Block library; Village library; and Smaller book deposit centers;
* Provision for three types of library funds, such as State Library Fund, District Library Fund, and City/Town/Block/Village Library Fund;
* Levy of Library cess in the form of surcharge on property tax and house tax as decided by the government from time to time;
* Provision to recognize state library associations, and co-operative institutions by the State Library Authority.

Before the creation of this separate state, some public libraries were already established, Guru Gobind Singh Municipal Library in 1926, Shri Parmeshwari Yuvak Librray in 1927, and Sri Bal Amar Samiti Library in 1932. A State Central Library was started in 1967 by th4 Government of Haryana. Besides it has started 12 District Libraries, 11 Sub-Divisional Libraries and 11 Municipal Libraries.

Many philanthropic trusts and local bodies/organizations had also established public libraries, which took active role in the promotion of reading habits and library services in the state. The Haryana Library Association was founded in 1967. The Haryana Public Libraries Bill was passed in 1989 and independent Directorate of Libraries was established in January 1993.

Mobile library services to reach the interior of the remote villages with reading facilities were started and the people are very much encouraged for the development of libraries at villages and panchayat levels as a social education center and community information center as well.

Mizoram

Mizoram is the ninth state of India to have library legislation.

Preamble of this Act stated its objective as, "An Act to provide for the establishment, maintenance and development of comprehensive public libraries system in the State of Mizoram".

Important features of this Act are:

* Constitution of State Library Council to advise the Government on all matters relating to libraries and also in regard to promotion and development of libraries in the State;
* Constitution of the Department of Public Libraries to control and supervise the public library system in the State;
* Constitution of State Library, District Library, Sub-Divisional Library and Village Libraries;
* Provision of grant-in-aid to recognized libraries;
* No library cess. All expenses shall be made from the Government funds.

Goa

Goa is the tenth state to have library legislation in India. Preamble of this Act stated that, "An Act to provide for the establishment, maintenance and development of Public Libraries in the State of Goa and for the matters ancillary hereto".

Important salient features of this Act are:

* Constitution of State Library Council with the Minister-in-charge a the Chairman to advise the Government on all matters arising under the Act;
* Constitution of State Library Directorate for controlling and directing the public library system in the State;
* Organization of State Library, District Library, Taluk Library, and Village library;
* Creation of Public Library employees similar to the employees of State Government;
* Recognition of one State Library Association as co-operating institution;
* State library fund from different sources, *viz.* Government contribution, Government Grants, and any other contribution from the public;
* Levy of Library Cess in the form of a surcharge on

Indian Made Foreign Liquor at the rate of 50 paise per bulk litre of beer.

Under the order of the Viceroy, *Dom Manuel de Portugal e Castro*, a public library, Publica Livraria was opened and attached to Academia Militar in 1832 and it was named as Bibliotheca Nacional de Goa in 1959 and came under the administration of Education and Health Services department. The Government of Goa constituted a State Level Expert Committee in 1978 and State Library Advisory Board in 1983 for the development of library services in the state. The public libraries of Goa can be categorized into five levels, as State Library, Taluka Libraries, Village Libraries, Government Aided Libraries, and Municipal Libraries. Goa is the tenth state in India with Public Library Act in 1993.

Orissa

The establishment of Diamond Jubilee Library at Kendrapara in 1897 and at Baripada in 1898 started the development of public library and followed by establishment of other libraries in the state. Three Government functionaries, Department of Information and Public Relations, Department of Sports and Culture, and Department of Housing and Urban Development operated public libraries in the state for some times.

In 1975, the Department of Cultural Affairs, Government of Orissa took complete charge of Public Libraries from the Department of Education. There is one State Library, 13 District Libraries, four Sub-Divisional libraries, six Ex. District Board Libraries, and four Memorial Hall Libraries.

Gujarat

Objective of Gujarat Public Libraries Act provided in its preamble is to provide for the promotion and development of public libraries in the State of Gujarat and for that purpose to constitute State Library development Council and for the matters connected therewith or incidental thereto.

Important features of this act are:

* Constitution of State Library Council with Minister—in-charge of Libraries as its Chairman;

* Establishment of Public Library Department with Director as its head of office;
* Establishment of District and Taluka Libraries at the headquarters of taluka;
* Constitution of District and Taluka Library Advisory Committee;
* Formation of State Library Development Fund;
* Recognition of libraries run by voluntary organizations.

The first considered public library in Gujarat was called, "Himabhai Institute of Library" established in 1849 in Ahmedabad. Other pioneer public libraries are Andrews Library established in 1850, Lang Library in 1857, Lakhajirao Pusthakalaya in 1868, Bhagavatsihji Library in 1884, State Library in 1865, Barton Library in 1882, Takhsinhi Library in 1877, and Victoria Jubilee Library in 1891.

There are two State Central libraries, 18 District Libraries in all the districts, 45 Taluka Libraries, 129 Mahila Libraries run by voluntary organizations, more than 300 Book Service Centers and Mobile Library service.

Uttarakhand

Uttarakhand is the 27th State of Indian Union, separated from Uttar Pradesh and coming into existence on 9.11.2000. The State comprises ten districts, namely Uttarkashi, Dehradun, Tehri Garhwal, Chamoli, Pithoragarh, Nainital, Uddam Singh Nagar, Pauri Garhwal and Hardwar. Public Libraries within these districts were automatically came under the Uttarakhand administration.

The State literacy rate is 72.28%. The state government is very interested to serve the people through public libraries and the Uttaranchal Public Libraries Bill was enacted in 2005 to become the thirteenth state in India with Library legislation. Some of the well established libraries by the state government of Uttar Pradesh were taken over while coming up into existence.

Rajasthan

Libraries were established in Rajasthan as early as 14th. Century and maintained in the form of *Pothi-Khanas* consisting rich collections of manuscripts on different disciplines. Rana Kumbha's Saraswati Bhandar Library was established in 1448. Raja Man Singh established library, *Pothi-Khana* in 1592 by keeping rare and important manuscripts.

Pioneer Public Libraries were established in Bharatpur in 1907, Sikar in 1908, Kota in 1910, Fatehpur in 1910, and Jodhpur in 1915. There are 5 Divisional libraries, 24 District Libraries, and 8 Tehsil Libraries with 600 Book Deposit Centers on 15 August 1956. Mobile van was also provided to Division Libraries to supervise library services in the state.

STATES/UTs WITHOUT LIBRARY LEGISLATION

Public library systems and services of Indian states and Union Territories are highlighted hereunder.

Arunachal Pradesh

Arunachal Pradesh, formerly known as North East Frontier Agency, introduced library service since 1950s. During the Seventh Five Year Plan period, the state government took up the scheme of developing libraries in the state and set up a number of libraries at block and circle levels. Mobile library system was introduced in the state capital. The state has six categories of library, such as – one State Library, two Branch Libraries, 13 District Libraries, 2 Sub-Divisional Libraries, 20 Block Libraries, and 45 Circle Libraries.

Assam

In 1865, George Williamson, a tea-planter of Golaghat bequeathed 10,000 pounds for the purpose of educational and set up of libraries in Assam and the government taken up as an experiment measure to established public libraries at the initiatives of British government in 1902-1903 at Dhubri, Guwahati, Nagaon, Jorhat, Tezpur, Shillong, Sibsagar, Goalpara, Dibrugarh, Hailakandi, etc. and then handed over to the Local Boards.

The people were awakened and established rural libraries in some areas. The Assam Library Association came into existence in 1938 and extended all possible help to established public libraries in different areas. The Central Library, established in 1954 at Shillong and the Assam Government Public Library established in 1903 was amalgamated in 1956 and renamed as the State Central Library.

In 1955, seven District Libraries were set up at Guwahati, Nagaon, Jorhat, Dibrugarh, Tezpur, Dhubri and Silchar. Book Mobile Service along with 70 Deposit Centers for Circulation of Books was organized to villages in 1959. Assam is running one State Library, one Branch Library, 22 District Libraries, 14 Sub-Divisional Libraries, and one Children Library.

Bihar

The ancient Educational and Cultural Centers like Nalanda, Vikramshala, Patiliputra and Taxila had magnificent libraries and Bihar Library Association was founded on 15 October 1936. The Association popularized importance of libraries and in 1937 prepared a Draft Scheme for the development of libraries in Bihar.

There is one State Central Library at Patna, having seven wings, *viz.*, State Reference Library, State Lending Library, State Library for Blind, State Bureau of Inter-Library Loan, State Bibliographical Bureau, State Bureau of Technical Service, and State Institute of Library Training and Research.

At present, there is one State Central Library, six Divisional Libraries, seven Special Libraries, 17 District Central Libraries, two State Libraries, 11 Sub-Divisional Libraries, 328 Block Libraries, and 4422 Village Libraries in Bihar. The library service is at the government level is under the control and supervision of the Commissioner of Education. In the state of Jharkhand area, there are five District Libraries, four Sub-Divisional Libraries and other Village Libraries are under the public library sector. The state of Jharkhand came into existence on 15 November 2000 by separating some areas of Bihar state.

Himachal Pradesh

Under the scheme of Integrated Library Service formulated by the Union Ministry of Education, a small library system was introduced in 1952. A State Central Library was established in

Solan in 1959, and within two years sic District Libraries were opened. The State Central Library created four departments, namely, reference, Lending, Periodicals, and Children Section for the benefit of the readers.

Membership registration is free of charge to all the residents of Himachal Pradesh. It has one State Central Library, 11 District Libraries, 15 Community Central Public Libraries, and 101 Senior Secondary School Libraries in the state. The School Libraries are also used as public libraries after the school hours. Two Mobile units are set up in 1961 to cater the needs of the community particularly in the rural areas of the state.

Jharkhand

The state of Jharkhand, separated from Bihar, is having 18 public libraries established by the state government.

These public libraries may be classified into four groups as below:

* Three State Public Libraries, one each at Ranchi, Chaibasa, Dhanbad and Dumka.
* One Divisional Library at Hazaribagh;
* Five District Libraries, one each at Gumla, Lohardaga, Daltonganj and Godda; and
* Eight Sub-Divisional Libraries, one each at Garhwa, Lahetar, Pakur, Simdega, Chatra, Sahebganj, Saraikela, and Khunti..

The library building are, generally, not functional to cater more readers at a time. Furniture is inadequate and water supply system is poor. No electricity connection was available to some of them due to non-payment of bills. Collection and subscription of periodicals/newspapers are not adequate to serve the library users as well.

Jammu and Kashmir

The state is divided into 14 districts. The Christian missinaries started education. Until 1947, the state has only two public libraries, namely, Sri Pratap Singh Library in 1893 in the city of Srinagar and Sri Ranbir Singh Library in Jammu.

The State government establishes the department of public Libraries in 1961 for the establishment and promotion of public library services in the state. The state has 2 Central Libraries, one each in the province of Jammu and Kashmir, 14 District Libraries, 51 Tehsil Libraries, and 18 Block Libraries.

Madhya Pradesh and Chhattisgarh

The state of Madhya Pradesh including Chhattisgarh lies in the heart of the country came into existence on 1 November 1956. Madhya Pradesh was divided into two states, *viz.*, Madhya Pradesh and Chhatisgarh on 1 November 2000; hence the state of Chhattisgarh came into existence.

It has 5 Regional Libraries in Bhopal, Gwalior, Jabalpur, Rewa, and Indore, 42 District Libraries, 6 Information Centers, 80 Private Public Libraries, and 15800 Gram Panchayat Libraries. The Madhya Pradesh Library Association was formed in 1957.

Meghalaya

Meghalaya has taken up the State Library of Assam established in Shillong in 1903 as its State Central Library. It has one State Central Library, four District Libraries, and Libraries run by voluntary organizations in different localities. The Meghalaya Library Association was established in 1994.

Nagaland

Nagaland has established a State Central Library at Kohima in 1981 functioning under the Directorate of Art and Culture. It offers computer facilities and reprographic services to its readers. There are eight district libraries and four of them have completed computerization. 330 Rural libraries are registered under the department of Art and Culture.

Punjab

The first public library in Punjab, known as Punjab Public Library was established at Lahore in 1884. Other pioneer libraries are Dyal Singh Public Library was established at Lahore in 1896 through a trust created in the name of Dyal Singh, Sir Ganga Commercial Public Library established in 1923, and Dwarka Das Public Library at Lahore in 1921.

Pioneer Municipality Libraries in the state were established in Ludhiana in 1878, Lahore in 1884, Patiala in 1897, Amritsar in 1900, Kapurthala in 1904, and Sangrur in 1912. There are 2 State Central Libraries at Chandigarh and Patiala, 14 District Libraries, and 97 Municipal Libraries. Dr. A.C.Wooner founded the Punjab Library Association in 1915 at Lahore. The Association organize training, seminar, conferences and also publish some library literatures.

Sikkim

Sikkim public libraries came into existence under the influence of academic libraries in the state. After 1975 the Government of Sikkim realised the importance of public libraries and has started a few libraries but public libraries have not made much progress in a systematic way. All the four districts have a separate District Library at the district headquarters. These libraries were controlled, supervise and administered by the Cultural Department of the Government of Sikkim.

Tripura

From the nucleus of "Ujjayanta Palace Library", the then Maharaja Birchandra Manikya established a library in the Royal Palace in the year 1896 in Agartala was called as "Birchandra Library" and declared open to the public. This library was taken over by the government in 1953 and named as Birchandra Public Library and from 1977; it was designated as a State Central Library and renamed as Birchandra State Central Library.

Libraries are look after by the Government of Higher and Technical Education and at present the position of public library in Tripura is – one State Central Library, 3 District Libraries, seven Sub-Divisional Libraries, 10 Block Level Public Libraries, two Rural Libraries, and 1 Children Library. The departments of Social Education and Panchayat Raj also run some public libraries in the state.

Uttar Pradesh

Uttaranchal state came into existence on 9 November 2000 separating some areas from the state of Uttar Pradesh. Some libraries were established in the early days, such as, Raza Library, Rampur in 1750, Allahabad Public Library, Allahabad in 1763, Maulana Azad Library, Aligarh in 1877, Bharati Bhawan Library, Allahabad in 1889 and Lyall Library, Aligarh in 1899. The state has a State Central Library at Allhabad, 69 District level libraries, 62 other prominent public libraries run by voluntary organizations..

Andaman and Nicobar Island

Andaman and Nicobar Island, one of the Union Territories of India, have never experienced the services of libraries until a small library was set up in the cellular jail in the early 1930s. The prisoners were allowed to read books, newspapers and magazines in this library. The Government took initiatives in establishing school libraries. In 1957 an Information Centre was set up at Port Blair.

In 1964, this Information Centre was converted into District Library and later on considering the public interest the District Library was enlarged and reorganized into the State Library in 1977. Library service is under the Department of Education and financed by the Andaman and Nicobar Administration and the department came forward with an idea of spreading education through the libraries. At present, there is one State Central library, one State Library, two District Libraries, 12 Zonal Libraries, and three Public Libraries..

Dadra and Nagar Haveli

In the Union Territory of Dadra and Nagar Haveli, there is a State Central Library at the capital city Silvasa and Public Library, known as Central Libariy at Naroli, Kanvel, Randha, Kilvani, Dapido, Amoli, Dushni and Mandoni. The Central Library at Silvasa and Naroli were established in 1954 and 1965 respectively.

Central Libraries at Silvasa, Dadra and Kanvel are functioning in their own buildings whereas the remaining libraries were in a rented building and primary schools. There are no public libraries run by voluntary organizations in this Union Territory. The library services were under the control and supervision of the Director of Education..

Daman and Diu

The Assistant Director of Education under the control of the Department of Education supervises library services in the Union Territory of Daman and Diu. There are 3 Municipal Libraries at Moti Daman, Nani Daman, and Diu. Establishment of a Central library, 2 District libraries, and 1 Mobile Library is under consideration..

Lakshadweep

There was no library service in this Union Territory before independence. The first public library was established at Karavati in 1951. However, the island has the apex library of this Union Territory established in 1958 as Freedom Fighters Central Library, which was subsequently named as Lakshadweep Central Library.

It has well organized public library system in which Lakshadweep Central Library serves as the State Central Library and each of the ten constituent inhabited islands Androtti, Amini, Agatti, Bitta, Chetlat, Kadmat, Kalpeni, Karavatti, Kilton, and Minicoy is provided with a public library by the Administration of Lakshadweep. These libraries were earlier known as Reading Room-cum-Library.

Library services are looked after by a Library Development Officer who performs the supervision function under the overall control of the Director of Social Welfare and Culture. To develop and sustain library movement, the administration has constituted a state level committee known as 'Lakshadweep State Library Committee' in 1994 comprising 10 members including Library Development..

Pondicherry

The history of Library in Pondicherry began with the establishment of a *'Bibliotheque Publique'* in 1827 with a modest stock of books collected from several Government establishments functioning in this region. The British Indian Government also donated some books to this library from time to time.

It was renamed as *'Romain Rolland Library'* in 1967 after the French scholar Romain Rolland. The General Assembly, in 1892, authorized the opening of the library at Karaikal and constituted a Commission to advise the administration on measures to be taken for the development of the Library.

The Library was originally named as *'Bibliotheque Coloniale'*. This library was renamed as *'Bibliotheque Publique'* in 1952 and subsequently categorized as Regional Library and called as Government Public Library. The first library was actually started by the 'Association of Old Students' in 1918 at Mahe.

The Old Boys Association donated all the books and furniture of Mahe Public Library. In 1964, the Union Territory Administration has evolved a policy of opening Branch Libraries at rural areas of the territory and the number of Branch Libraries opened in four regions are, 46 in Pondicherry region, 14 in Karaikal region, 3 in Mahe region, and 2 in Yanam region.

The Director of Education from 1954 to 1991 controlled the library services. Since 1991, Director of Art and Culture is the head of the Library services. There are three Assistant Library and Information Officers to look after the library services under the Director of Art and Culture..

National Capital Territory of New Delhi

Before the independence, Delhi was very poor in library services, particularly in public libraries, due to political structures, lack of educational facilities, and attitude of the authorities. Harding Library was established in 1862 and housed in a portion of the Town Hall.

In 1942, Delhi Municipal Committee changed the name of the library to the Harding Municipal Public Library, which was further rechristened in 1970 as the Hardayal Municipal Public Library after the famous freedom fighter and intellectual Lala Hardayal.

The British Council Library and American Information resource Centre are also being developed for the public and function with the latest technology which enrich public library services in Delhi. Marwari Seth Kedar Nath Goenka in the Chandi Chawk area of Delhi set up the Marwari Library, the first of any type founded through community awareness in Modern India, in 1915.

Under the UNESCO's Pilot Project, the Ministry of Education, Government of India, founded Delhi Public Library in 1951. It was very much developed and became one of the depository libraries in India. The Delhi Public Library consists of the Central Library, Zonal Libraries, Branch Libraries, and Sub-Branch Libraries in addition to the Community libraries, Resettlement Colonies libraries, Sports libraries, and an adequately good network of Mobile Library Services to link up the remote urban and rural areas spread over the Union Territory of Delhi.

CONTRIBUTION OF RAJA RAMMOHUN ROY LIBRARY FOUNDATION

1972 was a significant year in the history of library movement in India. The country was celebrating the silver jubilee of its independence from the British Administration in 1972. Coincidentally it was an International Book Year with the slogan of 'Books For All' emphasizing promotion of reading habits among the masses. Not only that, it was the auspicious occasion of the bicentennial birth anniversary of an Indian social reformer, who stressed the need of modern education for the development of the nation.

In this august year, Raja Rammohun Roy Library came into being in May 1972. It is the nodal agency of Government of India to support public library services and systems and promote public library movement in the country. Raja Rammohun Roy Library Foundation is an autonomous organization, established and sponsored by the Department of Culture, Government of India.

It is registered under the West Bengal Societies Registration Act, 1961. Its headquarters is located at Kolkata. In view of the expanding activities, the Foundation has opened zonal offices under the Assistant Field Officers for monitoring the impact and implementation of the assistance rendered by the Foundation such as-Eastern Zonal Office at Calcutta; Northern Zonal Office at New Delhi; Southern Zonal Office at Chennai and Western Zonal Office at Mumbai.

Objectives

Raja Rammohun Roy Library Foundation is a national agency for the promotion of library services in general and public library services in particular. The main objective of the Foundation is to promote and support public library movement in the country by providing adequate library services and by developing reading habits all over the country with the active cooperation of State Government and Union Territories and of Voluntary Organizations operating in the filed of library services, cultural activities, adult education and the like.

Objectives of the Foundation may be listed as below:

* To promote library movement in the country;
* To enunciate a national library policy and to help build up a national library system;
* To provide financial and technical assistance to libraries;
* To provide financial assistance to organizations, regional or national engaged in the promotion of library development;
* To publish appropriate literature and to act as a clearing house of ideas and information on library development in India and abroad;
* To promote research in problems of library development;
* To advise the government on all matters pertaining to the library development in the country; and
* To propagate the adoption of library legislation in the country.

Assistance Programme

The Foundation promotes public library services rendering book and financial assistance to the public libraries under different schemes of assistance. The scheme of assistance is of two types, *viz.*, Matching and Non-Matching schemes.

Matching Schemes

Assistance under Matching Scheme is given from the resources shared on matching basis with the States/Union Territory Administrations on the basis of developed states 50;50; developing and lagging states 60;40 and North-Eastern States 90;10. This revised matching scheme is effective from 2005.

The Matching assistance can be given to achieve its main objectives for:

* Assistance towards building up of adequate stock of books and reading materials.

* Assistance towards development of rural book deposit centers and mobile library services.
* Assistance towards organization of seminars, workshops, training courses and book exhibition.
* Assistance towards storage and display of books including reading room furniture.
* Assistance to public libraries below district level for increasing accommodation.
* Assistance to public libraries below State Central Libraries to acquire TVcum-VCP sets for educational purposes/Computer for library application.
* Assistance towards Networking of Public Libraries.

Non-Matching Schemes

The Foundation fully gives assistance under this scheme from his own resources to implement its objectives for:

* Assistance towards building up of adequate stock of books through central selection.
* Assistance to voluntary organizations providing public library Services
* Assistance to children libraries or children's section of general public libraries including women section and senior citizen section.
* Assistance to public libraries towards celebration of 50 years, 100 years and 125 years.
* Assistance towards collection and compilation of library statistics through official and non-official agencies.
* Assistance to centrally sponsored libraries.
* Assistance towards organization of seminars/ conferences by national level library organizations.
* Assistance towards establishment of children's corner.

Promotion of **District Youth Resource Centres** *(DYRCs)*

The development of DYRCs is being made commensurate with the decision of the inter Ministerial Steering Committee constitutes for the purpose with the representative from Ministry of Sports and Youth Affairs, Ministry of Culture, Raja Rammohun Roy Library foundation and Nehru Yuvak Kendra Sanghatana.

The DYRCs are assisted for the following purpose:

* Towards building up adequate stock of books.
* Towards acquiring storage materials and library furniture.
* Towards construction of library building.
* Towards acquisition of computers with accessories.

Promotional Activities

RRRLF has undertaken a number of promotional activities for qualitative improvement of library services. It is associated and interacts with different national and international library professional associations like IFLA, ILA, IASLIC and different state level library associations.

Some of the promotional activities taken up by the Foundation for the qualitative improvement of library services may be given as below:

* It organizes seminars and conferences on the topics related to the development of public libraries in India.
* It plays a major role in the preparation of National Policy on Library and Information Systems and also issued guidelines on public library systems and services.
* It instituted 'RRRLF Fellowship' to eminent men and women in the field of library services who have contributed significantly to the library movement particularly, public library movement in the country through active involvement in the movement, organizational initiative, intellectual leadership or are dedicated to the propagation of the reading habit among the mass. Fellowship carries a cash award of Rs. 25,000 besides a plaque and a citation detailing the services rendered by the Fellow in the country.
* 'RRRLF Best Library Award' for the Best State Central Library in India. The Award carries a Citation and a cash incentive of Rs. 1 lakh.
* 'RRRLF Best District Library Award' in each of the six regions. The Award carries a Citation and cash incentive of Rs. 50,000.

* The Foundation instituted 'RRRLF Best Rural Library Awards' one for each state since 2005.
* 'Raja Rammohun Roy Award' was introduced annually to the best contributor of an article covering the area of development of Public Library Systems and Services or suggesting measures for the promotion of reading habits.

Research Cell and Special Library

A research cell along with a special library on Library and Information Science and statistics unit supported by a computer unit are providing necessary input to its various activities. About 5000 important books and journals on Library and Information Science and allied fields have been acquired in the library. Besides carrying on Research Projects on public library or allied subject, the Research Cell renders advisory and consultancy services whenever required. It has prepared and published a report on loss of books in libraries for the Government of India.

Publications

The Foundation has brought out many useful publications for the promotion and development of public library services in the country.

Some of its significant publications are:

* Indian Libraries; Trends and Perspectives
* Raja Rammohun Roy and the New Learning
* Directory of Indian Public Libraries
* RRRLF Newsletter
* Granthana-Indian Journal of Library Studies
* Annual Report
* Books for the Millions at their Doorsteps..

Modernization Programme

The Foundation is taking steps to meet the new technologies of information for the promotion of library services. It has a Computer Section for building-up data bank of Public Libraries for the country. This section is planned to give information storage, retrieval and data processing support for all the application areas. It has keen interest with enthusiasm to computerized state libraries in India. It gave computers to the state and district libraries to carry out Foundations' zeal to computerize such libraries. The work is going on to computerized shortly.

Achievement

The Foundation has taken pains in promoting and developing library services in the country since its inception. Central Government's grant allotment is increasing over the last years and state contributions for matching scheme is also increasing as well. This increased shows that the works carried out by the Foundation is growing and the State Government gives emphasis for the promotion of public libraries through the Foundation.

During the VIII Five Year Plan period the total plan grant from the Government of India was Rs.1175.50 lakhs with an average annual plan grant of Rs. 235.10 lakhs and contribution of States under matching scheme reaches Rs. 645.97 lakhs. The Government of India allotted an amount of Rs. 3233 lakhs as plan grant during IX Five Year Plan period. The annual average plan grant was Rs. 646.60 lakhs and the state contribution reaches Rs. 1977 lakhs.

During the last three years of the X Five Year Plan period, the plan grant stepped up to Rs. 1150.21 lakhs including a special grant of Rs. 150.21 lakhs for North-Eastern States and contributions received from various state governments also reaches Rs. 769.59 lakhs. Plan grants and State contribution of matching scheme may be given in Table 5.1 and Graph 5.1 as below:

Table 5.1. Plan Grant and State Contributions.

Rupees in lakhs

Five Year Plan	Plan Grant	Average Annual Plan Grant	State Contribution
VIII	1175.70	235.10	645.97
IX	3233.00	646.60	1977.00
X	1150.21	383.40	769.59

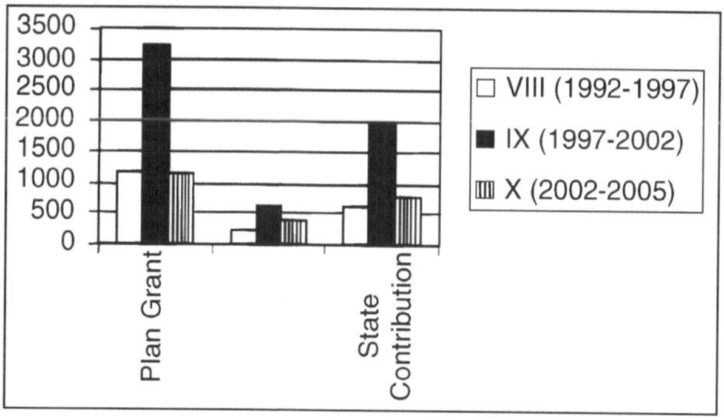

Fig 5.1. Plan Grant and State Contributions.

Over the last thirty-two years, the Foundation has covered about a little thirty-one thousand libraries at different levels for assistance. The RRRLF assistance to libraries/kendras is illustrated in Table 5.2 and Graph 5.2 as below:

Table 5.2. Assistance to Libraries Cover by RRRLF.

Category of Libraries/Kendras, etc.	No of Libraries Covered
State Central Libraries	28
Divisional and District Libraries	451
Sub-divisional/Taluka/Tehsil Libraries	501
Towns and Rural Libraries	30134
Nehru Yuvak Kendras	272
Jawahar Bal Bhavans	49
Others	128
Total	31563

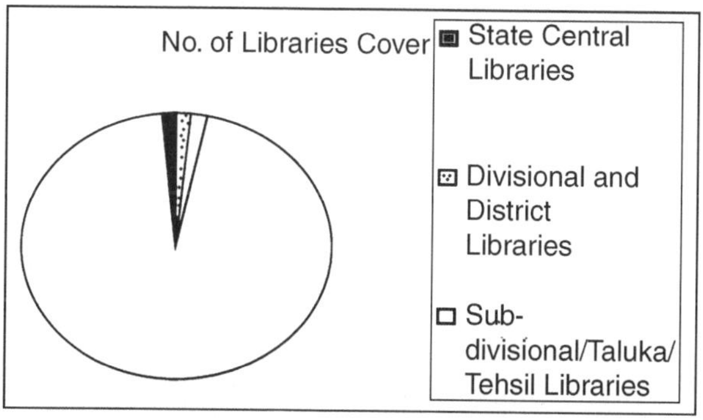

Fig 5.2. Assistance to Libraries Cover by RRRLF.

State Library Committee

The Foundation renders matching as well as non-matching assistance to support and promote public library services in the States and Union Territories in accordance with rules and procedures. Every State/Union Territory Administration are advised to set up State Library Committee (SLC) consisting of the following members and will meet at least twice a year:

* Secretary/Director or person nominated by the Department controlling library services-Chairman
* Director or Officer-in-Charge of the Department, if he is not the Chairman
* Director of the Foundation or his representative
* Nominee of the Chairman of the Foundation;
* President or Secretary of the State Library Association;
* A representative of the Education Department, if library service is controlled by a separate department;
* An educationist or an author or a person representing the state level organization connected with book production to be nominated by the State Government; and
* Librarian of the State Central Library or any other public library nominated by the State Government shall be the Convener of the State Library Committee. Where this is not feasible, the State Government will nominate a suitable official looking after library service as the Convener.

The functions of the State Library Committee shall be:

* To prepare perspective and annual plan of library services in the State with particular reference to the assistance programmes of the Foundation;
* To ensure payment of State Government/UT Administration contribution and availing of the matching grant from the Foundation;
* To select books according to the felt need of the community and in conformity with the guidelines prescribed by the Foundation;
* To scrutinize and recommend proposals for other schemes of assistance to the Foundation;

* To ensure proper utilization of assistance by the Foundation; and
* To perform any other activity conducive to the development of library in the State or Union Territory.

Foundation's assistance is available for all categories of public libraries, *viz.*, State Central Library, Regional/Divisional Libraries, District Central Libraries, Subdivisional Libraries, Tehsil Libraries, Taluka Libraries, Block Libraries, Branch Libraries, Municipal Libraries, Town Libraries, Rural Libraries, Panchayat Libraries, Village Libraries, etc. directly maintained or aided or recognized by the State Government.

State Library Committee will decide number and categories of libraries for assistance under different schemes and consolidated list of books for different categories of libraries. However, Textbooks, costly books and foreign publications should not ordinarily be selected. The maxim "the best reading for the largest number at the least cost' should be the guiding principle for selection of books.

The Foundation buys books at a graded rate of discount as mentioned below:

1	to	10 copies	-	10% discount
11	to	25 copies	-	15% discount
26	to	100 copies	-	20% discount
101	to	200 copies	-	25% discount
201	to	500 copies	-	30% discount
501	and above		-	35% discount

The Foundation also gives assistance to Public Libraries to acquire new computer or upgrade as the case may be for either of the following items, with accessories for educational purposes once in 10 years:

* One TV-cum-VCP sets with accessories together with five educational videocassettes
* Computer System
  - One Server
  - Three clients for State Central Library
  - UPS in capacity rage of 0.5 kva to 3 kva
  - One Laser Printer and one Dot Matrix Printer; one

Laser Printer, one Inkjet Printer and two Dot Matrix Printer for State Central Library.

- Library Software
- Network Equipments
- Others;
  a. One Web Camera
  b. Two Barcode Reader
  c. Two Speaker
  d. One CD-Writer
  e. One Scanner
- Cost of power cabling and installation of LAN
- Cost of Retro Conversion of total holdings.

Assistance is also given to both Government and Non-government libraries for construction of a new building or extension of the existing building. Maximum amount given to District Level Library is ₹10 lakh and ₹8 lakh for Sub. Division/ Town Level Library once in ten years. For other libraries ₹ 4 lakh can be given for construction of library building.

NATIONAL POLICY ON LIBRARY AND INFORMATION SYSTEM

John Martin said, "Policy is a statement of a specific goal or goals which are to be achieved, or to be pursued; a statement of the means by which realization of the goals will be brought about; an assignment of the responsibilities for implementation of the means, and a set of rules or guidelines regulating the activity".

National Policy on Library and Information Science is to "provide a framework for properly planned and co-coordinated development of library and information structure in a country, resulting thereby in an enhanced and user-oriented information services to its user population".

The need for the formulation of National Policy on Library and Information Systems was brought to the notice of the Government of India by Indian library profession since 1950s by Dr. S.R.Ranganathan and in the recommendations of the Library Advisory Committee Report, 1958. Afterwards, professional organizations, like RRRLF, NISSAT and National Library urged upon the Government the necessity of enunciating such policy.

The matter was discussed in the annual conference of IASLIC

in 1979 at Roorkee and ILA in 1984 at Jaipur. Consequently, Indian Library Association submitted a draft policy statement to the Government in 1985. The Planning Commission Working Group in its report Modernization of Library Services and Informatics for the 7th Five-Year Plan emphasized the need of such policy.

The Raja Rammohun Roy Foundation, after nine years of its inception, took up the task in 1981 and after careful deliberations submitted a Draft National policy on Library and Information Systems to the government in July 1984.

On the basis of the draft policy submitted by the Raja Rammohun Roy Library Foundation and Indian Library Association, the Government of India, Ministry of Human resources Development, Department of Culture, set up a Committee in October 1985 under the Chairmanship of Professor D.P.Chattopadhyaya for the formulation of a National Policy on Library and Information Systems and the final report was submitted in May 1986 which includes:

* The Public Library system;
* The Academic Library System;
* Special Libraries and Information Systems;
* The National Library System and the Bibliographical Services;
* Manpower Development and Professional Status; and
* Modernization of Library and Information Systems.

Though the government has not adopted the recommendations as the official policy, but it serves as suggestive model for the development of libraries as a whole.

The recommendations under the Public Library System are as follows:

* The most important task before the government is to establish, maintain and strengthen the free public libraries in the country and enable them to work as a system.
* The main thrust in this area should go to the rural public library. A village or a village cluster with an adequate population should have a community library, which will also serve as an information center. Resources of different agencies engaged in the work

of public health, adult education, local selfgovernment and such others may be pooled to build up this composite center.

* An important link should be established between the community library of the village and the village primary school. If the school does not have a library of its own, the community library should provide the children with an adequate book-corner.
* The community library should also importantly cater for adult education and make adequate audio-visual aids available to attract the illiterate villagers.
* The district library should serve as an apex library for each district with public libraries at city, town and village levels constituting important components in the district library system. In addition to the usual services to be rendered by it, it should also provide for learning facilities and recreation for the handicapped. Wherever possible, district libraries and comparable city public libraries should provide literature in Braille. The district library and branch libraries should also arrange mobile and circulating library services within its area wherever it is necessary and feasible. Special services should be rendered to hospitals, prisons, and the infirm in their homes.
* Libraries for special groups should be built in areas of tribal concentration or minority communities to develop their distinctive cultures. The government will provide all encouragement for such communities to develop their own libraries through voluntary effort.
* Each public library should have a section for children and, in addition, separate libraries for children with attractive books and audio-visual supporting materials should be established wherever possible.
* The district library will take the leadership in establishing linkages between all other public libraries of the district and work towards resource sharing within the area.
* The key role of public libraries as chief sustaining

agencies of distance education should be recognized and they should be adequately equipped with the relevant resources for this purpose.

* All the libraries within a state should form part of a network extending from the community library of the village through intermediary levels to the district and to the State Central Library. This State network should eventually connect with the national level.
* The role of the State Central Library is crucial in networking and the establishment of uniform library procedures within the States. The State Central Library/Directorate of Public Libraries has to perform as the coordinating agency for public libraries in the State.
* To bring about the development of the public libraries in a State it is vital that each State enact its own library legislation. The Central Government should revise the Model Public Library Bill, which it has already prepared, in the light of experience gained in recent years and urge upon the States the importance of enacting such legislation. Finances for library development should be found by each State either from its general revenues or from local taxation.
* The Central Government should assist the State in the development of public libraries in a larger way than it has done so far. The Raja Rammohun Roy Library Foundation as the national agency for co-coordinating and assisting the development of public libraries be suitably strengthened enabling it to discharge its responsibilities effectively.

NATIONAL KNOWLEDGE COMMISSION

National Knowledge Commission was set up by the Prime Minister of India, Manmohan Singh to prepare a blueprint to tap into the enormous reservoir of our knowledge base so that our people can confidently face challenges of the 21st. Century. The Commission has a designated time frame of three years from 2nd. October 2005 to 2nd. October 2008.

The Commissions' Terms of References are:

* Build excellence in the educational system to meet the knowledge challenges of the 21st. century and increase India's competitive advantage in fields of knowledge.
* Promote creation of knowledge in Science and Technology laboratories.
* Improve the management of institutions engaged in Intellectual Property Rights.
* Promote knowledge applications in Agriculture and Industry.
* Promote the use of knowledge capabilities in making government an effective, transparent and accountable service provider to the citizen and promote widespread sharing of knowledge to maximize public benefit.

The Commission headed by Mr. Sam Pitroda as its Chairman and there are other 5 members, who are renowned persons in different fields of knowledge. It is a high-level advisory body to the Prime Minister of India, with a mandate to guide policy and generate reforms. The Commission is the world's first body of its kind.

The prime focus of the Commission is on five key areas of the knowledge paradigm, such as:

* Access
  - Literacy
  - Language
  - Translation
  - Libraries
  - Networks
  - Portals
* Concepts
  - School Education
  - Vocational Education
  - Higher Education
  - Medical Education
  - Legal Education
  - Management Education
  - Engineering Education
  - Open and Distance Education

* Creation
    - Science and Technology
    - Intellectual Property Rights
    - Innovation
    - Entrepreneurship
* Application
    - Traditional knowledge
    - Agriculture
* Services
    - E-governance

Besides the Working Group on Libraries, other four Committees were set up with specialists and professionals in different areas of Libraries under the Chairmanship of Mrs. Kalpana Dasgupta.

Such Committees are:

* Committee on database creation and networking;
* Committee on private collections;
* Committee to set standards and modalities for collection development, systems and services;
* Committee on staffing pattern and staff requirement of libraries.

Terms of References of the Working Group on Libraries are given below:

* To redefine the objectives of the country's Library and Information Service sector;
* To identify constraints, problems and challenges relating to the sector;
* To recommend changes and reforms to address the problems and challenges to ensure a holistic development of information services in all areas of national activity;
* To take necessary steps to mobilize and upgrade the existing library and information systems and services, taking advantage of the latest advances in Information Community Technology;
* To explore possibilities for innovation and initiate new programmes relevant to our national needs, especially to bridge the gap between the information rich and the information poor within society;

* To suggest means of raising standards and promoting excellence in Library and Information Science education including re-orientation and training of working professionals;
* To assist in setting up facilities to preserve and access to indigenous knowledge and the nation's cultural heritage;
* To set up adequate mechanisms to monitor activities for securing the benefits of acquisition and application of knowledge for the people of India;
* To examine any other issues that may be relevant in this context..

The Notional Knowledge Commission's Working Group on Libraries, after consultations of more than 20 state representatives and NGOs and many more interest groups and professionals in the field, ready its first recommendations for submission to the nation.

Moreover, the Commission submitted its first recommendations to the Prime Minister in December 2006 on the following areas:

* Libraries
* Translation
* Language
* Knowledge Networks
* Right to Education
* Vocational education
* Higher Education
* National Science and Social science Foundation
* E-governance.

The Commission argued Libraries as Gateways to knowledge and continued that a "Library is not a building stacked with books-it is a repository and source of information and ideas, a place for learning and enquiry, and for the generation of thought and the creation of new knowledge.

Public libraries in particular have the potential to bridge the gap between the 'information poor' and the 'information rich' by ensuing that people from all sectors and settings of society and the community across India have easy access to knowledge seek".. The Commission clearly incorporated roadmap for the execution of its recommendations on libraries under different points of consideration. It gave a Library Charter that is incorporated below.

Recognising that the library's objectives are to:

* Disseminate knowledge as widely as possible;
* Serve as a major vehicle to facilitate creation of new knowledge;
* Facilitate optimal use of knowledge by all sectors, such a government, industry, rural sector and civil society;
* Ensure that people from all sectors and all parts of the country have easy access to knowledge relevant to their needs, in their own language.

The library undertakes to:

* Serve as local center of information and a gateway to national and global knowledge providing fair access to knowledge and information to as many as users as possible;
* Offer an inviting and attractive physical space with clean drinking water and toilet facilities;
* Offer proactive services to its user communities;
* Ensure that users are treated with courtesy and respect by library staff;
* Pay attention to the needs of children, women, senior citizens and the physically challenged;
* Optimize its potential to provide access to information and knowledge to all;
* Help users developed information skills to make optimum use of resources;
* Improve its collections and services on continuing basis in consultation with users;
* To work more effectively and efficiently by undertaking every activity in a professional manner;
* To bridge the gap between the information poor and the information rich.

The Commission is organizing discussion forum at different areas for the preparation of its final report, which is expected to be submit to the nation within its stipulated time.

LIBRARY ASSOCIATIONS

The term 'association' is used to denote a group or body of individuals or institutions associated with a common purpose revolving generally for the two main purposes, viz.,:

* Advancement of the service oriented goals of the association, and
* Protection of the interests of the members.

Association may be of different kinds with different objectives and categories, professional or non-professional. However, by considering its nature, Pandey S.K.Sharma defined library associations as 'a group or body of libraries or librarians and users of libraries formed with the common purpose of advancement of library profession including service and also for protection of interests of the members including raising their capabilities to serve more effectively'.

There are more than seventy professional organizations and associations at state level in India. William A Borden went to Baroda in 1910 at the invitation of Maharaja Sayajirao Gaekwar of Baroda and organized the first professional organization of librarians in the country, the Baroda Library Club in 1912. Other professional associations came up afterwards and some of the national level associations worth to be mentioned for their contributions in public library developments in the country.

NATIONAL LIBRARY OF INDIA

The National Library of India at Belvedere, Kolkata, is the largest library in India by volume and India's library of public record. It is under the Department of Culture, Ministry of Tourism and Culture, Government of India. The library is designated to collect, disseminate and preserve the printed material produced in India. The library is situated on the scenic 30 acre Belvedere Estate, in Kolkata. The Library is the largest in India, with a collection in excess of 2.2 million books.

AIMS

* Acquisition and conservation of all significant national production of printed material, excluding ephemera.

* Collection of printed material concerning the country, no matter where it is published, and as a corollary, the acquisition of photographic records of such material that is not available with in the country
* Acquisition and conservation of foreign material required by the country.
* Rendering of bibliographical and documents services of current and retrospective material, both general and specialised.
* Acting as a referral centre purveying full and accurate knowledge.

HISTORY

The Calcutta Public Library

The history of the National Library began with the formation of Calcutta Public Library in 1836. That was a non-governmental institution and was run on a proprietary basis. People contributing ₹300 in subscription became the proprietors. Prince Dwarkanath Tagore was the first proprietor of that Library. ₹300 at that time was a significant amount, so poor students and others were allowed free use the library for some period of time.

Lord Metcalfe, the Governor General at that time, transferred 4,675 volumes from the library of the College of Fort William, Calcutta to the Calcutta Public Library. This and donations of books from individuals formed the nucleus of the library. Both Indian and foreign books, especially British, were purchased for the library. Donations were regularly made by individuals as well as by the government.

The Calcutta Public Library had a unique position as the first public library in this part of the world. Such a well-organized and efficiently run library was rare even in Europe during the first half of the 19th century. Because of the efforts of the Calcutta Public Library, the present National Library has many extremely rare books and journals in its collection.

The Imperial Library

Built after the model of the Town Hall at Ypres. A fine

example of the Public Buildings in Calcutta.The Imperial Library was formed in 1891 by combining a number of Secretariat libraries in Calcutta. Of those, the most important and interesting was the library of the Home Department, which contained many books formerly belonging to the library of East India College, Fort William and the library of the East India Board in London. But the use of the library was restricted to the superior officers of the Government.

Amalgamation of the Calcutta Public Library and Imperial Library

In 1903, Lord Curzon, the Governor-General of India, conceived the idea of opening a library for the use of the public. He noticed both the libraries—Imperial Library and Calcutta Public Library were under-utilized because of limited access and lack of amenities. He decided to amalgamate the rich collection of both of these libraries. The new amalgamated library, called Imperial Library, was formally opened to the public on January 30, 1903 at Metcalfe Hall, Kolkata.

Metcalfe Hall had earlier been the residence of the Governor-Generals Wellington, Cornwallis and Warren Hastings:

* "It is intended that it should be a library of reference, a working place for students and a repository of material for the future historians of India, in which, so far as possible, every work written about India, at any time, can be seen and read."—*The Gazette of India*

Declaring the Imperial Library as the National Library

After Independence the Government of India changed the name of the Imperial Library to the National Library, with the enactment of the Imperial Library Act, 1948, and the collection was shifted from the Esplanade to the present Belvedere Estate. On February 1, 1953, the National Library was opened to the public, inaugurated by Maulana Abul Kalam Azad. B. S. Kesavan was appointed the first Librarian of the National Library.

Discovery of Hidden Chamber

In 2010, the Ministry of Culture, the owner of the library,

decided to get the library building restored by the *Archaeological Survey of India* (ASI). While taking stock of the library building, the conservation engineers discovered a previously unknown room. The ground-floor room, about 1000 sq. ft. in size, seems to have no opening of any kind. The ASI archaeologists tried to search the first floor area for a trap door, but found nothing.

Since the building is of historical and cultural importance, ASI decided to bore a hole through the wall instead of breaking it. There was speculations about the room being a punishment room used by Warren Hastings and other British officials, or a place to store treasure. After six months of study, it was determined to be not a room at all, but merely "a block stuffed with mud, perhaps constructed by the British architects to strengthen the base of the building."

COLLECTION

Indian Languages Collection

The National Library receives books and periodicals in almost all Indian languages. These are received under the *Delivery of Books and Newspapers Act 1954*. Language divisions acquire, process and provide reading materials in all major Indian languages. Hindi, Kashmiri, Punjabi, Sindhi, Telugu and Urdu language divisions maintain their own stacks. Other language books are stacked in the Stack division.

Language divisions are also responsible for answering reference queries. The library has separate Indian language divisions for Assamese, Bengali, Gujarati, Hindi, Kannada, Kashmiri, Malayalam, Marathi, Oriya, Punjabi, Sanskrit, Sindhi, Tamil, Telugu and Urdu. Sanskrit language division also collects and processes Pali and Prakrit books. English books published in India are collected under D.B. Act.

Assamese Language Collection

In 1963, a separate division was established in the National Library to collect and process Assamese books. At present the division has 12,000 books. This collection has some works published between 1840 and 1900. Some of the important publications are Asamiya Larar Mitra by Anandaram Dhekiyal

Phukan, Larabodh Byakaran by Dharmeswar Goswami, Prakrit Bhugol by Lambodara Datta and several volumes of Sri Sankardev's Kirattan, Gunamala, Srimad Bhagavad, Bargit, Rukmini Haran Nat, and Ankiyanat. Volumes of the periodical Arunodoi are also available in the collection.

Bengali Language Collection

The library has 85,000 books in its Bengali collection. The collection contains very rare and valuable books as well as periodicals published from the last quarter of the 18th century. Early Bengali plays and novels are well represented. The collection has many rare items such as the manuscripts of Sarat Chandra Chattopadhaya, Bibuti Bhushan Bandao padhaya, Jibanananda Das and Bisnu De.

154 letters of Netaji *Subhas Chandra Bose* written to his nephew Sri *Asok Nath Bose* and letters to *Sarat Chandra Bose* are also available in the collection. The collection has the complete set of Rabindranath Tagore's works, except a few of his early works. This includes 190 first editions of Tagore's works.

Some of the rare and important works in this collection are: A Grammar of the Bengal Language by Nathaniel Brassey Halhed, which is the earliest printed book in Bengali, Henry Forster's A Vocabulary in Two parts, English and Bangalee, William Carrey's Dialogues, Intended to Facilitate the Acquiring of the Bengali Language, Ram Ram Basu's Raja Pratapaditya Charitra, Mrityunjay Vidyalankar's Batris Simhansan, Ramayana translated by Krittibas and published in five volumes, Mahabharat translated by Kashi Ram Das, Chandicharan Munshi's Tota Itihas, Jayanarayan Ghosal's Sri Karunani-dhanavilasa, William Carey's Dictionary of the Bengali Language, 2 volumes.

There are 400 titles of Bengali periodicals including many rare 19th century periodicals such as Digdarshan first Bengali monthly and the first issue of Samachar Darpan—the first Bengali weekly.

Gujarati Language Collection

The library has 37,000 Gujarati books. 1100 of them are titles published prior to 1900. This collection also has 30 albums of paintings by Kanu Desai published between 1936 and 1956. Ancient Jaina miniature paintings are well reproduced in Sri Jaina Chitravali, Sri Jaina Chitra Patavali and other valuable books edited by Sarabhai Nawab.

The authentic editions of the poetic works of medieval Gujarati poets such as Narsinh Meheta, Mirabai, Premanand and Symal Bhat are also part of the holdings. The rare titles include Robert Drummond's Illustrations of Grammatical Parts Guzerattee, Maratta and English Languages, translations of Aesop's Fables by Bapushastri Pandya Raykaval, Edalji Patel's Suratani Tavarikh and Jnana Chakra—a Gujarati encyclopaedia in 9 volumes.

Hindi Language Division

Hindi is one of the official languages of India. The collection building of Hindi books has been continuing since the time of the Imperial Library, and a separate division was established in 1960. At present 80,000 Hindi books are in the library collection. The collection has rare works published during the last decades of the 18th Century. Many of the publications published by Lulloo Lal, the first printer, publisher and writer of Kolkata, are represented in this collection.

The following rare books published by Lulloo Lal are in the library: Braja Bhasha Grammar, Lataife Hindi, Rajaniti, and Prem Sagur. In addition, the library has The Oriental Linguist with an Extensive Vocabulary English and Hindoostanee and Hindoostanee and English by John B. Gilchrist, Hindi-Roman Orthoepigraphical Ultimatum by John B. Gilchrist, Rajneeti by Narayana Pandit, Sudamacaritra by Haldhara Dasa, Raga Kalpadruma, Baital Pachisi by Duncan Forbes, Dictionary of Hindee and English by J. T. Thompson, Yavan Bhasa ka Vyakaran by Hooper William, Siva Simha Saroja by Siva Simha Senagar, Hindi Pradipa edited by Balkrishna Bhatt, Brief Account of the Solar System in Hindi, and a microfilm copy of Bal Bodhini—a monthly journal for women edited by Bharatendu Harischandra. There are also about 1200 rare first issues of important journals.

Kannada Language Collection

A separate Kannada division was set up in 1963 in the

National Library. In 1960, the library purchased the personal collection of H. Channakeshava Ayyangar. It consists of 1300 books published between the last two decades of the 19th century and the first three decades of the 20th century. An important contribution towards building the collection was the efforts of *G. P. Rajaratnam*, a noted Kannada author.

Immediately after the enactment of the D.B. Act, Rajaratnam toured the erstwhile Mysore State to create awareness among the publishers about the Act. He collected about 1500 books without any expense to the library. The Kannada collection in the library is particularly useful for the study of the cultural history of Karnataka. At present there are 32,000 Kannada books in the library.

Kashmiri Language Collection

The Kashmiri division was formed in 1983. Currently the library has 500 Kashmiri books. Some of the important items in this collection are Muhammad Yusuf Teng's Shirin Qalm, Wiyur edited by Ghulam Muhammad Rafiq, Ghulam Nabi Khyal's Akah Nandun, Nurnama and compiled by Muhammad Amin Kaim, Fazil and Kashmiri's Krishna Lila.

Malayalam Language Collection

The Malayalam division was established as a separate division in 1963, with around 5000 books. Now the collection has 34,500 books. The earliest printed book, Centum Adagia Malabarica, a Latin translation of Malayalam proverbs, dates back to 1791. The Latin translations are printed alongside the Malayalam originals

Rare and old books include Robert Drummond's Grammar of the Malabar Language, Dr Gundart's Malayalam-English Dictionary Vartamanapu-stakam by Parammachkal Govarnno-doracchan, Appu Nedungadi's Kundalata and Chantu Menan's Indulekha. Apart from these, many works representing earlier periods are part of this collection. A few of these are Ramacaritam, works of Niranam, Cerussery's Krishnagatha, Vatakkan Pattukal, Ezuttachan's Adhyatama Ramayana, Ramaprattu Variyar's Kucelavrtam, and Kuncan Nampyar's Tullol.

Marathi Language Collection

The Marathi division was established in 1963 with a

collection of 8900 volumes. The division now has 37,000 books in its collection. In 1954 the National Library purchased the library of the Bengal Nagpur Railway Indian Institute, Kharagpur, which had a good number of Marathi books. Sir Jadunath Sarkar collection also has about 350 Marathi books, mostly on the history of the Marathas. The division has many rare and old Marathi publications.

These include William Carey's A Grammar of the Mahratta Language and Dictionary of the Maharatta Language, Simhasana Battisi, Raghuji Bhonsalyaci Vanshavali, Vans Kennedy's A Dictionary of Maratta Language, Nava Karar, A Short Account of Railways by K. Bhatwadekar, Charles Hutton's Bijaganit, Tukaram's Abhangachi Gatha edited by Vishnu Parashuram Pandit and Shankar Pandurang Pandit, Itihasaprisiddha Purushanche va Striyanche Povade edited by H. A. Acworth.

Oriya Language Collection

A separate Oriya division was established in 1973. The Imperial Library had only 133 books; later the collection was increased to 425 books. Currently, the division has 19,500 books. The oldest publication available in the Oriya collection dates back to 1831. It is Rev.

Amos Sutton's Introductory Grammar of Oriya Language. Some of the other rarities in the collection are Jayadeva's Gitagovinda, translated by Dharanidhara, Amos Sutton's An Oriya Dictionary, 3 volumes, Dharmapustakara Adibhaya, and Purnacandra Odiabhasa Kosh, a lexicon of the Oriya language compiled by Gopalachandra Praharaj.

Punjabi Language Collection

A separate division for the acquisition and processing of Punjabi language books was established in 1974. Most of the works in this collection are of recent origin. There are a few old and rare Punjabi books, such as William Carey's A Grammar of Punjabee Language, Samuel Starkey's A Dictionary of English Punjabee, Geographical Description of the Panjab, Bhai Santosh Singh's Guru Paratap Suraj Granthavali and Gurudas Bhai's Vars.

Sanskrit, Pali and Prakrit Languages Collection

Sanskrit has a rich literature in many fields of knowledge. A separate division in the library collects and processes Sanskrit books. At present the division has over 20,000 Sanskrit books, printed in the Devanagari script. Almost all Indian language divisions possess Sanskrit works printed in their respective language scripts.

The library also has a rich collection of Sanskrit works edited or translated with original scripts, in English and many other foreign languages. The collection attracts scholars from India and abroad. Apart from Sanskrit, books in Pail and Prakrit languages are also collected and processed by this division. At present the library has about 500 books in Pali and a comparable collection of books in Prakrit.

Sindhi Language Collection

Since 1957, the library has been building a collection of Sindhi books. At present the library has 2100 Sindhi books. Shah Abdul Latif's Shah Jo Rasalo and Shah Jo Sher are the rare items in this collection.

Tamil Language Collection

The Tamil division was formed in 1963. The division currently has 57,000 books. Apart from this, the library has 1000 Tamil books and 300 Tamil manuscripts in the Vaiyapuri Pillai collection. There are many rare and old works among the Tamil titles.

Early printed Tamil books in the library include the Tamil Bible, John Philip Fabricius's A Malabar and English Dictionary, a Tamil translation of John Bunyan's Piligrim's Progress, and Caldwell's Comparative Grammar of DravidianLlanguages. The collection also includes standard editions of five great Sangam Classics.

Telugu Language Collection

The Telugu division was started in the National Library in 1963. The collection has a good number of old Telugu books published since the earlier decades of the 19th century. Some of the rarities in Telugu available in this collection are William Carey's Grammar of Telugu Language, C.P. Brown's A Vocabulary of Gentoo and English, Vakyavali, Catalogue of Telugu books in the British Library, London compiled by L. D. Barnett.

Urdu Language Collection

Like Arabic and Persian, the Urdu collection was substantial since the days of Imperial Library. Special collections such as the Buhar Library, Hidayat Husain collection, Zakariya collection and Imambara collection have some Urdu books and manuscripts. In 1968 a separate Urdu division was set up formed in the library. At present it has more than 20,000 books. Some of the oldest are Uklakhi Hindee or Indian Ethics, and Mir Muhamad Taki's Kulliuat-e-Mir.

English Language Collection

The National Library has an invaluable collection of books in the English language, because of the systematic development by Calcutta Public Library and the Imperial Library. Way back in 1848, an attempt was made to acquire journals issued by the foreign learned institutions.

Serious works were purchased in larger numbers than light literature. The same policy has been pursued in recent times. Although the library has English books and other reading materials in almost all subjects, the collection is especially rich in the humanities, British and Indian history and literature

Foreign Languages Collections

One of the aims of the National Library is to collect all the books published on India, anywhere in the world and in any language. At the same time it collects reading materials on other subjects in different languages for the use of the country. The Imperial Library had a good number of Arabic and Persian works and a few other foreign language books. In 1985 the European Languages Division was reorganized and five separate divisions were formed.

These are East Asian Languages Division, Germanic Languages Division, Romance Languages Division, Slavonic

Languages Division, West Asian and African Languages Division. The foreign language works are mainly acquired through purchase, gift and exchange. The divisions mentioned are responsible for collection development, collection organisation and information dissemination to the readers in the respective languages. They also maintain their own stacks and provide reading facilities.

East Asian Languages Collection

A separate division collects, processes and preserves Chinese and other East Asian languages. At present the collection has 15,000 Chinese books and one thousand each in Japanese, Korean, Tibetan, Nepali and Thai languages.

Germanic Languages Collection

The Germanic Languages division was formed in the library in the year 1985. The division has books in German, Dutch, Norwegian and Swedish. But the largest number of books is in German. The division has book exchange agreements with seven Germanic language-speaking countries. Berliner Zeitung, a newspaper published from former East Germany is available in this collection.

Romance Languages Collection

Romance Languages division came into existence in 1985, along with other foreign languages divisions. Although the collection includes books and other materials in languages belonging to the Romance group, the largest number of books is in French, about 5000. About 2000 Romanian and a handful of books in Italian and Spanish are also available.

Slavonic Languages Collection

The collection has books in Slavonic languages, spoken in Russia, Poland, Bulgaria, the Czech Republic, Slovakia, former Yugoslavia and other countries and peoples of the region. It deals with reading materials in 28 languages. But the largest collection is in the Russian language. At present the division has 65,000 books.

West Asian and African Languages Collection

The Buhar Library may be considered the nucleus of West Asian and African languages collection. The division has a handful of books in other West Asian languages such as Hebrew and Amharic. The largest number of books is in Persian and Arabic, approximately 12,000 in Arabic and 12,000 in Persian. The collection includes the lexicons compiled and prepared by Indians authors of the past and edited by the 'native' scholars of the College of Fort William and European orientalists of the said college.

The division also holds a large numbers of historical works published under the Bibliotheca Indica series of the Asiatic Society of Bengal in the 19th century. A large number of Arabic and Persian books and manuscripts can also be found in Sir Abdur Rahim Collection, Hidayat Husain Collection, Zakaria Collection and Imambara Collection. Sir Jadunath Sarkar Collection also has 200 Persian manuscripts. These manuscripts relate mainly to the later Mughal period and the early years of British rule.

Rare Books

The National Library has an impressive number of rare books and other reading materials. In 1973, a separate Rare Books division was established. At present the books published prior to 1860 are considered rare books, along with limited and first editions, books distinguished by their design, illustration or history, and a few other criteria. Along with rare books, manuscripts and microfilms of the library are also stacked in this division. The division also provides reading facilities to the users who wish to consult these items. At present the division has 4700 monographs, 3000 manuscripts and 1500 microfilms

Manuscripts

National Library has about 3600 rare and historically important manuscripts in different languages. These manuscripts are preserved separately along with other important and rare books in the Rare Books division.

Science and Technology Collection

Following the recommendations of the Reviewing Committee, the Science and Technology division was set up in 1972. The basic function of this division is to collect and disseminate the core material in science and technology. At present the division holds about 17,000 books and monographs and 800 current print periodicals. The division provides reading facilities and has an open access stack system.

Indian Official Documents

All the publications of Government of India, State Governments, Union Territories, Government Undertakings, Autonomous Bodies are collected, processed and preserved separately. A separate division for this purpose was established in 1972. The library owns a rich collection of Indian official documents from the days of the East India Company to the present.

The collection also includes the documents published by the Government of Great Britain relating to India. A good collection of Myanmarese documents and few documents of Aden, Sri Lanka, Persian Gulf Political Residency are also part of this collection. At present, the division holds around 4,90,000 documents.

Foreign Official Documents

The National Library is one of the repository libraries for United Nations Organisation and its agencies. Thus all the publications of UNO and its agencies are received by the library free of cost. These documents are processed and stacked separately.

The library also receives publications of the governments of the United States of America, Great Britain, Canada, the Commonwealth nations, and the publications of the European Economic Committee.

Almost all the volumes of the sessional sets of British Parliamentary papers since the beginning of the 19th century are available. Apart from the depositary copies, the library acquires selected foreign publications through purchase. At present the library has around 400,000 foreign official documents.

Newspapers and Periodicals

All the newspapers and periodicals in Indian languages are received and processed in their respective language divisions. But English newspapers and periodicals, both the Indian and foreign, are acquired and processed separately. A separate Serials division is responsible for acquiring and processing of English newspapers and periodicals.

The library has a rich collection of late 19th and early 20th century newspapers and periodicals, but almost all of them are incomplete sets. There are catalogues for periodicals, newspapers and gazettes available in the library up to 1953.

Maps and Prints

The library has an extensive collection of maps from the 17th century onwards. Indian topographical sheets of earlier days and maps of natural resources, population, transport and communication systems, agricultural production, soil, vegetation and the geology of India form the major part of the collection. At present the library has 85,000 printed maps, 54 cartographic manuscripts, and 280 atlases

Microforms

The library has around 500 rolls of Microfilms and 1000 Microfiches. These are preserved in the Rare Books division. The Census of India is one of the most important and rare document available in the form of Microfiches...

CONSERVATION ACTIVITIES

One of the basic functions of the National Library is to conserve the printed heritage for future generations.

For this purpose the library has separate divisions for physical, chemical, reprographic and digital conservation:

* *Physical Conservation*: Books damaged by human error or by natural causes are mended, repaired and bound in the Binding division. Journals are bound by volume.
* *Chemical Conservation*: The Laboratory division of the library, established in 1968, is taking care of the chemical treatment of books. Advanced procedures of chemical

treatment are adopted to restore brittle and damaged books. The library is in the process of developing non-chemical treatment system for the preservation of printed materials. An indigenously developed fumigation chamber is being used to destroy the eggs and larvae of insects and termites. Encapsulation is another method of preservation that has been developed by the library.

* *Reprographic Preservation*: Most of the 19th century newspapers, Arabic, Persian and Sanskrit manuscripts have already been microfilmed. 5000 rolls of microfilms are already produced so far by the Reprography division.
* *Digitisation*: The scanning and archiving of rare and brittle books and other documents on compact disc has started. English books and documents published before 1900 and Indian publications preceding 1920 are considered for digitisation. 9140 selected books in Indian and English languages have already been scanned and stored—a total of over 3.2 million pages.

ACADEMIC LIBRARY

An academic library is a library that is attached to academic institutions above the secondary level, serving the teaching and research needs of students and staff. These libraries serve two complementary purposes: to support the school's curriculum, and to support the research of the university faculty and students.

The support of teaching requires material for class readings and for student papers. In the past, the material for class readings, intended to supplement lectures as prescribed by the instructor, has been called reserves.

In the period before electronic resources became available, the reserves were supplied as actual books or as photocopies of appropriate journal articles. Traditionally, one copy of a book was made available for each 10 students—this is practical for large classes only if paperback copies are available, and the books reused from term to term.

Academic libraries must decide what focus they take in collecting materials since no single library can supply everything.

When there are particular areas of specialization in academic libraries these are often referred to as niche collections. These collections are often the basis of a special collection department and may include original papers, artwork, and artifacts written or created by a single author or about a specific subject.

ACADEMIC LIBRARIES IN INDIA: A PRESENT-DAY SCENARIO

Education aims to impart knowledge and makes good citizens. Libraries are the repositories of knowledge and form an integral part of education. Libraries have a long history, starting with the chained and closed-access libraries of earlier times to the present-day hybrid, digital, and virtual libraries that use the latest technology for provision of information through various services.

Librarians have also changed from storekeepers who were concerned with protection of books against theft, mutilation, and pilferage, to that of information officers, navigators, and cybrarians who find themselves in the vast ocean of reading material and are busy in satisfying their clients who want anytime and anywhere information.

With the advent of computers, the nature of libraries has changed dramatically. Computers are being used in libraries to process, store, retrieve and disseminate information. As a result, the traditional concept of library is being redefined from a place to access books to one which houses the most advanced media including CD-ROM, Internet, and remote access to a wide range of resources.

Libraries have now metamorphosed into digital institutions. Gone are the days when a library was judged by its quantitative resources. Today, libraries are surrounded by networked data that is connected to a vast ocean of Internet-based services. Moreover, electronic resources relevant to the professions are developing at an unprecedented pace.

Academic libraries are considered to be the nerve centres of academic institutions, and must support teaching, research, and other academic programmes. The situation in academic libraries of India is the same as that of academic libraries the world over; however, Indian libraries must provide maximum information with limited resources.

The Educational System of India

India has a large higher education system. The growth rate of educational institutions in India was very slow before independence in 1947.

Today there are a total of 237 universities, including 116 general universities, 12 science and technology universities, 7 open universities, 33 agricultural universities, 5 women's universities, 1 language universities and 11 medical universities along with 12,600 colleges that provide education in all disciplines. The number of teachers is 3.1 million, and 7.8 million students are enrolled in higher education.

University Grants Commission (UGC)

UGC, established by an act of parliament in 1956, coordinates and monitors the higher education system in India and provides grants to the universities and colleges. Two hundred ninety four universities/institutions in the country are directly under the purview of UGC.

It also advises the union and state governments on measures to university education. It frames rules and regulations for overall teaching and research at higher education. As a result, it also looks after the academic libraries, *i.e.*, sets various standards for library education, library staff, library services, etc. A number of committees have been set up by the UGC for the support of higher education in general and the library services in academic libraries in particular.

UGC has also set up three information centres covering different disciplines—the *National Centre for Science Information* (NCSI) at Indian Institute of Science Bangalore, SNDT Women's University Mumbai, and National Social Science Information Centre at M.S. University at Baroda, to provide the document delivery services to students, teachers, and researchers.

Information and Library Network

The University Grants Commission has set up an autonomous Inter-University Centre in 1991 called INFLIBNET. It is involved in modernizing university libraries in India and connects them through a nation-wide high-speed data network.

It promotes automation of libraries, develops standards, creates union catalogues of serials, theses, books, monographs and non-book materials; provides access to bibliographic information sources; creates database of projects, institutions, specialists; provides training, etc.

Almost all academic libraries, especially university libraries, are members of INFLIBNET. It has also developed library automation software called SOUL (*Software for University Libraries*) and has distributed the same free of cost to its member libraries.

Other Networks

Besides INFLIBNET, a number of other national networks and various library networks have also been developed including:

* NICNET (National Informatic Center's network),
* INDONET,
* ERNET,
* CALIBNET,
* DELNET:
  - ADINET is associated with INFLIBNET,
  - DELNET with NIC and
  - MALIBNET with CFTRI.

A number of educational institutions are members of such networks. These networks, especially DELNET are engaged in compiling union catalogs, creating various databases of experts, providing training to library staff, ILL, online facilities, reference service, assistance in retrospective conversion, etc.

Library Consortia

Due to a financial crunch and the rising costs of journals, many Indian university and college libraries cannot subscribe to all the required journals and databases. To overcome this problem, libraries are forming consortia.

Some special libraries and organizations like the Indian Institute of Astrophysics Library, Inter-university Centre for Astronomy and Astrophysics Library, *National Centre for Radio Astrophysics* (NCRA) Library, Physical Research Laboratory (PRL) Library, Raman Research Institute (RRI) Library, Tata

Institute of Fundamental Research (TIFR) Library, Council of Scientific and Industrial Research, Department of Atomic Energy, etc., have established consortia to share electronic access to journal literature.

NISCAIR (formed by the merger of INSDOC and NISCOM) is developing a consortium for CSIR labs for accessing e-journals. Consortia in India are still a new concept that requires proper guidelines and methodologies. In a survey by UGC in 2001, it was noted that although 142 university libraries had computer and Internet facilities and were interlinked to INFLIBNET, they were subscribing to printed journals only.

In order to solve this problem, UGC launched a major initiative called UGC-INFONET that provides high speed Internet connections so as to have electronic access to professional literature including research journals, abstracts, review publications, and databases from all areas in science and technology, as well as in social sciences and humanities.

Today, a number of professional journals are available over UGC-INFONET to all universities. The e-subscription initiative under UGC-Infonet is an important portal for sharing print as well as electronic resources amongst university libraries. INFLIBNET functions as a resource center with an aim to cater to the needs of its members for resources not accessible to them in electronic media or are available in print media.

INDEST Consortium

The Ministry of Human Resource Development (MHRD) has set up the "Indian National Digital Library in Science and Technology Consortium". The ministry provides funds required for the subscription to electronic resources for 38 academic institutions, including the Indian Institute of Sciences, Indian Institute of Technology, Regional Engineering Colleges, Indian Institute of Managements, and about 60 centrally-funded/aided government institutions through the consortium.

The INDEST consortium is the most ambitious initiative so far in the area of engineering and technology disciplines. The primary objective of libraries is to organize and provide access to information, and it remains the same although the format and methods have changed drastically.

Under the present scenario of declining budgets and higher subscription costs of journals in India, it is becoming very difficult to meet the demands of library/information users. The only solution to the problem is the pooling and sharing of resources—print as well as electronic—by way of consortia.

New technology has provided great opportunities for delivery of services within consortia. More and more libraries must unite, which of course requires a change in the attitudes, practices, and policies to get the maximum benefit.

SCHOOL LIBRARY

A school library is a library within a school where students, staff, and often, parents of a public or private school have access to a variety of resources. The goal of the school library media center is to ensure that all members of the school community have equitable access "to books and reading, to information, and to information technology."

A school library media center "uses all types of media... is automated, and utilizes the Internet for information gathering." School libraries are distinct from public libraries because they serve as "learner-oriented laboratories which support, extend, and individualize the school's curriculum... A school library serves as the center and coordinating agency for all material used in the school."

Researchers have demonstrated that school libraries have a positive impact on student achievement. More than 60 studies have been conducted in 19 U.S. states and one Canadian province. The major finding of these studies is that students with access to a well-supported school library media programme with a qualified school library media specialist, scored higher on reading assessments regardless of their socio-economic statuses.

In addition, a study conducted in Ohio revealed that 99.4% of students surveyed believed that their school librarians and school library media programmes helped them succeed in school. A report that reported similar conclusions was compiled by Michele Lonsdale in Australia in 2003.

HISTORY OF SCHOOL LIBRARIES

The later part of the 19th century marked the beginning of the modern American library movement with the creation of the American Library Association (ALA) in 1876 by a group of librarians led by Melvil Dewey. At these beginning stages of development, the school libraries were primarily made up of small collections with the school librarian playing primarily a clerical role.

1920 marked the first effort by the library and education communities to evaluate school libraries with the publication of the *Certain Report,* which provided the first yardstick for evaluating school libraries.

School libraries experienced another major push following the launch of *Sputnik* in 1957, which forced the United States to re-evaluate its priorities for math and science education. As a result, the 1960s were one of the greatest periods of growth and development for school libraries due to an increased flow of money and support from the private sector and public funding for education. Most notable during this time was the *Knapp School Libraries Project* which established model school library media centers across the country.

Hundreds of new school libraries were expanded and renovated during this time. Most recently, school libraries have been defined by three major guidelines documents: *Information Power* and *Information Power II.* Globally important mission statement is the Unesco School library Manifesto.

THE PURPOSE OF THE SCHOOL LIBRARY

The school library exists to provide a range of learning opportunities for both large and small groups as well as individuals with a focus on intellectual content, information literacy, and the learner.

In addition to classroom visits with collaborating teachers, the school library also serves as a place for students to do independent work, use computers, equipment and research materials; to host special events such as author visits and book clubs; and for tutoring and testing.

The school library media center programme is a

collaborative venture in which school library media specialists, teachers, and administrators work together to provide opportunities for the social, cultural, and educational growth of students. Activities that are part of the school library media programme can take place in the school library media centre, the laboratory classroom, through the school, and via the school library's online resources.

THE SCHOOL LIBRARY COLLECTION

School libraries are similar to public libraries in that they contain books, films, recorded sound, periodicals, realia, and digital media. These items are not only for the education, enjoyment, and entertainment of the all members of the school community, but also to enhance and expand the school's curriculum.

STAFFING OF THE SCHOOL LIBRARY

In many schools, school libraries are staffed by librarians, teacher-librarians, or school library media specialists who hold a specific library science degree. In some jurisdictions, school librarians are required to have specific certification and/or a teaching certificate.

The school librarian performs four leadership main roles: teacher, instructional partner, information specialist, and programme administrator. In the teacher role, the school librarian develops and implements curricula relating to information literacy and enquiry. School librarians may read to children, assist them in selecting books, and assist with schoolwork.

Some school librarians see classes on a "flexible schedule". A flexible schedule means that rather than having students come to the library for instruction at a fixed time every week, the classroom teacher schedules library time when library skills or materials are needed as part of the classroom learning experience.

In the instructional partner role, school librarians collaborate with classroom teachers to create independent learners by fostering students' research, information literacy, technology, and critical thinking skills.

As information specialists, school librarians develop a resource base for the school by using the curriculum and student interests to identify and obtain library materials, organize and maintain the library collection in order to promote independent reading and lifelong learning. Materials in the library collection can be located using an *Online Public Access Catalog* (OPAC).

This role also encompasses many activities relating to technology including the integration of resources in a variety of formats: periodical databases; Web sites; digital video segments; podcasts; blog and wiki content; digital images; virtual classrooms, etc. School librarians are often responsible for audio-visual equipment and are sometimes in charge of school computers and computer networks. Many school librarians also perform clerical duties. They handle the circulating and cataloging of materials, facilitate interlibrary loans, shelve materials, perform inventory, etc.

RESEARCH LIBRARIES

A research library contains an in-depth collection of material on one or more subjects. A research library supports scholarly research and will generally include primary as well as secondary sources; it will maintain permanent collections and attempt to provide access to all necessary material.

A research library is most often an academic or national library, but a large special library may have a research library within its special field and a very few of the largest public libraries also serve as research libraries. A large university library may be considered a research library; and in North America they may belong to the *Association of Research Libraries*.

A research library can be either a reference library, which does not lend its holdings, or a lending library, which does lend all or some of its holdings. Some extremely large or traditional research libraries are entirely reference in this sense, lending none of their material; most academic research libraries, at least in the U.S., now lend books, but not periodicals or other material.

REFERENCE LIBRARIES

A reference library does not lend books and other items;

instead, they must be read at the library itself. Typically such libraries are used for research purposes, for example at a university. Some items at reference libraries may be historical and even unique. Examples of reference libraries include the British Library in London and the Bodleian Library at Oxford University.

Many libraries contain a "reference section", which holds books, such as dictionaries, which are common reference books, and are therefore not lent out. Such references sections may be referred to as "reading rooms", which may also include newspapers and periodicals.

SPECIAL LIBRARIES

All other libraries fall into the "special library" category. Many private businesses and public organizations, including hospitals, museums, research laboratories, law firms, and many government departments and agencies, maintain their own libraries for the use of their employees in doing specialized research related to their work.

Special libraries may or may not be accessible to some identified part of the general public. Branches of a large academic or research libraries dealing with particular subjects are also usually called "special libraries": they are generally associated with one or more academic departments. Special libraries are distinguished from special collections, which are branches or parts of a library intended for rare books, manuscripts, and other special materials.

ARCHIVE, MUSEUM AND RECORDS MANAGEMENT

ARCHIVE

An archive is a collection of historical records, or the physical place they are located. Archives contain primary source documents that have accumulated over the course of an individual or organization's lifetime, and are kept to show the function of an organization.

In general, archives consist of records that have been selected for permanent or long-term preservation on grounds of their enduring cultural, historical, or evidentiary value. Archival records are normally unpublished and almost always unique, unlike books or magazines for which many identical copies exist. This means that archives are quite distinct from libraries with regard to their functions and organization, although archival collections can often be found within library buildings.

A person who works in archives is called an archivist. The study and practice of organizing, preserving, and providing access to information and materials in archives is called archival science.

When referring to historical records or the places they are kept, the plural form *archives* is chiefly used. Archivists tend to prefer the term "archives" as the correct terminology to serve as both the singular and plural, since "archive," as a noun or a verb, has acquired meanings related to computer science.

The use of keeping official documents is very old. Archeologists have discovered archives of hundreds of clay tablets going back to the IIIrd and IInd millennia BC in sites like Ebla, Mari, Amarna, Hattusas, Ugarit, Pylos. And these discoveries have been fundamental to know ancient alphabets, languages, literatures and politics.

Archives were well developed by the ancient Chinese, the ancient Greeks, and ancient Romans. However, they have been lost, since documents were written on organic materials like papyrus and paper.

On the contrary, many archives founded since Middle Age by churches, kingdoms and cities survive and often have kept their official status uninterruptedly till now. They are the basic tool for historical research on these ages.

Modern archival thinking has many roots in the French Revolution. The French National Archives, who possess perhaps the largest archival collection in the world, with records going as far back as A.D. 625, were created in 1790 during the French Revolution from various government, religious, and private archives seized by the revolutionaries.

Users and Institutions

Historians, genealogists, lawyers, demographers, film-makers, and others conduct research at archives. The research process at each archive is unique, and depends upon the institution in which the archive is housed. While there are many different kinds of archives, the most recent census of archivists in the United States identified five major types: academic, business, government, non-profit, and other.

There are also four main areas of enquiry involved with archives:

* Material technologies,
* Organizing principles,
* Geographic locations, and
* Tangled embodiments of humans and non-humans.

These areas help to further categorize what kind of archive is being created.

Academic

Archives in colleges, universities, and other educational facilities are typically housed within a library, and duties may be carried out by an archivist. professors may also run a smaller archive. Academic archives exist to preserve and celebrate the history of their school and academic community.

An academic archive may contain items such as the administrative records of the institution, papers of former professors and presidents, memorabilia related to school organizations and activities, and items the academic library wishes to remain in a closed-stack setting, such as rare books or thesis copies.

Access to the collections in these archives is usually by prior appointment only; some have posted hours for making enquiries. Users of academic archives can be undergraduates, graduate students, faculty and staff, scholarly researchers, and the general public.

Many academic archives work closely with alumni relations departments or other campus institutions to help raise funds for their library or school. Because of their library setting, a degree certified by the American Library Association is preferred for employment in an academic archive in the United States.

Business

Archives located in for-profit institutions are usually those owned by a private business. Examples of prominent business archives in the United States include Coca-Cola, Procter and Gamble, Motorola Heritage Services and Archives, and Levi Strauss and Co. These corporate archives maintain historic documents and items related to the history and administration of their companies.

Business archives serve the purpose of helping their corporations maintain control over their brand by retaining memories of the company's past. Especially in business archives, records management is separate from the historic aspect of archives.

Workers in these types of archives may have any combination of training and degrees, from either a history or library background. These archives are typically not open to the public and only used by workers of the owner company, although some will allow approved visitors by appointment. Business archives are concerned with maintaining the integrity of their company, and are therefore selective of how their materials may be used.

Government

Government archives include those maintained by local and state government as well as those maintained by the national government. Anyone may use a government archive, and frequent users include reporters, genealogists, writers, historians, students, and people seeking information on the history of their home or region. Many government archives are open to the public and no appointment is required to visit.

In the United States, *National Archives and Records Administration* (NARA) maintains central archival facilities in the District of Columbia and College Park, Maryland, with regional facilities distributed throughout the United States.

Some city or local governments may have repositories, but their organization and accessibility varies widely. State or province archives typically require at least a bachelor's degree in history for employment, although some ask for certification by test as well.

In the UK the National Archives, formerly known as the

Public Record Office, is the government archive for England and Wales. The National Monuments Record is the public archive of English Heritage. The National Archives of Scotland, located in Edinburgh, serve that country while the Public Record Office of Northern Ireland in Belfast is the government archive for Northern Ireland.

A network of local authority-run record offices and archives exists throughout England, Wales and Scotland and holds many important collections, including local government, landed estates, church and business records. Many archives have contributed catalogues to the national Access 2 Archives programme and online searching across collections is possible.

In France, the French Archives Administration in the Ministry of Culture manages the National Archives which possess 406 km. of archives as of 2010 with original records going as far back as A.D. 625, as well as the departmental archives, located in the *préfectures* of each of the 100 *départements* of France, which possess 2,297 km. of archives, and also the local city archives, about 600 in total, which possess 456 km. of archives.

Put together, the total volume of archives under the supervision of the French Archives Administration is the largest in the world:

* In India the National Archives are located in New Delhi.
* In Taiwan the National Archives Administration are located in Taipei.

Most intergovernmental organisations keep their own historical archives. However, a number of European organisations, including the European Commission, choose to deposit their archives with the European University Institute in Florence.

Museum

A museum is an institution that cares for a collection of artifacts and other objects of scientific, artistic, cultural, or historical importance and makes them available for public viewing through exhibits that may be permanent or temporary.

Most large museums are located in major cities throughout the world and more local ones exist in smaller cities, towns and even the countryside. The continuing acceleration in the digitization of information, combined with the increasing capacity of digital information storage, is causing the traditional model of museums to expand to include virtual exhibits and high-resolution images of their collections for perusal, study, and exploration from any place with Internet connectivity.

Purpose

Museum purposes change from institution to institution. Some favour education over conservation, or *vice-versa*. For example, in the 1970s, the Canada Science and Technology Museum favoured education over preservation of their objects. They displayed objects as well as their functions.

One exhibit featured a historic printing press that a staff member used for visitors to create museum memorabilia. Some seek to reach a wide audience, such as a national or state museum, while some museums have specific audiences, like the LDS Church History Museum or local history organizations.

Generally speaking, museums collect objects of significance that comply with their mission statement for conservation and display. Although most museums do not allow physical contact with the associated artifacts, there are some that are interactive and encourage a more hands-on approach.

In 2009, Hampton Court Palace, palace of Henry VIII, opened the council room to the general public to create an interactive environment for visitors. Rather than allowing visitors to handle 500 year old objects, the museum created replicas, as well as replica costumes. The daily activities, historic clothing, and even temperature changes immerse the visitor in a slice of what Tudor life may have been

Management

The roles associated with the management a museum largely depends on the size of the institution, but every museum has a hierarchy of governance with a Board of Trustees serving at the top. The Director is next in command and works with the Board to establish and fulfil the museum's mission statement and to ensure that the museum is accountable to the public.

Together, the Board and the Director establish a good system of governance that is guided by various other documents such as an institutional or strategic plan, institutional code of ethics, bylaws, and collections policy.

The *American Association of Museums* (AAM) has also formulated a series of standards and best practices that help guide the management of museums. Unfortunately, many small, local museums lack this guidance since accreditation with AAM requires a museum to operate on an annual budget of at least $25,000.

A change in leadership may ultimately effect changes at the museum, as new directors commonly have new ideas for the institution they work for. For instance, the Los Angeles County Museum of Art's Director and CEO, Michael Govan, has made great strides for the museum since he started in 2006.

Undertaking elaborate building projects, acquiring large collections of objects, and creating new relationships with contemporary artists are just some of his accomplishments. While change and growth is often good for a museum, they should not reach outside the original mission statement of the institution.

Museum professionals Hugh H. Genoways and Lynne M. Ireland, "Administration of the organization requires skill in conflict management, interpersonal relations, budget management and monitoring, and staff supervision and evaluation. Managers must also set legal and ethical standards and maintain involvement in the museum profession."

Various positions within the museum carry out the policies established by the Board and the Director. These positions include but are not limited to curators, collections managers/ registrars, public programmers/educators, exhibition designers, and building operators.

These positions and all other employees should work together towards the museum's institutional goal:

* *Curator:* Research the collection and most often write the text labels for exhibitions. In larger institutions, there may be a curator assigned to each collection of objects the museum holds. Ex: Curator of Modern Art, Curator of Natural History, Curator of History, etc.

* *Collections Management/Registrar*: Responsible for the care and maintenance of all objects in the museum's collection, tracks movement of objects in and out of the museum on loan or on exhibition, records information about objects in databases-such as an object's provenance. Registrars oversee the accessioning process, which formally accepts objects into the museum's collection with an accession number and detailed record. Collections Managers and Registrars uphold the Collections Policy, which guides what is and is not accepted into the museum collection.
* *Public Programmer/Educator:* Creates programmes for the public and designs interactives for exhibitions. This position also oversees volunteers and docents at the museum. Depending on the institution, educators may also research the collections and write text for exhibitions. Educators work with the Board, Director, and Curator to ensure that the needs of the public are met as laid out in the institution's mission statement.
* *Exhibition Designer*: Designs and installs the exhibition under the supervision of the curator and collections manager. They have the vital role of creating exhibition space that is navigable by the visitor.
* *Building Operators:* Oversee security and maintenance of the museum. In larger museums, building operators will work with Collections Managers to maintain appropriate levels of temperature and humidity which can affect the stability of the objects.

Records Management

Records management, or RM, is the practice of maintaining the records of an organization from the time they are created up to their eventual disposal. This may include classifying, storing, securing, and destruction of records

A record can be either a tangible object or digital information: for example, birth certificates, medical x-rays, office documents, databases, application data, and e-mail. Records management is primarily concerned with the evidence of an organization's activities, and is usually applied according to the value of the records rather than their physical format.

In the past, 'records management' was sometimes used to refer only to the management of records which were no longer in everyday use but still needed to be kept-'semi-current' or 'inactive' records, often stored in basements or offsite. More modern usage tends to refer to the entire 'lifecycle' of records-from the point of creation right through until their eventual disposal.

* *The ISO 15489-1:* 2001 standard defines records management as " field of management responsible for the efficient and systematic control of the creation, receipt, maintenance, use and disposition of records, including the processes for capturing and maintaining evidence of and information about business activities and transactions in the form of records".
* *The ISO 15489-1:* 2001 defines records as "information created, received, and maintained as evidence and information by an organization or person, in pursuance of legal obligations or in the transaction of business". While there are many purposes of and benefits to records management, as both this definition highlights, a key feature of records is their ability to serve as evidence of an event. Proper records management can help preserve this feature of records.

It should be noted that the format and media of records is generally irrelevant for the purposes of records management. The ISO considers management of both physical and electronic records. Also, section DL1.105 of the United States Department of Defence standard DoD 5015.02-STD defines Records Management as "[t]he planning, controlling, directing, organizing, training, promoting, and other managerial activities involving the life cycle of information, including creation, maintenance, and disposal, regardless of media."

Practising Records Management

A Records Manager is someone who is responsible for records management in an organization.

Section 4 of the ISO 15489-1:2001 states that records management includes:

* Setting policies and standards;
* Assigning responsibilities and authorities;
* Establishing and promulgating procedures and guidelines;
* Providing a range of services relating to the management and use of records;
* Designing, implementing and administering specialized systems for managing records; and
* Integrating records management into business systems and processes.

Thus, the practice of records management may involve:

* Planning the information needs of an organization
* Identifying information requiring capture
* Creating, approving, and enforcing policies and practices regarding records, including their organization and disposal
* Developing a records storage plan, which includes the short and long-term housing of physical records and digital information
* Identifying, classifying, and storing records
* Coordinating access to records internally and outside of the organization, balancing the requirements of business confidentiality, data privacy, and public access.
* Executing a retention policy on the disposal of records which are no longer required for operational reasons; according to organizational policies, statutory requirements, and other regulations this may involve either their destruction or permanent preservation in an archive.

Records management principles and automated records management systems aid in the capture, classification, and ongoing management of records throughout their lifecycle. Such a system may be paper based or may be a computer system, such as an electronic records management application.

Managing Physical Records

Managing physical records involves different disciplines and may draw on a variety of forms of expertise. Records must be identified and authenticated.

This is usually a matter of filing and retrieval; in some circumstances, more careful handling is required.

* *Identifying Records*: If an item is presented as a legal record, it needs to be authenticated. Forensic experts may need to examine a document or artifact to determine that it is not a forgery, and that any damage, alteration, or missing content is documented. In extreme cases, items may be subjected to a microscope, x-ray, radiocarbon dating or chemical analysis. This level of authentication is rare, but requires that special care be taken in the creation and retention of the records of an organization.
* *Storing Records:* Records must be stored in such a way that they are accessible and safeguarded against environmental damage. A typical paper document may be stored in a filing cabinet in an office. However, some organisations employ file rooms with specialized environmental controls including temperature and humidity. Vital records may need to be stored in a disaster-resistant safe or vault to protect against fire, flood, earthquakes and conflict. In extreme cases, the item may require both disaster-proofing and public access, such as the original, signed US Constitution. Civil engineers may need to be consulted to determine that the file room can effectively withstand the weight of shelves and file cabinets filled with paper; historically, some military vessels were designed to take into account the weight of their operating procedures on paper as part of their ballast equation. In addition to on-site storage of records, many organizations operate their own off-site records centers or contract with commercial records centres.
* *Circulating Records:* Tracking the record while it is away from the normal storage area is referred to as circulation. Often this is handled by simple written recording procedures. However, many modern records environments use a computerized system involving bar

code scanners, or *radio-frequency identification technology* (RFID) to track movement of the records. These can also be used for periodic auditing to identify unauthorized movement of the record.

* *Disposal of Records:* Disposal of records does not always mean destruction. It can also include transfer to a historical archive, museum, or private individual. Destruction of records ought to be authorized by law, statute, regulation, or operating procedure, and the records should be disposed of with care to avoid inadvertent disclosure of information. The process needs to be well-documented, starting with a records retention schedule and policies and procedures that have been approved at the highest level. An inventory of the records disposed of should be maintained, including certification that they have been destroyed. Records should never simply be discarded as refuse. Most organizations use processes including pulverization, paper shredding or incineration.

Commercially available products can manage records through all processes active, inactive, archival, retention scheduling and disposal. Some also utilizes RFID technology for the tracking of the physical file.

Managing Electronic Records

The general principles of records management apply to records in any format. Digital records, however, raise specific issues. It is more difficult to ensure that the content, context and structure of records is preserved and protected when the records do not have a physical existence. This has important implications for the authenticity, reliability, and trust-worthiness of records.

Much research is being conducted on the management of electronic records. The International Research on Permanent Authentic Records in Electronic Systems Project is one example of such an initiative. Based at the School of Library, Archival and Information Studies at the University of British Columbia, in Vancouver, British Columbia, Canada, the InterPARES Project is a collaborative project between researchers all across the world committed to developing theories and methodologies to ensure the reliability, accuracy, and authenticity of electronic records.

Functional requirements for computer systems to manage electronic records have been produced by the US Department of Defence, the National Archives of England and Wales and the European Commission, whose MoReq (Model Requirements for the Management of Electronic Records) specification has been translated into at least twelve languages and is used beyond the borders of Europe.

Development of MoReq was initiated by the DLM Forum, funded by the European Commission. Particular concerns exist about the ability to access and read electronic records over time, since the rapid pace of change in technology can make the software used to create the records obsolete, leaving the records unreadable.

A considerable amount of research is being undertaken to address this, under the heading of digital preservation. The Public Record Office Victoria (PROV) located in Melbourne, Australia published the Victorian Electronic Records Strategy (VERS) which includes a standard for the preservation, long-term storage and access to permanent electronic records.

The VERS standard has been adopted by all Victorian Government departments. A digital archive has been established by PROV to enable the general public to access permanent records. Archives New Zealand is also setting up a digital archive.

Electronic Tax Records

Electronic Tax Records are computer-based/non-paper versions of records required by tax agencies like the Internal Revenue Service. There is substantial confusion about what constitutes acceptable digital records for the IRS, as the concept is relatively new. The subject is discussed in Publication 583 and Bulletin 1997-13, but not in specific detail.

Businesses and individuals wishing to convert their paper records into scanned copies may be at risk if they do so. For example, it is unclear if an IRS auditor would accept a JPEG, PNG, or PDF format scanned copy of a purchase receipt for a deducted expense item.

Current Issues in Records Management

As of 2005, records management has increased interest among corporations due to new compliance regulations and statutes. While government, legal, and healthcare entities have a strong historical records management discipline, general record-keeping of corporate records has been poorly standardized and implemented.

In addition, scandals such as the Enron/Andersen scandal, and more recently records-related mishaps at Morgan Stanley, have renewed interest in corporate records compliance, retention period requirements, litigation preparedness, and related issues.

Statutes such as the US Sarbanes-Oxley Act have created new concerns among corporate "compliance officers" that result in more standardization of records management practices within an organization. Most of the 1990s has seen discussions between records managers and IT managers, and the emphasis has expanded to include the legal aspects, as it is now focused on compliance and risk.

Privacy, data protection, and identity theft have become issues of interest for records managers. The role of the records manager to aid in the protection of an organization's records has often grown to include attention to these concerns. The need to ensure that certain information about individuals is not retained has brought greater focus to records retention schedules and records destruction.

The most significant issue is implementing the required changes to individual and corporate culture to derive the benefits to internal and external stakeholders. Records management is often seen as an unnecessary or low priority administrative task that can be performed at the lowest levels within an organization.

Publicised events have demonstrated that records management is in fact the responsibility of all individuals within an organization and the corporate entity. An issue that has been very controversial among records managers has been the uncritical adoption of Electronic Document and Records Management Systems.

One well known RM thinker, Steve Bailey, has stated:

- "As far as the average user is concerned, the EDRMS is something they didn't want, don't like and can't use. As such, its no wonder that so few users accept them–as one person once said to me "making me use an EDRMS is like asking a plasterer to use a hammer!
- "And now, finally, it is time to turn our eyes to the records management profession itself. In my opinion, we have come within a whisker of allowing our blind obsession with EDRMS to turn us into an intellectually-sterile, vendor-led profession. For the best part of a decade we have allowed others to do the thinking for us and have come to rely on EDRMS as our intellectual-crutch. But make no mistake about it, the blame for this rests squarely with us. Like children following the Pied Piper, we allowed ourselves to be so enchanted by the tune being played that we were led, without question or debate, wherever the technology took us."

Another issue of great interest to records managers is the impact of social media, such as wikis, Facebook and Twitter, on traditional records management practice, principles, and concepts.

6

Library Co-operation

RESOURCE SHARING

The sharing is a need-based activity framed around the age-old concept of give and take. In general it is as old as the civilization. In "the field of libraries we might trace the history of resource sharing since their inception in various forms *viz.*, shared cataloguing, library cooperation, interlibrary loan and union catalogue etc.

The term library resources include any and all of the materials, functions and services, which constitute a modern library system. It is amalgamation of people, processes, ideas, materials and money which forms the substance of a library and can be described as its resources.

Resource sharing is a sort of implied agreement amongst participating libraries wherein each participant willing to share its resource to other members and in turn are privileged to share the resources of its partners as and when the need arises.

At present time when the Computer and Communication Technology has gained the central role in all walks of life and drastically changed the way people think, communicate and do business, it became indispensable to computerise and network the libraries just to survive.

The entrance of these new technologies in library premises rescheduled the functioning of libraries and provided a new dynamic shape to the age-old concept of resource sharing. Lack of effective and efficient technology has been a major hurdle for resource sharing in India, besides the lack of co-operation among the participating libraries.

Now by the use of Information Technology, it became possible to create co-operative functional resource sharing library-network which is the—most important requirement at this juncture where the economic consideration, information explosion and specialized users needs are forcing the libraries to co-operate.

RESOURCE SHARING: NEED OF THE TIME

The increased growth, use and value of information generated the concept of information society or information oriented society. If we analyse the situation from invention of printing press to Internet, we find that the complete civilization is moving from generalisation to specialisation, whether it is growth and nature of subject, commodities or services.

In this era of specialization, the efficiency and efficacy of libraries will be measured by the services provided by them not by the physical collection they have. In this situation the sharing of the resources only may provide the variety of new information services, because in this era it is not possible for any library to accommodate the universe of knowledge physically within the library boundaries.

So the resource sharing became the need of the time to fulfill the ever-specialized user's information needs in cost effective manner as the main objectives of resource sharing are:

* Reduction in all round cast.
* Avoidance of unnecessary duplication of information materials and efforts.
* Possibility of developing specialised activities specifically concentrating on some particular area. Maximum accessibility to information without losing the individual identity of libraries.

At present, specifically in case of Indian academic libraries, which are planning and going to adopt the Information Technology, the resource sharing is needed for:

* Retrospective conversion of their bibliographical data to electronic form.
  - To help less equipped libraries.
  - To reudce the cataloguing cost.
  - To share the valuable resources

- Documents and information.
- Technical expertise.
- To decentralise information.
- To boost the distance learning and more.

PROBLEMS, PROSPECTS AND PREREQUISITES

If we look at the usefulness and strength of resource sharing among libraries, we find a very enthusiastic picture, but on the other hand when we analyse the ground realities of the present situation of our academic institutions and libraries, it seems worthless to talk about these services and activities. We have to accept the realities to reform them as soon as possible, because the growth of IT will not leave space to do anything after some years.

The major problems to be eliminated before may be identified as:

* The required technology and needed organisational structures are not presently available to provide the required level of service, comparable to that available today without the concept of resource sharing.
* Resource sharing will effect the economics of publishing by increasing unit pricing as library orders decline. A substantial part of the prospective saving from resource sharing will thus evaporate.
* A large library may become more and more of a lender of materials, causing resource sharing to be a drain rather than a source of additional material.
* If all libraries turn to resource sharing, none will acquire sufficiently and have books to lend.

In spite of these lacunae we have started to move in the direction. At this stage it is essential to develop some sort arrangements to stream line the movement. Followings might be recognized the prerequisites of a functional resource sharing system.,

Infrastructure

It includes the installation of required hardware and software to create bibliographical, contents pages, abstracts and full text electronic databases and their networking. It is also needed to create various union catalogues and to develop efficient software to handle on-line users query. In addition to these a sound document delivery system could also be needed to send the required information to its end user.

In nut shelta library wants to be part of resource sharing network should have to have computers, printers, modem, scanners, database creation and networking software of specified standards, telephone connectivity, network access, photocopying machines, fax and a reliable postal system. The cost effectiveness of resource sharing is diminished at the present, because it has to run in parallel with other running system.

Common Code of Conduct

Apart from similar software and networking protocols the participating libraries have to evolve a common code of conduct regarding the collection development and resource sharing. There are several basic agreements among libraries that must be developed to operate a co-operative resource-sharing network.

It includes:

* Agreement to share currently owned materials will protocols, limitations and priorities.
* Financial agreement, to safeguard the individual recognition of the libraries.
* Agreement on acquisition policies to ensure consistent development of holdings and to avoid redundancy.
* Agreement of record keeping to streamline and to ensure the smooth operations from acquisition to borrowing and lending.

Legal Copyright and Photo Copying Laws

It is noticeable that the resource sharing activities should violate the copyright and photocopying laws.

Trained Manpower

The establishment and organisation of resource sharing activities are not possible with out the competent, trained and dedicated manpower. At present it is needed to organise massive education and training programmes via different modes to fulfil the required need.

Aware Users

The user is the most important component of any system. Keeping in view this fact, participating libraries and nodal agency simultaneously have to develop and organise user education/orientation programmes in changing context, to ensure the maximum utilizations of the resource sharing activities.

In addition to above said prerequisites it is essential to adopt some professional ethics to run the system smoothly. There is no procedure to impose this idea on participating libraries, but it is worth noticeable that in future only those libraries will survive whose professionals will be guided by this idea.

CHARACTERISTICS OF A NETWORKED LIBRARY RESOURCE SHARING SYSTEM

Where there is a system there must be its users. The satisfaction of users should be the criteria to measure the effectiveness of the system. A sound library resource sharing system, whether it is automatic or manual should have following characteristics. These characteristics should be kept in mind to establish or remodel the networked system.

These checkpoints are also useful to measure the effectiveness of the existing resource sharing system:

* *Speed*: The resource sharing system should be speedy. It should be based on the latest means of data communication systems and programmes. It should be able to judge tile timeliness and urgency of user's information need, because the use of information depends on whether it is provided at right time or not.
* *Accuracy*: The resource sharing system should be able to locate and provide the accurate information. It should be reliable and error free.
* *Cost/Fee:* The information provided should be cost

effective. It must be less than the original cost of document.

* *Staff Courtesy/Knowledge/Assistance:* The professionals engaged in the resource sharing activities should be knowledgeable and prompt to handle the queries. The speed and accuracy of manual resource sharing system depends on these professionals.
* *Consistency of Service and Reliability:* It must be consistent and reliable. The resource sharing activity should be adopted as an important component of present library system.
* *Communication (Provision for Status Reports):* The union catalogues should be able to provide the status report regarding availability of the document.
* *Delivery and Request Options:* The resource center should be able to deliver the needed document! information through required mode of delivery *i.e.* via e-mail, fax, courier or by post.
* *Self-service Options:* It will be easy to use, so that user can handle it without any problem. These characteristics should be considered as guiding principals to establish a new resource sharing system and to measure the efficiency and efficacy of existing one.

LIBRARY NETWORKING

The world has been witnessing a knowledge and information explosion during the past few decades. Over 10 million journal articles are published every year besides news items, editorials and articles that are appearing in popular print media. Information professionals who would be the leaders in the twenty-first century depend on information for their work.

Access to information holds the key to development. Libraries which are store houses of knowledge and information, and information centers which disseminate knowledge and information, form two important components of present day society.

While there is a deluge of information on one hand, the cost of collecting, processing, storing and disseminating information has been spiraling up on the other hand. This calls for heavy budgets for libraries even to maintain a reasonable level of acquisition of journals, books and reports. Estimates show that a three to fourfold rise in library budgets will be needed by AD 2000 to maintain the same acquisition level as in 1990.

Information buying power of libraries has been declining year after year. Because of this, resource sharing and cooperative functioning through networking have become inescapable for libraries and information centres worldwide. India is no exception; for that matter, it is even more necessary to network libraries in newly developing countries like India than in the developed nations.

Efficient resource sharing can be achieved by using the recent advances in information technology for realising a network of libraries. Information technology signifies the coming together of the disciplines of electronics, computer hardware and software, communications, artificial intelligence and human/machine interface.

During the last six to seven years, library and information activities in the country have entered a new era. Individual libraries are coming out of the proverbial "Berlin Wall"around them. They are trying to form a larger community in an effort to tackle the ever increasing demands for better services, quantitatively and qualitatively, in an environment already over strained by financial pressures. Forced, motivated, or logic driven, the librarians are coming out of their shell in large numbers.

This has resulted in discernible change in the information scenario. Now a large number of library resource sharing networks like the Metropolitan Area Networks, such as Calibnet (Calcutta), Delnet (Delhi), Bonet (Bombay), Punenet (Pune), Malibnet (Madras), Mylibnet (Mysore), Hylibnet (Hyderabad), Adne (Ahmedabad), and countrywide ones like ERNET (Educational and Research Institutions), Sirnet (CSIR Laboratories), Inflibnet (Universities and Research Institutions) and Desinet (Defence Laboratories), and sectoral ones like BTISNET (Biotechnology) and TIFACLINE (Technology *per se*) are under various stages of conceptualization, design and development.

A host of agencies, like the National Information System for Science and Technology (NISSAT), Dept. of Electronics, INSDOC/CSIR, DESIDOC/DRDO, DBT, NIC, and TIFAC/DST, are involved. Looking from the participant's side, it is common to find an institution participating in more than one network.

The ultimate goal of information/library networks is to interlink information resources in a metropolitan area, so that that users could access information irrespective of its location, format, medium, language, script etc.

Further, the development of such networks requires actions in several areas such as training, rationalization of information resource acquisition, diffusion of standards, preparation of union lists, generation of database services apart from setting up hardware, software and communication facilities. The concept of library networking to aid information resource sharing and support activities in libraries has become a real necessity.

The shortcomings observed are mainly related to two aspects:

* Non-availability of materials and services, and
* Efficient administrative control.

In India, the need for resource sharing has been well recognized but the technology options available until now were limited. NISSAT has taken up networking of libraries in Calcutta (Calibnet), Delhi (Delnet), Madras (Malibnet), Mysore (Mylibnet), Hyderabad (Hylibnet), Ahmedabad (Adnet), Pune (Punenet), and Bombay (Bonet). The present study highlights only some of the major library networks in India.

Towards library networking activities in India NISSAT has taken the initiative for promoting resource sharing activities. These initiatives are aimed at ensuring better utilization of science and technology information resources, minimization of functional load of information centres and encouragement of motivational factors to a large extent by better means of communication.

NISSAT only goes to the extent of setting up general infrastructural facilities like network service centres including hardware, software, manpower and other organizational requirements, communication facilities etc. With a change in the development and implementation strategy, the participating institutions in a network are to arrange their own terminal hardware, software, manpower and data conversion.

DELNET

The limitation of financial resources and space for housing library collections in the libraries in Delhi led to the promotion of sharing of resources by automation and networking and establishment of the Delnet in 1988. NISSAT took the initiative in setting up Delnet. It has emerged as an important resource centre for the libraries in Delhi.

In Delhi the libraries have been growing very fast in number and site during the last four decades. They cater to specialized and general clientele and are of various types which include institutional libraries, research libraries, government libraries, public libraries, departmental libraries and libraries of the universities, colleges and schools.

During the recent years, cumulative information has been increasing at a very fast pace and with it the increase in demands of the users. It has been noticed that in the era of information explosion the libraries in India are generally ill equipped to handle and retrieve information effectively.

The financial resources and the space for housing library collections are limited in almost all of the libraries. The option left with the forward looking librarians has been to promote the sharing of resources by automation and networking.

Initially, 40 libraries were directly linked to the DELNET host system through e-mail to promote library mailing, interlibrary requests, transfer of files, exchange of messages, interlibrary services, etc. Side by side with the automation of participating libraries, the functions and services have also started.

Presently about 90 libraries are members of DELNET. Almost all participating libraries are now computerized by means of acquisition and fund accounting, cataloguing, circulation, serials control and local users services. Users are able to locate books and serials through Online Public Access Catalogue (OPAC).

A union catalogue of current periodicals available in Delhi

libraries, and a union list of current serials available in Indian libraries are available on online for Delnet participant libraries. A central database of Delnet has been created and made operational. This central database includes the library holdings of Delnet member libraries used as union catalogues of books/ monographs.

Delnet provides access to the central union catalogue for books and monographs, efficient electronic mailing facilities to access databases of member libraries. It also proposes to develop a network for accessing CD–ROM databases available at member libraries in the near future.

Delnet also provides CAS and SDI services, consultancy in library computerization, training and H.R.D. and assistance to libraries on standardization, local automation, retrospective conversion etc. Delnet is likely to emerge as a co–operative network incorporating all disciplines of science, technology, social sciences and humanities.

CALIBNET

The Calcutta Library Network (CALIBNET) was inaugurated on 21 December 1993. NISSAT, Department of Scientific and Industrial Research (DSIR), Government. of India, took the initiative in setting up CALIBNET, which has adopted a two way system for networking:

* The networking route with a library automation and networking through its own application software "Maitrayee" and
* The e-mail route connecting member libraries with on-line access to various databases within network and Internet access.

Calibnet established a high-tech resource base and provides the following services:

* Online/CDROM based global information search and retrieval services
* Full-text document delivery
* Database services

MALIBNET

The need for interconnecting libraries and information

centres in Madras was visualized in the Indian National Scientific Documentation Centre (INSDOC) in 1991. Initially six major academic institutions were directly linked to the Malibnet host system.

Two important databases have been created utilising the resources available in Madras libraries. One is a Directory Database of Current Serials in Madras covering 30 libraries, and the other is a Contents Database covering articles published in 300 journals available in Madras libraries.

Both these databases are continuously updated and also expanded. They are available for online-access to any user and the information is also supplied in diskettes and hard copy. Photocopies of articles from member libraries can be supplied within two days.

Madras has about 60 important libraries besides information centres like INSDOC. About 15 of these libraries have a holding of well over 100,000 items. These libraries act as good resource centres on the network. As of December 1993, all the 60 libraries together invest about Rupees 8,000,000 on acquiring journals and books every year.

It is estimated that 40% of the information acquired is redundant. With the libraries networked and resource sharing implemented, each user on the network can get access to a vast amount of literature, and redundancy can be brought down significantly.

A novel and unique feature of Malibnet is that the members will be permitted to offer their own innovative information services on the network. A membership in MALIBNET is open to universities, colleges, R&D institutions, industries and individuals.

Malibnet presently offers the following information services:

* Current serials acquired in about 60 libraries
* Full journal holdings of about 60 libraries
* Contents information of about 500 important journals
* Electronic mail including internet connectivity
* Door delivery system for document photocopies
* It also offers access to about 1000 international databases

MYLIBNET

It is the first library network established in a small city. The launching of MYLIBNET in association with Mysore city library consortium (MCLC) took place on 12th June 1995. There are 16 institutional members. The holding list of Mysore city libraries has been computerised and software has been developed to enable users to access the catalogue and information on-line. Mylibnet provides e-mail facilities to its members.

BONET

The Bombay Library Network (Bonet) was setup at the National Centre for Software Technology (NCST), Bombay, on 6 November 1992. The Network is sponsored by NISSAT. The aim of Bonet is to build a low cost library information system which can possibly be used as a model for future expansion of this service even outside Bombay.

Bonet also benefits significantly from the experience gained, and facilities created, by the Education and Research Networking (ERNET) project of the Department of Electronics, Govt. of India, assisted by the United Nations Development Programme (UNDP). Bonet is aimed at promoting cooperation between libraries in Bombay.

The focus is on inter-library activities, rather than on computerizing individual libraries, which will no doubt computerize their own operations and are likely to share their experiences with each other. Bonet offers training related to library computerization and networking, and speed up computerization of Bombay libraries. Bonet membership provides for access to its centralised catalogues and for E-mail among Bonet members. However, access to library related services outside Bombay in India and abroad would require use of ERNET.

The services offered through Bonet include the following:

* Consultation on standards
* Organized training for selected staff of participating libraries
* On-line catalogue of periodicals for the region
* On-line catalogue of books for the region

* On-line catalogue of preprints/reprints
* Inter-library lending of books and periodicals
* Inter-library request for photocopying
* Computer network support for book ordering
* Information retrieval services
* On-line document delivery of items (such as technical reports) made available by participating libraries in machine readable form
* On-line access to foreign databases, subject to the user's willingness to pay the costs incurred
* E-mail interface for inter–library queries
* E-mail facilities to order reprints from abroad, when necessary
* Dissemination of information, on new books etc, using E–mail, Bulletin boards, and SDI techniques
* Courier service for inter–library exchange of materials

Under Bonet the following databases were created:

* 25,000 items in a bibliographic database on computers and software technology
* Union catalogue of journals and other periodicals in libraries in the region
* Tables of contents of 250 Indian periodicals created by the national centre for information

** A number of CDROM databases have been mounted on a Novell Server for use to members

PUNENET

Presently, 30 libraries and 15 professionals from Pune city are accessing the Punenet through modem. The users not only access Punenet data, but also use the e-mail and internet facilities.

Following databases are available on Punenet for its members:

* Catalogues of holding of all member libraries
* Union catalogue of current periodicals in Pune libraries and information centres
* Publishers and book sellers database
* Database on international grants and fellowships in the health sciences

* Hard databanks in biotechnology
* Access to NICNET and databases available on NICNET *e.g.*, MEDLANS,AIDS database, US patent database
* Access to internet and various databases available on internet
* Patent information
* Union catalogue of books available in British libraries in India

ADINET

Ahmedabad Library Network (ADINET) was formally inaugurated in February 1995 when a memorandum of understanding was signed between NISSAT and ADINET at Ahmedabad. ADINET has ten institutional members, five associate institutional members and two professional members. A centralized database has been created at ADINET which contains institute master, journal master and book databases. It also organized six work and training programmes. ADINET provided e-mail connectivity to 30 libraries of Ahmedabad.

INFLIBNET

Information and Library Network (INFLIBNET), a programme of the University Grants Commission, was launched in May 1991. The main aim of INFLIBNET is to establish a national computer-communication network to link libraries and information centres in universities, colleges, universities, UGC information centres, institutions of national importance, R&D institutions, etc., and thereby improve capability in information handling and services.

It is a programme for academic excellence to be achieved through establishment of a mechanism for information transfer and access to support scholarship and academic work. It facilitates pooling, sharing and optimization of scarce library resources in the country. As a major programme it helps modernize libraries and information centres in the country through application of information technology.

The National Centre of INFLIBNET is located in Gujarat University campus at Ahmedabad. At present, INFLIBNET aims at computerizing and networking of university/college libraries. Every year, INFLIBNET programme is identifying a number of university libraries for automation depending on the budget allocation.

The selected institutions are given funds for procuring computer systems, retroconversion and networking. Application software for data entry and other library functions, library standards and formats, etc., are provided by INFLIBNET to the participating libraries.

Manpower development is an important part of the programme. Training courses for core library staff engaged in computerised library operations, have been conducted since 1992-93.

Development of suitable software, standards for various library operations and communication based services (*e.g.*, e-mail, bulletin boards) designing suitable network architecture and preparation of union catalogues of serials, books, non-book materials, and cooperation with other networking organisations like NISSAT, NICNET, etc., are other important activities.

Objectives of INFLIBNET

INFLIBNET is an autonomous institution and aims to provide a channel to the academicians and researchers for exchange of information from sources within the country and abroad:

* Modernize libraries/information centres in India
* Mechanization for information transfer and access
* Facilitate pooling, sharing and optimization of library resources
* Organize library services at macro level
* Speedy and efficient services to end users
* Promoting equity

The ultimate aim is to provide the end-users a mechanism for sharing and using information resources and for exploiting modern information technology.

Functions of INFLIBNET

* Aims to establish a nation-wide network for computer

communication linking academic libraries and information

* Aims to establish a mechanism for information transfer and access to support scholarship and academic work
* Aims to organize library services at macro levels at affordable cost and maximise benefits providing speedy and efficient services to end users.
* Will include participants from colleges, universities, R&D institutes, institutes of higher learning, information centres, institutes of national importance and document resource centres
* Covers all disciplines such as science, technology, medicine, agriculture, fine arts, humanities, social science
* Will provide networking to members using available communication infrastructure in the country.

CONCLUSION

Following the launching of Delnet and Calibnet, the library automation and networking movement in India is surely catching on.

The objectives which are:

* Better utilization of funds through sharing of resources by creation of commonly usable data-bases and communication between libraries.
* Automating the functions of individual libraries at a local level for effective and efficient services to the users.

A number of benefits are being offered to member libraries of the particular networks. First, one gets access to a very large volume of literature without increase in the library budget because of the sharing of resources among the members. Secondly, the library budget can now be diverted to acquire the most important (even if expensive) information required by an institution, the other peripheral information being available on the network.

Third, one gets near real time access to about 1000 international databases apart from the electronic mail and remote log in facilities. There are plans of these networks to connect and share the resources in the near future. Nevertheless, the growth of these networks is slow. It is taking a long time to create and provide bibliographic databases of recognisable size, *e.g.*, DELNET took already ten years in creating bibliographic databases of reasonably good size. Without the databases neither could networks be made effective to achieve the goals nor could resource sharing be effective.

Finally it appears that prospects are quite favourable for development of networks for better information services and resource sharing in India. In this direction lot of work has to be done. Some of the problems faced by other developing countries are common to India too, including financial constraints, inadequate communication, non-availability of equipments, less awareness of the value of information, reluctance to development and non-coordination of various kind of activities, resource building, resource sharing and exchange of information and ideas, non-standardization operational procedure, lack of dedication, motivation and knowledge on the part of available manpower.

7

Professional Associations in Library and Information Science

INDIAN LIBRARY ASSOCIATION (ILA)

Indian Library Association (ILA) was established on September 13, 1933, on the occasion of the First All India Library Conference held at Calcutta (now Kolkata). The ILA is the largest and renowned professional body in the field of Library and Information Science in India with a membership of more than 7000.

The main objectives of the Association are:

* Promoting library movement in the country,
* Developing Library and Information Science education,
* Training and research, betterment of library personnel,
* Cooperation at the national and international levels,
* Promotion of standards, norms, services and guidelines, and
* Providing a forum for professionals and publication of materials.

INDIAN ASSOCIATION OF SPECIAL LIBRARIES AND INFORMATION CENTRES (IASLIC)

The IASLIC, acronym for the Indian Association of Special Libraries and Information Centres, was established on 3 September 1955 as a non-profit making national, professional body to:

* Promote the quality of Library and Information Services
* Coordinate the activities, and

* Foster mutual cooperation and assistance among the special libraries, scientific, technological and research institutions, learned societies, commercial organizations, industrial research establishments as well as centres of studies in social sciences and humanities
* Improve the technical efficiency of the professionals
* Act as a centre of research and studies in special librarianship and documentation techniques
* Act as a centre of information in scientific, technical and other related fields of LIS in pursuance of the aforesaid objects.

INDIAN ASSOCIATION OF TEACHERS OF LIBRARY AND INFORMATION SCIENCE (IATLIS)

The idea of founding an association of library science teachers was floated at the Unesco Regional Seminar held at the University of Delhi in October 1960 and later on discussed at the following three seminars:

* All India Seminar on Education for Librarianship held at Banaras Hindu University (1963),
* All India Seminar on Education for Librarianship held at SNDT Women's University (1965), and
* All India Seminar on Teaching of Library Science held at Delhi University (1966). To elicit the opinion from teachers in library schools, a circular was issued by Prof Bashiruddin in collaboration with the late Prof. Das Gupta and P.N.Kaula from the Rajasthan School. At the Delhi Seminar in 1966, the same issue was reviewed but without yielding any result.

Mr *Derek Langridge,* principal lecturer, North Western Polytechnic School (England) delivered Sarada Ranganathan Endowment Lectures at DRTC, Bangalore on 'Teaching of Library Classification' from 15-19 December 1969. This provided a fortuitous opportunity to discuss the issue of having an organization for teachers of Library Science.

FORMATION OF THE ORGANIZATION

On 19th December 1969, a meeting of the teachers of library science attending the Sarada Ranganathan Endowment Lectures was convened by Mr. P. N. Kaula at DRTC with Mr. C. K. Langridge in the chair. This was attended by teachers from several Library schools.

Dr. D. B. Krishna Rao asked Mr. P.N. Kaula to give his opening Address stating the purpose of the meeting. Mr. P. N. Kaula described the structure of Library education in the country and the need for having an association of teachers of Library science.He also stated the efforts made in the past and the interest shown by the teachers at the seminar.

Dr. D. B. Krishna Rao declared that the Indian Association of Teachers of library science be formed with an ad-hoc committee constituted for this purpose. Mr. Ganesh Bhattacharya proposed a vote of thanks. In the end a Committee was formed with Dr. D. B. Krishna Rao as its Chairman and Mr. P. N. Kaula as the Secretary.

Thus was born the Indian Association of the Teachers of Library and Information Science (IATLIS) a national professional organization to further the cause of library education in India. The General Body meeting of IATLIS was held on 21st December 1970 to adopt the draft constitution circulated to members earlier with Mr. P. B. Roy in the chair. The constitution was discussed and adopted unanimously.

THE REVIVAL

After the foundation meeting in 1969, the first 'National Seminar' was held in 1970 at DRTC, Bangalore with the blessings of Dr Ranganathan and dynamic leadership of Prof P.N.Kaula. Dr D.B.Krishna Rao, Padmasri Bashiruddin, Prof A.Neela-meghan, Prof M.R.Kumbar played a key role in the formative years of the Association.

However, the Association was remained dormant from 1973-80. In March 1980, Prof Kaula conducted an All India Seminar on Relevance of LIS Education to the changing needs of the country at BHU. At this Seminar IATLIS was revived with Prof Kaula as President and Prof Kumar as General Secretary. Since 1981 it was active once again and IATLIS Communication and several other activities were initiated by Prof Kumar. National Seminars are being conducted regularly since 1986.

AIMS AND OBJECTIVES

To promote exchange of ideas on education in library and information science, To promote research in education in library and information science, To promote the publication of books and periodicals on education in library and information science.

To hold conferences, seminars, and colloquia for the development and propagation of ideas on education in library and information science, to give consultation service on education in library and information science, to promote training of the teachers of library and information science in India, and to promote welfare of teachers of library and information science in India.

AMERICAN LIBRARY ASSOCIATION (ALA)

The American Library Association (ALA) is a non-profit organization based in the United States that promotes libraries and library education internationally. It is the oldest and largest library association in the world, with more than 62,000 members.

Founded by Justin Winsor, Charles Ammi Cutter, Samuel S. Green, James L. Whitney, Melvil Dewey (Melvil Dui), Fred B. Perkins and Thomas W. Bicknell in 1876 in Philadelphia and chartered in 1879 in Massachusetts, its head office is now in Chicago.

During the Centennial Exposition in Philadelphia in 1876, 103 librarians, 90 men and 13 women, responded to a call for a "Convention of Librarians" to be held October 4–6 at the Historical Society of Pennsylvania. At the end of the meeting, "the register was passed around for all to sign who wished to become charter members," making October 6, 1876 to be ALA's birthday.

In attendance were 90 men and 13 women, among them Justin Winsor (Boston Public, Harvard), William Frederick Poole (Chicago Public, Newberry), Charles Ammi Cutter (Boston Athenaeum), Melvil Dewey, and Richard Rogers Bowker. Attendees came from as far west as Chicago and from England.

The aim of the Association, in that resolution, was "to enable librarians to do their present work more easily and at less expense." The Association has worked throughout its history to define, extend, protect and advocate for equity of access to information.

Library activists in the 1930s pressured the American Library Association to be more responsive to issues put forth by young members involved with issues such as peace, segregation, library unions and intellectual freedom. In 1931, the Junior Members Round Table (JMRT) was formed to provide a voice for the younger members of the ALA, but much of what they had to say resurfaced in the social responsibility movement to come years later.

During this period, the first Library Bill of Rights (LBR) was drafted by Forrest Spaulding to set a standard against censorship and was adopted by the ALA in 1939. This has been recognized as the moment defining modern librarianship as a profession committed to intellectual freedom and the right to read over government dictates. The ALA formed the Staff Organization's Round Table in 1936 and the Library Unions Round Table in 1940.

The ALA appointed a committee to study censorship and recommend policy after the banning of *The Grapes of Wrath* and the implementation of the LBR. The committee reported in 1940 that intellectual freedom and professionalism were linked and recommended a permanent committee – Committee on Intellectual Freedom.

The ALA made revisions to strengthen the LBR in June 1948, approved the Statement on Labeling in 1951 to discourage labeling material as subversive, and adopted the Freedom to Read Statement and the Overseas Library Statement in 1953.

In 1961, the ALA took a stand regarding service to African Americans and others, advocating for equal library service for all. An amendment was passed to the LBR in 1961 that made clear that an individual's library use should not be denied or abridged because of race, religion, national origin, or political views. Some communities decided to close their doors rather than desegregate. In 1963, the ALA commissioned a study, *Access to Public Libraries*, which found direct and indirect discrimination in American libraries.

In 1967 some librarians protested against a pro-Vietnam War speech given by General Maxwell D. Taylor at the annual ALA conference in San Francisco; the former president of Sarah Lawrence College, Harold Taylor, spoke to the Middle-Atlantic Regional Library Conference about socially responsible professionalism; and less than one year later a group of librarians proposed that the ALA schedule a new round table programme discussion on the social responsibilities of librarians at its next annual conference in Kansas City.

This group called themselves the Organizing Committee for the ALA Round Table on Social Responsibilities of Libraries. This group drew in many other under-represented groups in the ALA who lacked power, including the Congress for Change in 1969. This formation of the committee was approved in 1969 and would change its name to the *Social Responsibilities Round Table (SRRT) in 1971.*

After its inception, the Round Table of Social Responsibilities began to press ALA leadership to address issues such as library unions, working conditions, wages, and intellectual freedom. The Freedom to Read Foundation was created by ALA's Executive Board in 1969. The Black Caucus of the ALA and the Office for Literacy and Outreach were set up in 1970.

In June 1990, the ALA approved "Policy on Library Services to the Poor" and in 1996 the Task Force on Hunger Homelessness, and Poverty was formed to resurrect and promote the ALA guidelines on library services to the poor. The ALA archival materials, non-current records, are currently held in the University of Illinois archives. These materials can only be used at the University of Illinois.

MEMBERSHIP

ALA membership is open to any person or organization, though most of its members are libraries or librarians. Most members live and work in the United States, with international members comprising 3.5% of total membership.

GOVERNING STRUCTURE

The ALA is governed by an elected council and an executive board. Since 2002,Keith Michael Fiels has been the ALA executive director (CEO). Policies and programmes are administered by various committees and round tables.

One of the organization's most visible tasks is overseen by the Office for Accreditation, which formally reviews and authorizes American and Canadian academic institutions that offer degree programmes in library and information science.

The ALA's current President is Molly Raphael (2011-2012). Notable past presidents of the ALA include Theresa Elmendorf, its first female president (1911–1912), Clara Stanton Jones, its first African-American president (1976-1977), Loriene Roy, its first Native American president (2007-2008), Michael Gorman (2005-6), and Roberta Stevens..

Activities

The official purpose of the association is "to promote library service and librarianship." Members may join one or more of eleven membership divisions that deal with specialized topics such as academic, school, or public libraries, technical or reference services, and library administration. Members may also join any of seventeen round tables that are grouped around more specific interests and issues than the broader set of ALA divisions.

Notable Divisions

* ALA Editions (book publishing)
* American Association of School Librarians (AASL)
* Association for Library Collections and Technical Services (ALCTS)
* Association for Library Service to Children (ALSC)
* Association of College and Research Libraries (ACRL)
* Library Information Technology Association (LITA)
* Public Library Association (PLA)
* Reference and User Services Association (RUSA)
* Young Adult Library Services Association (YALSA).

Notable Offices

* Office of Intellectual Freedom (OIF)
* Office for Accreditation (OA)
* Office for Literacy and Outreach Services (OLOS)
* Office for Information Technology Policy (OITP).

Notable Sub-organizations

In 1970, the ALA founded the first lesbian, gay, bisexual and transgender professional organization, called the "Task Force on Gay Liberation", now known as the GLBT Round Table. On July 23rd, 1976, the Committee on the Status of Women in Librarianship was established as a Council Committee of the ALA on recommendation of the Ad Hoc Committee with the same name (which had been appointed by the President of the ALA in December of 1975) and of the Committee on Organization.

The Committee on the Status of Women in Librarianship works to "officially represent the diversity of women's interest within ALA and to ensure that the Association considers the rights of the majority (women) in the library field; to promote and initiate the collection, analysis, dissemination, and coordination of information on the status of women in librarianship; to coordinate the activities of ALA units which consider questions of special relevance for women; to identify lags, gaps, and possible discrimination in resources and programmes relating to women; in cooperation with other ALA units, to help develop and evaluate tools, guidelines, and programmes designed to enhance the opportunities and the image of women in the library profession, thus raising the level of consciousness concerning women; to establish contacts with committees on women within other professional groups and to officially represent ALA concerns at interdisciplinary meetings on women's equality; and to provide Council and Membership with reports needed for establishment of policies and actions related to the status of women in librarianship; and to monitor ALA units to ensure consideration of the rights of women."

In 1979 the Committee on the Status of Women in Librarianship received the Bailey K. Howard-World Book Encyclopedia-ALA Goal Award to develop a profile of ALA personal members, known as the COSWL Study. In 1980 the Committee on the Status of Women in Librarianship was awarded the J. Morris Jones-World Book Encyclopedia-ALA Goals Award with the OLPR Advisory Committee to undertake a special project on equal pay for work of equal value.

National Outreach

The ALA is affiliated with regional, state, and student chapters across the country. It organizes conferences, participates in library standards development, and publishes a number of books and periodicals. The ALA publishes the magazines *American Libraries* and *Booklist*. Along with other organizations, it sponsors the annual Banned Books Week the last week of September. Young Adult Library Services Association (YALSA) also sponsors Teen Read Week, the third week of each October, and Teen Tech Week, the second week of each March.

Awards and Honours

The ALA annually confers numerous book and media awards, primarily through its children's and young adult divisions (others are the Dartmouth Medal, Coretta Scott King Awards, Schneider Book Awards, and Stonewall Book Award).

The children's division ALSC administers the Caldecott Medal, Newbery Medal, Batchelder Award, Belpré Awards, Geisel Award, and Sibert Medal, all annual book awards; the Odyssey Award for best audiobook (joint with YALSA), and the (U.S.) Carnegie Medal and for best video. There are also two ALSC lifetime recognitions, the Wilder Medal and the Arbuthnot Lecture.

The young-adult division YALSA administers the Margaret Edwards Award for significant and lasting contribution to YA literature, a lifetime recognition of one author annually, and some annual awards that recognize particular works: the Michael L. Printz Award for a YA book judged on literary merit alone, the William C. Morris Award for an author's first YA book, the new "YALSA Award for Excellence in Nonfiction for Young Adults", and the "Alex Award" list of ten adult books having special appeal for teens.

Jointly with the children's division ALSC there is the Odyssey Award for excellence in audiobook production.

The award for YA nonfiction was inaugurated in 2012, defined by ages 12 to 18 and publication year November 2010 to October 2011. The first winner was '*The Notorious Benedict Arnold: A True Story of Adventure, Heroism and Treachery* by Steve Sheinkin (Roaring Brook Press, November 2010) and four other finalists were named.

Beside the Alex Awards, ALA disseminates some annual lists of "Notable" and "Best" books. The annual awards roster includes the John Cotton Dana Award for excellence in library public relations. From 2006 the ALA annually selects a class of Emerging Leaders, typically comprising about 100 librarians and library school students.

This minor distinction is a form of organizational outreach to new librarians. The Emerging Leaders are allocated to project groups tasked with developing solutions to specified problems within ALA divisions. The class meets at the ALA Midwinter and Annual Meetings, commonly January and June. Project teams may present posters of their completed projects at the Annual.

Conferences

The ALA and its divisions hold numerous conferences throughout the year. The two largest conferences are the annual conference and the midwinter meeting. The latter is typically held in January and focused on internal business, while the annual conference is typically held in June and focused on exhibits and presentations. The ALA annual conference is notable for being one of the largest professional conferences in existence, typically drawing over 25,000 attendees.

Political Positions

The ALA advocates positions on United States political issues that it believes are related to libraries and librarianship. For court cases that touch on issues about which the organization holds positions, the ALA often files amici curiae briefs, voluntarily offering information on some aspect of the case to assist the court in deciding a matter before it.

The ALA has an office in Washington, D.C., that lobbies Congress on issues relating to libraries, information and communication. It also provides materials to libraries that may include information on how to apply for grants, how to comply with the law, and how to oppose a law.

Intellectual Freedom

The primary documented expressions of the ALA's intellectual freedom principles are the Freedom to Read Statement and the Library Bill of Rights; the Library Bill of Rights urges libraries to "challenge censorship in the fulfillment of their responsibility to provide information and enlightenment." The ALA Code of Ethics also calls on librarians to "uphold the principles of intellectual freedom and resist all efforts to censor library resources."

The ALA maintains an Office for Intellectual Freedom (OIF) headed by Barbara M. Jones, former University Librarian for Wesleyan University and internationally known intellectual freedom advocate and author. She is the second director of the Office for Intellectual Freedom, succeeding Judith Krug, who headed the office for four decades.

The OIF is charged with "implementing ALA policies concerning the concept of intellectual freedom," that the ALA defines as "the right of every individual to both seek and receive information from all points of view without restriction. It provides for free access to all expressions of ideas through which any and all sides of a question, cause or movement may be explored." Its goal is "to educate librarians and the general public about the nature and importance of intellectual freedom in libraries."

The OIF compiles lists of challenged books as reported in the media and submitted to them by librarians across the country. Its actions are not without controversy; for example, Nat Hentoff noted "An issue facing all members of the ALA is their leaders' shameful exception of the Cuban people's freedom to read."

Hentoff's characterization contradicts the ALA's official position on Cuba, which urges the Cuban Government "to eliminate obstacles to access to information" and expresses "deep concern" for political dissidents in Cuba.

In 1999, radio personality Laura Schlessinger campaigned publicly against the ALA's intellectual freedom policy, specifically in regard to the ALA's refusal to remove a link on its web site to a specific sex-education site for teens. Sharon Presley said, however, that Schlessinger "distorted and misrepresented the ALA stand to make it sound like the ALA was saying porno for 'children' is O.K."

In 2002, the ALA filed suit with library users and the ACLU against the United States Children's Internet Protection Act (CIPA), which required libraries receiving federal E-rate discounts for Internet access to install a "technology protection measure" to prevent children from accessing "visual depictions that are obscene, child pornography, or harmful to minors."

At trial, the federal district court struck down the law as unconstitutional. The government appealed this decision, and on June 23, 2003, the Supreme Court of the United States upheld the law as constitutional as a condition imposed on institutions in exchange for government funding.

In upholding the law, the Supreme Court, adopting the interpretation urged by the U.S. Solicitor General at oral argument, made it clear that the constitutionality of CIPA would be upheld only "if, as the Government represents, a librarian will unblock filtered material or disable the Internet software filter without significant delay on an adult user's request."

Privacy

In 2003, the ALA passed a resolution opposing the USA PATRIOT Act, which called sections of the law "a present danger to the constitutional rights and privacy rights of library users". Since then, the ALA and its members have sought to change the law by working with members of Congress and educating their communities and the press about the law's potential to violate the privacy rights of library users.

ALA has also participated as an *amicus curiae* in lawsuits filed by individuals challenging the constitutionality of the USA PATRIOT Act, including a lawsuit filed by four Connecticut librarians after the library consortium they managed was served with a National Security Letter seeking information about library users.

After several months of litigation, the lawsuit was dismissed when the FBI decided to withdraw the National Security Letter. In 2007 the "Connecticut Four" were honoured by the ALA with the Paul Howard Award for Courage for their challenge to the National Security Letter and gag order provision of the USA PATRIOT Act.

In 2006, the ALA sold humourous "radical militant librarian" buttons for librarians to wear in support of the ALA's stances on intellectual freedom, privacy, and civil liberties. Inspiration for the button's design came from documents obtained from the FBI by the Electronic Privacy Information Center (EPIC) through a Freedom of Information Act (FOIA) request.

The request revealed a series of e-mails in which FBI agents complained about the "radical, militant librarians" while criticizing the reluctance of FBI management to use the secret warrants authorized under Section 215 of the USA PATRIOT Act.

Copyright

The ALA "supports efforts to amend the Digital Millennium Copyright Act (DMCA) and urges the courts to restore the balance in copyright law, ensure fair use and protect and extend the public domain". It supports changing copyright law to eliminate damages when using orphan works without permission; is wary of digital rights management; and, in ALA v. FCC, successfully sued the Federal Communications Commission to prevent regulation that would enforce next-generation digital televisions to contain rights-management hardware.

It has joined the Information Access Alliance to promote open access to research. The Copyright Advisory Network of the Association's Office for Information Technology Policy provides copyright resources to libraries and the communities they serve.

SPECIAL LIBRARIES ASSOCIATION

Special Libraries Association (SLA) is an international professional association for library and information professionals working in business, government, law, finance, non-profit, and academic organizations and institutions.

While Special libraries include law libraries, news libraries, corporate libraries, museum libraries, and medical libraries, many information professionals today do not actually work in a library setting. They actively apply their specialized skills to support the information needs of their organizations.

SLA was founded in 1909 in the United States. It is now an international organization with over 9,000 members in over 75 countries. SLA is organized by Chapters (geographic) and Divisions (topical) and special interest groups. The association has a CEO (employee of the association) and an elected President (mandate of one year).

Members of SLA typically possess a master's degree in library or information science. Given the rapid adoption of information technologies for selecting, analysing, managing, storing, and delivering information and knowledge, the average SLA member might be performing a range of services and employing a diverse mix of skills related to, but not exclusive of, library science. Association activities include conferences, professional education, networking and advocacy.

CHARTERED INSTITUTE OF LIBRARY AND INFORMATION PROFESSIONALS

The Chartered Institute of Library and Information Professionals (CILIP) is a professional body representing librarians and other information professionals in the United Kingdom.

It was formed in 2002 by the merger of the Library Association (abbreviated to LA or sometimes LAUK)–founded in 1877 as a result of the first International Conference of Librarians and awarded a Royal Charter in 1898–and the Institute of Information Scientists, founded in 1958.

Membership is not compulsory for practice, but members can work towards *Chartered Membership* which entitles them to the postnominal letters MCLIP, and subsequently towards *Fellowship* (FCLIP). Affiliated members can also obtain ACLIP upon completing certification.

Honourary Fellowship (HonFCLIP or FCLIP(hc)), a qualification akin to an honourary degree, is granted to a small number of people who have rendered distinguished service to the profession.

Functions

CILIP accredits degree programmes in library and information science at universities in the UK, including City University, London, Loughborough University, the Manchester Metropolitan University, the Robert Gordon University, the University of Sheffield and University College London.

CILIP is perhaps best known to the general public for awarding the Carnegie and Kate Greenaway Medals for children's books. CILIP publishes a monthly magazine, *CILIP Update with Gazette*, including listings of job vacancies. It also runs a publishing imprint, Facet Publishing.

There are several local branches across the United Kingdom, 28 special interest groups and over 20 organisations in liaison including such bodies as the African Caribbean Library Association, the Librarians' Christian Fellowship and the Society of Indexers.

CILIP hosts a conference every two years called "Umbrella" (containing 'LA' the acronym of the Library Association). Umbrella 2009 was held in Hertfordshire and so was Umbrella 2011 (July 12-13 at Hatfield). The title is abbreviated from "Under One UmbrelLA" a Library Association event held every two years.

Role in LIS Education

CILIP's policy is to improve all aspects of professional practice through its work in education, maintaining a framework of universally recognised qualifications and providing a wide range of opportunities for CPD. In 2002 CILIP undertook a review of its qualifications framework. The new *Framework of Qualifications* was launched in April 2005.

It is designed to be flexible and adaptable, as the areas will evolve and develop over time to accommodate changing needs. It is appropriate to library and information professionals across the sector as a whole. As such it has a degree of overlap with the knowledge base of other professions.

The framework consists of four levels – certification, chartership, revalidation and fellowship. Certification provides recognition from the association for library and information work by para-professionals. Those who gain admittance to the Register of Certified Members are entitled to work towards Chartered Membership.

There are two categories of applicant for Chartership:

* Firstly para-professionals with over five years experience;
* Secondly those who have some evidence of training and have been working for two years.

Chartership is CILIP's standard for information professionals. Chartered members are entitled to use post nominal letters and describe themselves as qualified library and information professionals. All candidates for Chartership must work with a Mentor and demonstrate through their portfolio that they meet the required criteria.

Chartership is not an academic qualification but a recognition of the highest standards of professional practice. The individual makes a commitment to continued professional development. Normally applicants will have completed a degree in LIS and have been working for at least one year.

INTERNATIONAL FEDERATION OF LIBRARY ASSOCIATIONS AND INSTITUTIONS

The International Federation of Library Associations and Institutions (IFLA) is the leading international association of library organisations. It is the global voice of the library and information profession, and its annual conference provides a venue for librarians to learn from one another.

The IFLA forum promotes international cooperation, research and development in all fields related to library activities. A very important and close partner of the IFLA is UNESCO. Several of the manifestos prepared by committees of the IFLA have been recognized as UNESCO manifestos.

The IFLA is part of the International Committee of the Blue Shield (ICBS), which works to protect the world's cultural heritage threatened by wars and natural disasters, and whose Director General is currently Mr Julien Anfruns from the International Council of Museums (ICOM).

The IFLA was founded in Edinburgh, Scotland, in 1927 when library associations from 14 European countries and the United States signed a resolution at the celebration of the 50th anniversary of the Library Association of the United Kingdom. Isak Collijn, head of the National Library of Sweden, was elected the first president. The first constitution was approved in Rome in 1929 during the World Congress of Librarianship and Bibliography.

During the 1930s the first library associations from outside Europe and the US joined, these being China, India, Japan, Mexico and the Philippines. By 1958 membership had grown to 64 associations from 42 countries. A permanent secretariat was established in 1962. By 1970 there were 250 members from 52 countries. The secretariat was moved to The Hague in 1971. By 1974 IFLA membership had become virtually global with 600 members in 100 countries.

Membership criteria were expanded beyond library associations in 1976 to include institutions, *i.e.* libraries, library schools and bibliographic institutes. At this time, the word *Institutions* was added to the organisation's name. Since then further new categories of membership have been created, including personal affiliates.

IFLA has now grown to over 1,700 members in 155 countries. It is headquartered in the Koninklijke Bibliotheek, the National Library of the Netherlands, in The Hague.

Mission

IFLA's objectives are:

* To represent librarianship in matters of international interest
* To promote the continuing education of library personnel
* To develop, maintain and promote guidelines for library services

Core Values

The objectives are informed by the following core values:

* The endorsement of the principles of freedom of expression embodied in Article 19 of the Universal Declaration of Human Rights
* The belief that people, communities and organizations need universal and equitable access to information, ideas and works of imagination for their social, educational, cultural, democratic and economic well-being
* The conviction that delivery of high quality library and information services helps guarantee that access
* The commitment to enable all Members of the Federation to engage in, and benefit from, its activities without regard to citizenship, disability, ethnic origin, gender, geographical location, language, political philosophy, race or religion.

Committee on Free Access to Information and Freedom of Expression (FAIFE)

One of the core activities of IFLA is the Committee on Free Access to Information and Freedom of Expression, which monitors the state of intellectual freedom within the library community worldwide, supports IFLA policy development and co-operation with other international human rights organisations, and responds to violations of free access to information and freedom of expression.

IFLA/FAIFE is a member of the International Freedom of Expression Exchange, a global network of non-governmental organisations that monitors freedom of expression worldwide. It is also a member of the Tunisia Monitoring Group, a coalition of 16 free expression organisations that lobbies the Tunisian government to improve its human rights record.

Bibliography

Alexander, John M.: *Information: The Last Variable,* Finland: United Nations University, Helsinki, 2003.

Anderson, B.: *Journal of the American Society for Information Science,* Toronto: Thomson Nelson, 2008.

Bertozzi, S.: *Special Libraries,* Maharashtra: Pune Publication, 2006.

Byres,T. J.: *Information Processing and Management,* New York: Orgone Institute Press, 2004.

Chakravati, V.: *Foundations of Information Science,* Mumbai: Rohit Publication, 2003.

Chambers, R.: *Library Research,* New York: Oxford University Press, 2000.

Jogdand Mahipal, P.: *Outline of a Theory of Information Science,* Mumbai: Kamal Publication, 2003.

Jose, J.: *Theory and Metatheory of Information Science,* New York: Oxford University Press, 2003.

Kapur, R.: *Library and Information Science Research,* Maharashtra: Pune Publication, 2001.

Kumar, Akash: *Information and Information Science,* Maharashtra: Pune Publication, 2006.

Manoranjan, Mohanty: *Proposed Ideology and Methodology for the Critical Information Scientist,* New York: Oxford University Press, 2003.

Narayan, D.: *Theory in library and Information Science,* New York: Oxford University Press, 2003.

Neera, Chandhoke: *Scientism and Academic Librarianship,* Maharashtra: Pune Publication, 2006.

Niaz, M.: *Documentation and the Organization of Knowledge,* India: IDB Working Paper, 2009.

Rao, A.: *Legitimization of Librarianship,* New York: Orgone Institute Press, 2003.

Rawat, Shruti: *The Social Construction of a Digital Library,* Mumbai: Rohit Publication, 2003.

Roemer, John: *Electronic Information Technologies and Resources in Library*: Harvard University Press, 2008.

Sardesai, S.G.: *Influence of the Card Catalog on Circulation in a Small Public Library,* Maharashtra: Vidnayak Sansod Prakashan, 2002.

Shah, Ghanshyam: *Library Resources and Technical Services,* Toronto: Thomson Nelson, 2008.

Singh, Sonu: *Library's Public,* Vidnayak Sansod Prakashan, 2002.

Thorat, S.: Libraries: *Communicating with Individuals,* New York: Orgone Institute Press, 2004.

Verma,Vishwanath Prasad: *Cataloging & Classification,* Mumbai: Rohit Publication, 2003.

Index

A

Abstracting 63
Accentuate 93, 127
Accreditation 226, 258, 269
Acronyms 21
Amalgamation 147, 208, 245
Ancillary 77, 167, 168
Antiquarian 48
Artifacts 11, 16, 87, 211, 227
Astronomicorum Libri 78, 83

B

Bibliotheque Coloniale 178

C

Chaotic 1, 128
Consolation 17
Conundrum 18

D

Dehumidifiers 74
Desideratum 48
Deteriorate 47
Disenfranchisement 16
DRM 15
DYRCs 182

E

EDRMS 234
Embodied 269
Entanglement 87
Enunciating 189
Epitomized 13
Evidentiary 220
Excavations 49
Explicitly 65, 101, 104, 105

F

Facsimile 36
Fortuitous 253
Fumigation 210

G

Germanic 206, 207
Glimpse 28, 74

H

HCI 13, 20, 21, 23, 28
Hinayana 51

I

IATLIS 253, 254
IFLA 152, 157, 182, 267, 268, 269
Incineration 231
Indigenously 210
Inexplicability 33
INFLIBNET 68, 213, 214, 215, 248, 249
Inflibnet 68, 69, 70, 241
Intensified 6
Internationalization 36

M

Madhyamkaratnapradipa 51
Mahayana 51, 81
Maktabs 42
Manifests 11
Metadata 14, 21, 22, 24, 25, 26, 33, 34, 35, 87

O

Ostensibly 16

P

PAHO 28
Ponderous 11

R

Redundancy 238, 245
Retrieval 12, 23, 72, 100, 101, 113, 115, 117, 119, 120, 121, 184, 230, 244, 247

S

Shredding 231
Slavonic 206, 207

T

Tremendous 45, 48, 57, 137, 143, 144, 159
Tripitakas 52

U

Unanimously 4, 254
UNHCR 28